WORLD HIS

myWorld
INTERACTIVE
Active Journal

 Pearson

Boston, Massachusetts   Chandler, Arizona
Glenview, Illinois   New York, New York

ISBN-13: 978-0-328-96012-5
ISBN-10: 0-328-96012-8

CONTENTS

CONTENTS

Topic 3
Ancient Egypt and Kush (3000 BCE—600 BCE)

Topic 4
Early Civilizations of India (3100 BCE—540 CE)

CONTENTS

Topic 5
Early Civilizations of China (1700 BCE—220 CE)

Topic 6
Ancient Greece (2000 BCE–300 BCE)

CONTENTS

Topic 7
The Roman Republic (800 BCE–30 BCE)

Topic 8
The Roman and Byzantine Empires (30 BCE—1453 CE)

CONTENTS

Topic 9
Life in Medieval Christian Europe (486–1300)

Topic 10
Struggle in Medieval Europe (962–1492)

CONTENTS

Topic 12
Civilizations of East Asia and Southeast Asia
(250 BCE—644 CE)

CONTENTS

Topic 15
The Renaissance and Reformation (1300–1648)

CONTENTS

Topic 16
Global Convergence (1415–1763)

Topic 17
Absolutism and Enlightenment (1516–1796)

CONTENTS

Topic 19
The Modern World (1914–Present)

TOPIC 1

Origins of Civilization Preview

Essential Question **How much does geography shape people's lives?**

Before you begin this topic, think about the Essential Question by completing the following activity.

1. List the geographical features of your hometown. Describe any that influence how people live in your region.

2. Preview the topic by skimming lesson titles, headings, and graphics. Then study this list of the developments that took place in prehistoric times. How does each relate to geography?

humans domesticate animals   sea levels rise

the first cities appear   rivers deposit fertile soil

societies become more complex   sea levels drop during Ice Age

Timeline Skills

As you read, write and/or draw at least three events from the topic. Draw a line from each event to its correct position on the timeline.

2 million years ago	300,000 years ago	200,000 years ago	100,000 years ago

Map Skills

Using the map in your text, label the outline map with the places listed.

Gulf of Aden	Red Sea	Lake Victoria
Ethiopia	Kenya	Tanzania
Olduvai Gorge	Indian Ocean	Hadar

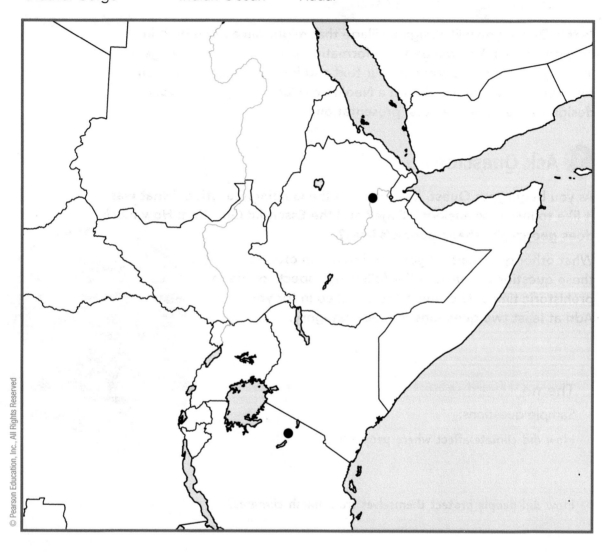

20,000 years ago	15,000 years ago	10,000 years ago	5,000 years ago

Quest
Project-Based Learning Inquiry

Design a Village

In this Quest, you will design a village that might have been built in Neolithic times. You will gather information about how early villagers lived by examining sources in your text and by conducting your own research. Then, you will design a Neolithic village and present your design to the class in an oral presentation.

① Ask Questions

As you begin your Quest, keep in mind the Guiding Question: **What was it like to live in an ancient village?** and the Essential Question: **How much does geography shape people's lives?**

What other questions do you need to ask in order to answer these questions? Consider the following aspects of life in prehistoric times. Two questions are filled in for you. Add at least two questions for each category.

Theme Location and Climate

Sample questions:

How did climate affect where people lived?

How did people protect themselves from harsh climates?

Theme Archaeology

Theme Social Organization

Theme Agriculture

Theme Building

Theme My Additional Questions

 INTERACTIVE

For extra help with Step 1, review the
21st Century Tutorial: **Ask Questions**.

② Investigate

As you read about the origins of civilization, collect five connections from your text to help you answer the Guiding Question. Three connections are already chosen for you.

Connect to Location

Lesson 3 When Did People Start to Farm?

Here's a connection! Look at the picture of a Neolithic settlement in Ireland in your text, and notice the settlement's location. What information does it give you about prehistoric life?

Why would people have chosen this spot to create a settlement in Neolithic times?

Connect to the Design of a Neolithic Village

Lesson 4 In-Text Primary Source The Houses of Çatalhöyük

Here's a connection! What does this Primary Source reveal about how the design of Çatalhöyük reflected villagers' priorities?

Why do you think the houses described in the Primary Source were packed so closely together, with no entrances at ground level?

Connect to Neolithic Shelters

Lesson 4 How Did the First Cities Begin?

What does the photo from your text show about how some ancient villagers built their shelters?

Why do you think these shelters are round?

It's Your Turn! **Find two more connections. Fill in the title of your connections, then answer the questions. Connections may be images, primary sources, maps, or text.**

Your Choice | Connect to

Location in text

What is the main idea of this connection?

What does it tell you about what it was like to live in an ancient village?

Your Choice | Connect to

Location in text

What is the main idea of this connection?

What does it tell you about what it was like to live in an ancient village?

③ Conduct Research

Use the ideas in the Connections to further explore the subject of Neolithic villages. Find more sources about the subject.

Be sure to find valid sources and take good notes so you can properly cite your sources. Record key information and brainstorm ways to enhance your points with visuals. Then, form teams based on your teacher's instructions. Meet to decide who will take on each role. Write who will do what in the chart below.

Role	Team Member
Research life during the Neolithic Era	
Research Neolithic village sites	
Collect photos of reconstructions and sites	
Create a plan and drawing of your village	
Present your village to the class	

👆 INTERACTIVE

For extra help, review the 21st Century Tutorials: **Work in Teams, Search for Information on the Internet,** and **Avoid Plagiarism.**

4 Design Your Village

Now it's time to apply your research into Neolithic village sites and use that information to create your own Neolithic village.

1. **List Village Features** You have gathered information about Neolithic villages and looked at photographs and reconstructions of village sites. Make a list of the features that your village should have, taking into consideration factors such as local climate, food sources, defense against animals and enemies, and building materials.

Features

2. **Meet with Your Team** Meet with your team to discuss the images of Neolithic sites and other information that you have found. Compare information about the various village sites and discuss how these villages differed from one another, as well as the features they have in common.

3. **Make a List of Essential Features** After your discussion, make a list of the essential features that your village should have.

4. **Create and Present Your Design** Create a rough draft of the plan of the village. Discuss the plan with members of your team and suggest improvements. You may need to follow this process several times before presenting the finished designs.

5. **Reflect on the Quest** Think about your experience completing this topic's Quest. What did you learn about Neolithic life and the villages that were built during this period? What questions do you still have about the Neolithic world? How will you answer them?

Reflections

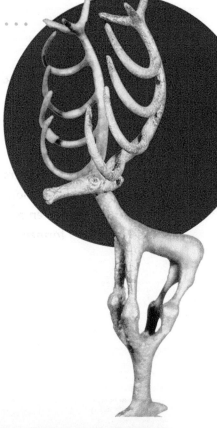

👆 **INTERACTIVE**

For extra help, review the 21st Century Tutorial: **Give an Effective Presentation**.

Take Notes

Literacy Skills: Main Idea and Details Use what you have read to complete the table. In each space, write one main idea and two details. The first one has been completed for you.

Studying Early Humans	Where Did Human Ancestors Live?	How Did Hunter-Gatherers Live?
Main Idea: Archaeologists use different methods for determining the ages of prehistoric objects.	Main Idea:	Main Idea:
Details: lower layers of soil are older; radioactive dating tells when an object was formed	Details:	Details:

INTERACTIVE

For extra help, review the 21st Century Tutorial: **Identify Main Ideas and Details**.

Practice Vocabulary

Word Map Study the word map for the word *artifact*. Characteristics are words or phrases that relate to the word in the center of the word map. Non-characteristics are words and phrases not associated with the word. Use the blank word map to explore the meaning of the word *culture*. Then make word maps of your own for these words: *anthropology, archaeologist, prehistory, fossil, geologist, technology,* and *hunter-gatherer*.

Characteristics
old, possibly buried,
museum object

Definition in your own words
objects made and used
by humans

artifact

Non-characteristics
new, produced by
natural forces

Picture or sentence
The museum had a display of
artifacts that were found in early
human settlements.

Characteristics

Definition in your own words

culture

Non-characteristics

Picture or sentence

Take Notes

Literacy Skills: Analyze Cause and Effect Use what you have read to complete the organizer. For each event, write the cause in the box to the left and the effect in the box to the right. The first one has been completed for you.

Cause	Event	Effect
200,000 years ago, the last new group of humans appeared: Homo sapiens.	Homo sapiens developed the skill of complex language.	Language skills gave these modern humans an advantage in the struggle to survive.
	Glaciers form.	
	Sea levels drop, exposing "land bridges."	
	About 15,000–18,000 years ago, humans enter North America by crossing a land bridge from Asia.	

INTERACTIVE

For extra help, review the 21st Century Tutorial: **Analyze Cause and Effect**.

Practice Vocabulary

Vocabulary Quiz Show Some quiz shows ask a question and expect the contestant to give the answer. In other shows, the contestant is given an answer and must supply the question. If the blank is in the Question column, write the question that would result in the answer in the Answer column. If the question is supplied, write the answer.

Question	Answer
1. What happens when people leave their homeland to live elsewhere?	1.
2.	2. environment
3. What do you call it when you change your way of life to suit a new environment?	3.

Take Notes

Literacy Skills: Sequence Use what you have read to complete the flowcharts to show the sequence of events. The first flowchart has been completed for you.

Humans live as hunter-gatherers.

↓

As Ice Age ends, some animals and plants cannot adapt.

↓

People search for new sources of food.

↓

Some people begin to depend on fishing.

Hunter-gatherers develop language.

↓

[ ]

↓

Other animals are domesticated and herded.

↓

Grains become a food source.

↓

Over time, domesticated plants produce more food.

↓

[ ]

↓

More efficient metal tools are developed.

↓

[ ]

INTERACTIVE

For extra help, review the 21st Century Tutorial: **Sequence**.

Practice Vocabulary

Sentence Builder Finish the sentences below with a key term from this section. You may have to change the form of the words to complete the sentences.

Word Bank

animism   nomad   revolution

domesticate   populate

1. Due to centuries of migrations, there were few places on Earth that humans did not

2. The adoption of farming led to so many changes that it has been called a(n)

3. The wolf was one of the first animals that humans were able to

4. The belief that the natural world is full of spirits is known as

5. A person with no permanent home who moves from place to place is known as a(n)

Quick Activity Explore Cave Paintings

With a partner or small group, study these prehistoric paintings.

Team Challenge! With your partner or group, answer these questions: What colors did the artists use? Why? What kinds of animals, people, or activities are shown in the paintings? What was important to the people who created these paintings? How do you know? Why do you think the artists created these paintings? Share your answers orally with the class.

Take Notes

Literacy Skills: Analyze Cause and Effect Use what you have read to complete the organizer. For each event, write the cause in the box to the left and the effect in the box to the right. The first one has been completed for you.

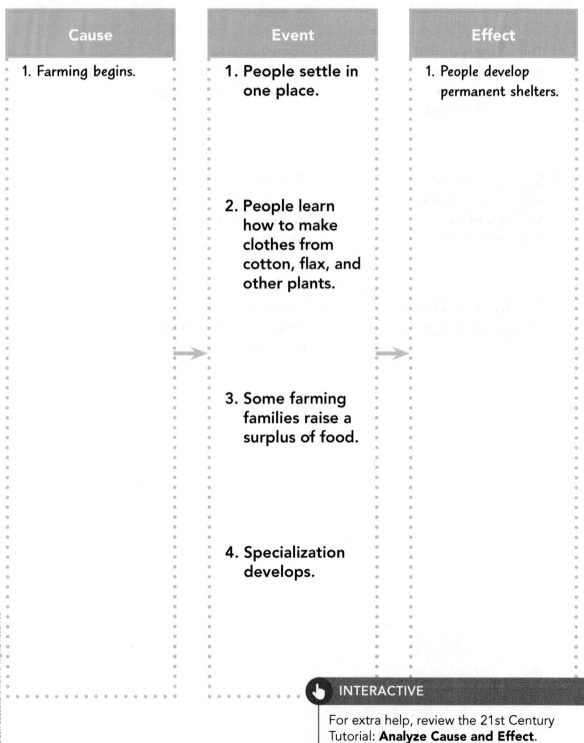

Cause	Event	Effect
1. Farming begins.	1. People settle in one place.	1. People develop permanent shelters.
	2. People learn how to make clothes from cotton, flax, and other plants.	
	3. Some farming families raise a surplus of food.	
	4. Specialization develops.	

👆 **INTERACTIVE**

For extra help, review the 21st Century Tutorial: **Analyze Cause and Effect**.

Practice Vocabulary

Matching Logic Using your knowledge of the underlined vocabulary words, draw a line from each sentence in Column 1 to match it with the sentence in Column 2 to which it logically belongs.

Column 1	Column 2
1. The villagers traded their <u>surplus</u> crops for pottery made in a nearby settlement.	Some people became skilled at weaving, pottery, or toolmaking.
2. <u>Specialization</u> led to a more complex society and an increase in trade.	The community had a system to produce and distribute goods and services.
3. The city of Uruk had a complex <u>economy</u>.	The good harvest supplied them with more than they could eat.

Quick Activity Explore Ancient Innovations

In prehistoric times, people developed new tools and practices that changed societies by increasing the population and improving the standard of living. What innovations do you see in the painting? Write you ideas in the space below.

My Ideas

Team Challenge! With a partner discuss the effect that one of the following innovations would have had on society: domestication of animals and plants; the ability to make tools; the ability to create art and music. Compare your ideas with classmates who discussed the same innovation.

Take Notes

Literacy Skills: Summarize Use what you have read to complete the flowcharts. Write a summary for each set of facts. The first flowchart has been completed for you.

As farming spread, settlements developed.

As settlements grew in size, specialization helped create complex societies.

Summary: Farming led to the development of complex societies.

Governments managed society's resources.

Governments also formed and trained armies to defend society from attack.

Summary:

The highest social class in most early societies was made up of priests and rulers.

Rulers of early civilizations claimed that their right to rule came from the gods.

Summary:

 INTERACTIVE

For extra help, review the 21st Century Tutorial: **Summarize**.

Practice Vocabulary

Words in Context For each question below, write an answer that shows your understanding of the boldfaced vocabulary term.

1. Why did different **social classes** emerge in the early cities?

2. What **resources** were important to farmers?

3. What are some characteristics of **civilization**?

4. What were some features of **religion** in early civilizations?

Writing Workshop Narrative Essay

Suppose you are visiting three different periods in the distant past to observe three different people: a hunter-gatherer, a herder, and a farmer. You will write a narrative essay describing the people you met and a few events in their lives. Although this assignment involves creative imagination, you should base the details and events on facts in the topic.

Lessons 1–3 Writing Task: Introduce Characters Imagine how each character's life was shaped by his or her environment, way of life, and the time in which he or she lived. Write your ideas in the chart.

Character	Details
Hunter-gatherer	
Herder	
Farmer	

Lesson 4 Writing Task: Organize Sequence of Events For each character, list the sequence of events you will include in your essay.

Character	Events
Hunter-gatherer	
Herder	
Farmer	

Lesson 5 Writing Task: Use Descriptive Details and Sensory Language
Imagine the sights, sounds, and tasks that would have been a familiar part of each character's world. Make a list of descriptive phases and adjectives that you can use for each character.

Character	Descriptive Details and Sensory Language
Hunter-gatherer	
Herder	
Farmer	

2 Civilizations and Peoples of the Fertile Crescent Preview

Essential Question **How do societies preserve order?**

Before you begin this topic, think about the Essential Question by answering the following questions.

1. What does *order* mean? In the space provided, write what order means for human societies in your own words. Then, write what it does not mean. You may list related words and phrases or write complete sentences.

What Order Means	What Order Does Not Mean

Timeline Skills

As you read, write and/or draw at least three events from the topic. Draw a line from each event to its correct position on the timeline.

4000 BCE	3000 BCE	2000 BCE

Map Skills

Using the map in your text, label the outline map with the places listed. Then color in water, desert, mountains, and the Fertile Crescent.

Egypt	Canaan	Phoenicia	Mesopotamia
Persia	Babylon	Nineveh	Jerusalem
Persepolis	Tigris River	Euphrates River	

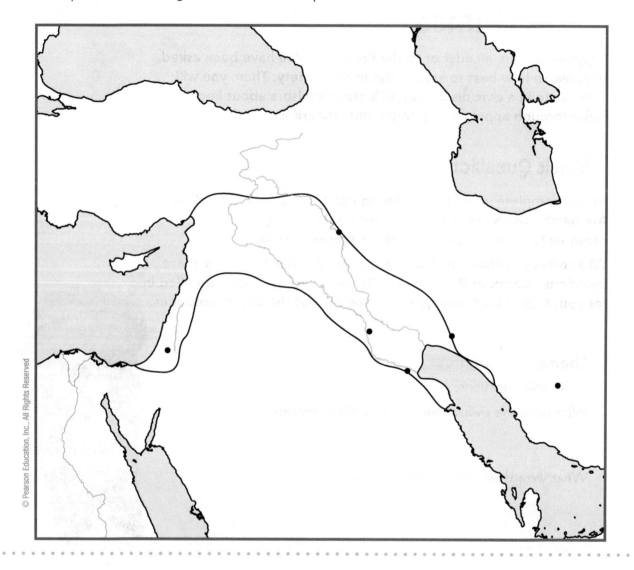

1000 BCE

1 CE

Quest
Discussion Inquiry

Debate Punishments for Crimes

Suppose you are an advisor to the President. You have been asked to research how best to keep order in our society. Then, you will participate in a civic discussion with other advisors about keeping order through appropriate punishments for crimes.

1 Ask Questions

As you complete your Quest, keep in mind the Guiding Question: **Are harsh punishments necessary for a safe society?** and the Essential Question: **How do societies preserve order?**

What other questions do you need to ask in order to answer these questions? Consider the following themes. Two questions are filled in for you. Add at least two questions for each of the other categories.

Theme Government

Sample questions:

Who ruled the civilizations of the Fertile Crescent?

What were their accomplishments?

Theme Economy and Trade

Theme Social Order

Theme Laws

Theme Religion

Theme My Additional Questions

 INTERACTIVE

For extra help with Step 1, review the
21st Century Tutorial: **Ask Questions**.

Quest CONNECTIONS

2 Investigate

As you read about the civilizations and peoples of the Fertile Crescent, collect five connections from your text to help you answer the Guiding Question. Three connections are already chosen for you.

Connect to Mesopotamian Contracts

Primary Source Contracts in Ancient Mesopotamia

Here's a Connection! Read and think about written contracts in ancient Mesopotamia. How would agreements like these contribute to social order?

What do you think the punishment should be for breaking contracts such as these?

Connect to Social Order in Persia

Lesson 3 Cyrus the Great

Here's another connection! Look at the biography of Cyrus the Great in your text and review what you've read about Cyrus and other Persian rulers. How did these rulers try to establish social order?

Do you think that punishments for crimes under Cyrus the Great's rule were harsh or mild? Explain your answer.

Connect to Teachings of Judaism

Lesson 6 Key Teachings of Judaism

Here's another connection! Study the infographic on the key teachings of Judaism. What does this connection tell you about how the basic teachings of Judaism support social order?

How do you think people accused of wrongdoing were treated under Judaism?

It's Your Turn! Find two more connections. Fill in the title of your connections, then answer the questions. Connections may be images, primary sources, maps, or text.

Your Choice | Connect to

Location in text

What is the main idea of this connection?

What does it tell you about social order and justice in the Fertile Crescent?

Your Choice | Connect to

Location in text

What is the main idea of this connection?

What does it tell you about social order and justice in the Fertile Crescent?

③ Examine Sources

One way societies create order is for citizens to know that there are possible punishments for their crimes. After a person has been convicted of a crime, judges today decide how harsh or mild the punishment should be. Some crimes have mandatory, or required, minimum sentences, however. Many lawmakers believe that people will stop committing crimes only if they are harshly punished.

Examine the primary and secondary sources provided online or from your teacher. Fill in the chart to show how these sources provide further information about whether harsh punishments are necessary for a safe society.

Are Harsh Punishments Necessary for a Safe Society?	
Source	Yes or No? Why?
J. Randy Forbes Testimony	
Sally Quillian Yates Testimony	
Mark Mauer Testimony	
"Mandatory Minimum Sentences"	

INTERACTIVE

For extra help with Step 1, review the 21st Century Tutorials: **Analyze Primary and Secondary Sources** and **Evaluate Existing Arguments**.

 **FINDINGS**

4 Discuss!

Now that you have collected clues and explored documents about harsh punishments, you are ready to discuss with your fellow advisors the Guiding Question: **Are harsh punishments necessary for a safe society?**

You will work with a partner in a small group of advisors. Try to reach consensus, a situation in which everyone is in agreement, on the question. Can you do it?

1. **Prepare your Arguments** You will be assigned a position on the question, either YES or NO.

   My position:

   Work with your partner to review your Quest notes from the Quest Connections and Quest Sources.

   - If you were assigned YES, agree with your partner on what you think were the strongest arguments from Forbes and Yates.

   - If you were assigned NO, agree on what you think were the strongest arguments from Mauer, Bernick, and Larkin.

2. **Present Your Position** Those assigned YES will present their arguments and evidence first. As you listen, ask clarifying questions to gain information and understanding.

What is a Clarifying Question?	
These types of questions do not judge the person talking. They are only for the listener to be clear on what he or she is hearing.	
Example: Can you tell me more about that?	Example: You said [x]. Am I getting that right?

 INTERACTIVE

For extra help with Step 4, review the 21st Century Tutorial: **Participate in a Discussion or Debate.**

While the opposite side speaks, take notes on what you hear in the space below.

3. **Switch!** Now NO and YES will switch sides. If you argued YES before, now you will argue NO. Work with your same partner and use your notes. Add any arguments and evidence from the clues and sources. Those *now* arguing YES go first.

When both sides have finished, answer the following:

Before I started this discussion with my fellow advisors, my opinion was that	*After* I started this discussion with my fellow advisors, my opinion was that
_____harsh punishments are necessary. _____harsh punishments are not necessary.	_____harsh punishments are necessary. _____harsh punishments are not necessary.

4. **Point of View** Do you all agree on the answer to the Guiding Question?

- ____ Yes

- ____ No

If not, on what points do you all agree?

Take Notes

Literacy Skills: Identify Main Ideas and Details Use what you have read to complete the tables. The column headings in the tables match the headings in your textbook. For each topic, write the main idea and some details that support it. The first one has been completed for you.

Agriculture in Mesopotamia	City-States of Sumer	Sumerian Religion
Main idea: Mesopotamia's rich soil allowed farmers to grow grains and vegetables and raise livestock. **Details:** • Tigris and Euphrates rivers carried silt across plains. • Sumerians used technology to irrigate crops. • Farmers developed a seed funnel to make planting faster and easier.	Main idea: Details:	Main idea: Details:

Sumerian Writing	Sumerian Government	Sumerian Achievements
Main idea: Details:	Main idea: Details:	Main idea: Details:

👆 **INTERACTIVE**

For extra help, review the 21st Century Tutorial: **Identify Main Ideas and Details**.

Practice Vocabulary

Use a Word Bank **Choose one word from the word bank to fill in each blank. When you have finished, you will have a short summary of important ideas from the section.**

Word Bank

Fertile Crescent	bartering	Mesopotamia	polytheism
irrigate	ziggurats	city-states	cuneiform

The _____ is a region of the Middle East that

stretches from the Persian Gulf to the Mediterranean Sea. This region

includes _____, where several independent

states known as _____ developed. As these

communities developed, ancient Sumerians used technology to improve

agriculture. They learned how to _____, or

supply water to, their crops. They also exchanged goods without using

money in a trading system known as _____.

Sumerians practiced _____, or the belief in

more than one god. To honor their gods, they built pyramid-shaped

temples called _____. Sumerians also

developed a writing system in which scribes made wedge-shaped marks in

wet clay. This writing system was called _____.

Take Notes

Literacy Skills: Analyze Cause and Effect Use what you have read to complete the table. Write four causes and four effects of the listed event. The first one has been completed for you.

Causes	Event	Effects
• Sumerian city-states struggle for power.	• Sargon builds the world's first empire.	• Akkadians and Sumerians share cultural traits.
•	• The Akkadian empire ends.	•
•	• Hammurabi becomes king of Babylon.	•
•	• Hammurabi establishes a code of law.	•

INTERACTIVE

For extra help, review the 21st Century Tutorial: **Analyze Cause and Effect**.

Practice Vocabulary

Vocabulary Quiz Show Some quiz shows ask a question and expect the contestant to give the answer. In other shows, the contestant is given an answer and must supply the question. If the blank is in the Question column, write the question that would result in the answer in the Answer column. If the question is supplied, write the answer.

Question	Answer
1. What is the term for a state containing several countries or territories?	1.
2. What phrase describes an idea or way of doing things that is common in a certain culture?	2.
3.	3. rule of law
4.	4. Hammurabi's Code
5. What is the word for an independent state that works with other states to achieve a shared military or political goal?	5.

Quick Activity An Eye for an Eye?

You might have heard the phrase "an eye for an eye" used to justify punishments, revenge, and other harsh actions. The phrase is derived from Hammurabi's Code, a set of laws nearly 4,000 years old. The code was remarkable in its time for providing a written rule of law—but would you want the laws of ancient Babylon in effect today? Below are excerpts from Hammurabi's Code.

Hammurabi's Code	Level of Agreement
If any one bring an accusation of any crime before the elders, and does not prove what he has charged, he shall, if it be a capital offense charged, be put to death.	
If any one steal cattle or sheep, or an ass, or a pig or a goat, if it belong to a god or to the court, the thief shall pay thirtyfold therefor; if they belonged to a freed man of the king he shall pay tenfold; if the thief has nothing with which to pay he shall be put to death.	
If a man put out the eye of another man, his eye shall be put out.	
If he break another man's bone, his bone shall be broken.	
If during a quarrel one man strike another and wound him, then he shall swear, "I did not injure him wittingly," and pay the physicians.	

Team Challenge! Do these laws seem fair? Rank the degree to which you agree or disagree with each law: 1 = Strongly Agree, 2 = Agree, 3 = Unsure, 4 = Disagree, 5 = Strongly Disagree. Then, for each law, form groups of students with the same rankings. Discuss your reasoning and decide on one argument in favor of your position. Share your argument with the class.

Take Notes

Literacy Skills: Summarize Use what you have read to complete the table. Summarize the most important ideas from each section of the lesson in the appropriate column. The first one has been completed for you.

Section	Main Ideas
The Assyrian and Neo-Babylonian Empires	• The Assyrians fought against a steady stream of invaders, becoming fierce warriors with some of the earliest cavalry. • Nebuchadnezzar became king of Babylon, capturing Jerusalem and restoring Babylon to form the Neo-Babylonian empire.
Rise of the Persian Empire	
Persia's Government and Religion	
Arts of Mesopotamia	

Summary Statement:

 INTERACTIVE

For extra help, review the 21st Century Tutorial: **Summarize**.

Practice Vocabulary

Matching Logic Using your knowledge of the underlined vocabulary words, draw a line from each sentence in Column 1 to match it with the sentence in Column 2 to which it logically belongs.

Column 1	Column 2
1. The Assyrian army relied on its <u>cavalry</u> to defend and expand its empire.	Professional soldiers devoted to service protected the Persian Empire.
2. Cyrus the Great maintained a powerful <u>standing army</u>.	Darius introduced the use of gold coins as a medium of exchange.
3. Under Darius, the Persian empire used <u>tribute</u> money to fund great public works projects.	Soldiers rode into battle mounted on horses.
4. The Persian economy benefited from having a common <u>currency</u>.	Hammurabi's Code appears carved in stone beneath a relief showing Hammurabi and the Babylonian god Shamash.
5. Ancient Sumerians carved relief sculptures on <u>stele</u>.	Conquered peoples paid money to the emperor based on their wealth.

Take Notes

Literacy Skills: Summarize Use what you have read to complete the table. For each section in the lesson, write three sentences that summarize the section. Remember that a summary restates the most important information and ideas. The first one has been completed for you.

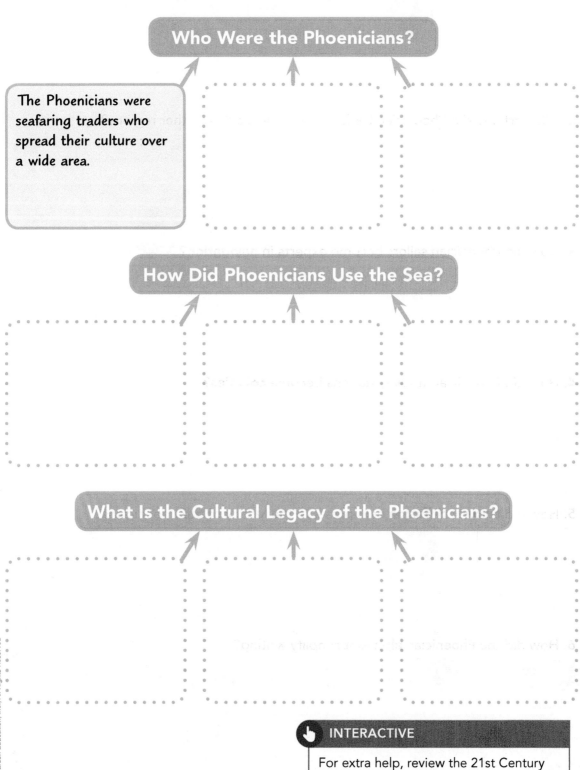

Who Were the Phoenicians?

The Phoenicians were seafaring traders who spread their culture over a wide area.

How Did Phoenicians Use the Sea?

What Is the Cultural Legacy of the Phoenicians?

INTERACTIVE

For extra help, review the 21st Century Tutorial: **Summarize**.

Practice Vocabulary

Words in Context For each question below, write an answer that shows your understanding of the boldfaced vocabulary term.

1. Why did the Phoenician traders bring back so many **imports**?

2. What articles did Phoenician traders send as **exports** to other regions?

3. How did Phoenician sailors become experts in **navigation**?

4. How did Phoenician trading stations become **colonies**?

5. How did **cultural diffusion** help preserve the legacy of the Phoenicians?

6. How did the Phoenician **alphabet** simplify writing?

Quick Activity The Power of Invention

With a partner or small group, discuss the ways in which the invention of the wheel in ancient Mesopotamia impacted the peoples who lived there as well as later societies. Then make a list in the space below of other inventions that originated in the Fertile Crescent. Circle those that had an impact on later societies.

Team Challenge!   Many societies have benefited from tools, weapons, medical advances, and other innovations. Consider what inventions you enjoy and depend on. Using three index cards or sticky notes, write three inventions that you consider the most important to your life. Post the notes on a class message board. As a class, identify the items that appear most often. Vote on which ones have had the most impact on our society or on humanity in general. Form groups according to votes, discuss your reasoning, and then debate with the other groups.

Take Notes

Literacy Skills: Summarize Use what you have read to complete the table. Summarize in the appropriate column each section's most important information. The first one has been completed for you. Then, use those ideas to write a summary statement.

Section	Main Ideas
The Early Israelites	• belief in one God • emphasis on ethics • The Torah tells the story of the origins of Judaism. • God makes a covenant with Abraham to lead his people to the Promised Land.
The Exodus	
The Ten Commandments	
The Promised Land	

Summary Statement:

 INTERACTIVE

For extra help, review the 21st Century Tutorial: **Summarize**.

Practice Vocabulary

Use a Word Bank Choose one word from the word bank to fill in each blank. When you have finished, you will have a short summary of important ideas from the lesson.

Word Bank

commandments	covenant	ethics
Exodus	monotheism	Torah

Unlike many other religions that originated in the Fertile

Crescent, Judaism is a belief in only one God, which is known as

.... The first five books of the Bible, called

the ...., tell how Judaism began. These

books describe how God told the Israelites to practice proper behavior,

or .... The Torah tells that God made a

.... with Abraham, whom Jews consider

to be the founder of their religion. According to the Bible, the Israelites

ended up in Egypt, where they became slaves. Moses became their

leader and helped them in an escape from slavery, in what is known as the

.... The Bible describes how God told Moses

to give the Israelites a series of ten .... to

teach them how to act toward God and toward other people.

Take Notes

Literacy Skills: Analyze Cause and Effect Use what you have read
to complete the chart. In the Text column, you will see a type of
Jewish religious text, including the three sections of the Hebrew Bible.
In the Effect column, write ways in which that body of texts has
affected Jewish beliefs. The first one has been completed for you.

Text	Effect on Jewish Beliefs
The Torah	contains many of the rules and laws by which the Jewish people live
The Prophets	
The Writings	
Talmud/Commentaries	

 INTERACTIVE

For extra help, review the 21st Century
Tutorial: **Analyze Cause and Effect.**

Practice Vocabulary

Vocabulary Quiz Show Some quiz shows ask a question and expect the contestant to give the answer. In other shows, the contestant is given an answer and must supply the question. If the blank is in the Question column, write the question that would result in the answer in the Answer column. If the question is supplied, write the answer.

Question

1.

2. Who is a person chosen by God to bring messages to the people?

3.

4. What is the name of the collection of teachings and commentaries about the Bible and Jewish law?

5.

6.

Answer

1. justice

2.

3. rabbi

4.

5. righteousness

6. Sabbath

Take Notes

Literacy Skills: Sequence Use what you have read to complete the timeline. Record key events from the lesson in the appropriate space on the timeline. The first one has been completed for you.

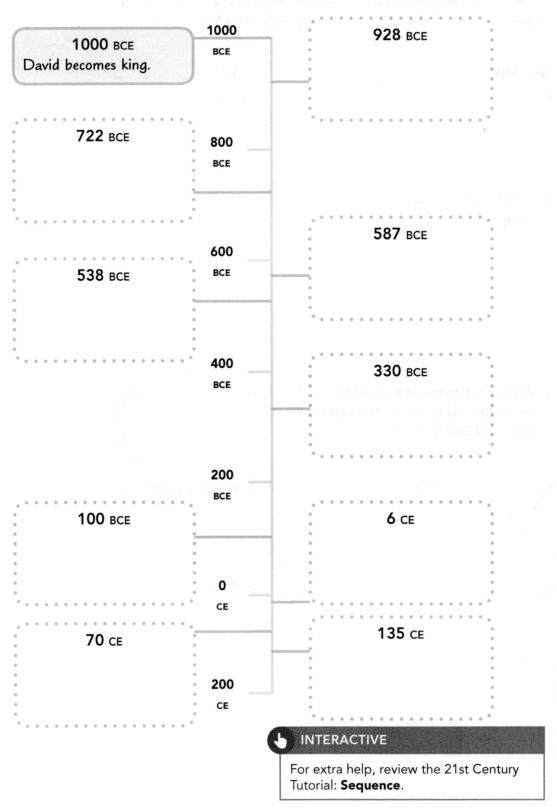

1000 BCE
1000 BCE
David becomes king.

928 BCE

722 BCE
800 BCE

587 BCE
600 BCE

538 BCE

330 BCE
400 BCE

200 BCE

100 BCE
6 CE

0 CE

70 CE
135 CE

200 CE

👆 **INTERACTIVE**

For extra help, review the 21st Century Tutorial: **Sequence**.

Practice Vocabulary

Words in Context For each question below, write an answer that shows your understanding of the boldfaced key term.

1. What is a **synagogue** used for?

2. What were the original causes of the **Diaspora**?

3. What did the Jews do when the king of the Persians, Cyrus the Great, ended the Babylonian **Exile**?

4. What role did **judges** play among the Israelites, according to the Bible?

Writing Workshop Narrative Essay

What was life like for people in ancient Mesopotamia? How did the environment affect the ways people lived? What technologies did they use to overcome challenges and solve problems? The prompts below will help walk you through the process of preparing to write your narrative essay about the life of someone living in ancient Mesopotamia.

Lessons 1 and 2 Writing Task: Introduce Characters Identify different groups of people who lived in ancient Mesopotamia. Then, circle one group about whom you want to write and imagine a character to represent them. Compose a sentence in which you describe your character's age, sex, and social class. Describe his or her profession and explain where and with whom your character probably lived. Brainstorm a name!

With which groups would your character interact? Write down three characters, identify their role in society, and explain what relationship they would have had with your character.

Lesson 3 Writing Task: Establish Setting Did your character live in Sumer, in Akkadia, in Babylon, or in Assyria? Did he or she live in a city, such as Ur, or outside of a city? Where would your character have spent the most time—on a farm, in a palace, in a temple, at a market, or in battle? Write two to three sentences to describe the setting of your narrative essay.

Lessons 4 and 5 Writing Task: Organize Sequence of Events What would life be like for your character over the course of a day? What would he or she do? What other characters would he or she meet, where would he or she go, what work and what fun things might he or she do, and what challenges would he or she face? List a sequence of at least four events or activities for your character's day.

Lesson 6 Writing Task: Use Narrative Techniques Consider the mood and tone that you will use. You might write your narrative to be exciting, scary, funny, or dramatic and serious. Brainstorm what narrative techniques you can use to make your story interesting to read. Decide whether you will write in first or third person and whether you will write in past or present tense.

Lesson 7 Writing Task: Use Descriptive Details and Sensory Language What people, plants, food and drink, music and sounds, weather, clothing, and tools or weapons might your character experience? What does he or she see, hear, feel, taste, and smell?

Writing Task Use your ideas to write a first draft for your essay. Ask yourself: Does the essay reflect what life might have been like for the character? Does it contain details about the setting? Does it show the effects of environment? Does it show how people use technology to solve problems? Revise your draft, being sure to use proper grammar and punctuation.

Ancient Egypt and Kush Preview

Essential Question **What makes a great leader?**

Before you begin this topic, think about the Essential Question by completing the following activity.

1. List three qualities of a great leader. Then, circle the one leadership quality that you think is the most important.

2. Preview the topic by skimming lesson titles, headings, and graphics. Then, place a check mark next to the qualities that you predict will be true about the leaders of ancient Egypt and Kush.

__ powerful   __ weak   __ concerned about the afterlife

__ wealthy   __ respected   __ uninterested in the arts

__ religious   __ monument builders

Timeline Skills

As you read, write and/or draw at least three events from the topic. Draw a line from each event to its position on the timeline.

4000	3000
BCE	BCE

Map Skills

**Using the map in your text, label the outline map with the places listed.
Then color in water, desert, and areas of fertile land.**

Western Desert	Eastern Desert	Lower Egypt	Upper Egypt
Africa	Asia	Sinai Peninsula	Red Sea
Nile River	Nile Delta	Mediterranean Sea	Kush

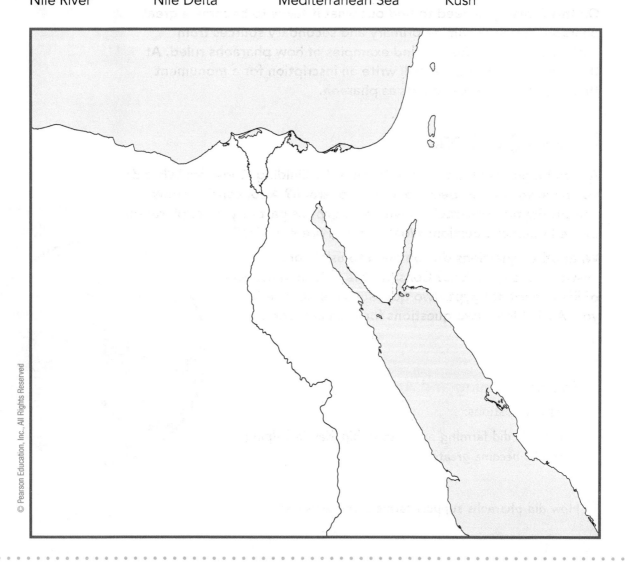

2000	1000	1
BCE	BCE	BCE

Quest
Document-Based Writing Inquiry

Become a Pharaoh-in-Training

On this Quest, you need to find out what it takes to become a great pharaoh. You will examine primary and secondary sources from ancient Egypt and Kush to find examples of how pharaohs ruled. At the end of the Quest, you will write an inscription for a monument that records your great deeds as pharaoh.

1 Ask Questions

As you begin your Quest, keep in mind the Guiding Question: **What do you need to learn to become a great pharaoh?** Also, consider how ancient Egyptian pharaohs governed Egypt as part of your exploration of the Essential Question: **What makes a great leader?**

What other questions do you need to ask in order to answer these questions? Consider the following aspects of life in ancient Egypt. Two questions are filled in for you. Add at least two questions for each category.

Theme Farming and Artisanship

Sample questions:

What role did farming and artisanship play in helping pharaohs become great?

How did pharaohs support farmers and artisans?

Theme Architecture and Building

Theme Science and Medicine

Theme Religion, Art, and Literature

Theme Trade and Warfare

Theme My Additional Questions

 INTERACTIVE

For extra help with Step 1, review
the 21st Century Skills Tutorial:
Ask Questions.

Quest CONNECTIONS

2 Investigate

As you read about ancient Egypt and Kush, collect five connections from your text to help you answer the Guiding Question. Three connections are already chosen for you.

Connect to Egypt's Social Pyramid

Lesson 1 How Was Egyptian Society Organized?

Here's a connection! Look at the social pyramid diagram in your text. The pharaoh is at the top. What roles do people on the other levels fulfill? How do they support you, the pharaoh? What does this diagram tell you about being a great pharaoh?

How do you, as pharaoh, benefit the people?

Connect to The Victory of Ramses II

Primary Source The Victory of Ramses II

Here's another connection! What does this primary source tell you about the power of a pharaoh in ancient Egypt? According to the poem, how does Ramses II prove his worthiness to be pharaoh?

What questions would you ask Ramses II if you could talk to him?

Connect to The Great Pyramid of Giza

Lesson 2 Architecture and Art

What does this connection tell you about Egyptian society during the reign of Khufu? What does the pyramid say about Khufu as a pharaoh?

What were Egyptian pharaohs trying to accomplish by building pyramids?

It's Your Turn! **Find two more connections. Fill in the title of your connections, then answer the questions. Connections may be images, primary sources, maps, or text.**

Your Choice | Connect to

Location in text

What is the main idea of this connection?

What does it tell you about how you, as pharaoh, should use your power?

Your Choice | Connect to

Location in text

What is the main idea of this connection?

What does it tell you about how you, as pharaoh, should use your power?

③ Examine Primary Sources

Examine the primary and secondary sources provided online or from your teacher. Fill in the chart to show how these sources provide further information about how to become a great pharaoh. The first one is completed for you.

Source	I am a great pharaoh because . . .
Hymn to the Nile	I fulfill all of my duties to worship the gods and keep them sending the flood waters to nourish the crops and feed the people.
Tomb of Tutankhamun	
Edwin Smith Surgical Papyrus	
Judgment of the Dead	
Luxury Products Imported by Ancient Egypt	

INTERACTIVE

For extra help with Step 3, review the 21st Century Skills Tutorials: **Analyze Primary and Secondary Sources** and **Analyze Images**.

Quest FINDINGS

4 Write Your Monument Inscription

Now it's time to put together all of the information you have gathered and use it to write your inscription.

1. **Prepare to Write** You have collected connections and explored primary and secondary sources that show how to be a great pharaoh. Look through your notes and decide which accomplishments you want to highlight in your monument inscription. Record them here.

Accomplishments

2. Write a Draft Using evidence from the clues you found and the documents you explored, write a draft of your inscription. Introduce yourself in character as pharaoh, then describe your accomplishments. Be sure to use vivid details that spring from evidence in the documents you've studied in this Quest.

3. Share With a Partner Exchange your draft with a partner. Tell your partner what you like about his or her draft, and suggest any improvements.

4. Finalize Your Inscription Revise your inscription. Correct any grammatical or spelling errors. Finally, make a sketch of your monument showing your inscription.

5. Reflect on the Quest Think about your experience completing this topic's Quest. What did you learn about ancient Egypt and its pharaohs? What questions do you still have about ancient Egypt? How will you answer them?

Reflections

 INTERACTIVE

For extra help with Step 4, review the 21st Century Skills Tutorial: **Write an Essay**.

Take Notes

Literacy Skills: Main Idea and Details Use what you have read to complete the table. In each space, write one main idea and two details. The first one has been completed for you.

The Nile River Valley	How Did Egyptian Civilization Develop?	The Kingdoms of Egypt
Main Idea: The Nile River strongly affected life in ancient Egypt. **Details:** Strips of fertile land between deserts supported farming. Unpredictable flooding could lead to crop failure and widespread hunger.	**Main Idea:** **Details:**	**Main Idea:** **Details:**

How Was Egyptian Society Organized?	Egyptian Religion	Great Rulers
Main Idea: **Details:**	**Main Idea:** **Details:**	**Main Idea:** **Details:**

INTERACTIVE

For extra help, review the 21st Century Skills Tutorial: **Identify Main Ideas and Details.**

Practice Vocabulary

Word Map Study the word map for the word *cataract*. Characteristics are words or phrases that relate to the word in the center of the word map. Non-characteristics are words and phrases not associated with the word. Use the blank word map to explore the meaning of the word *pharaoh*. Then make word maps of your own for these words: *mummy, dynasty, bureaucracy, delta,* and *artisan*.

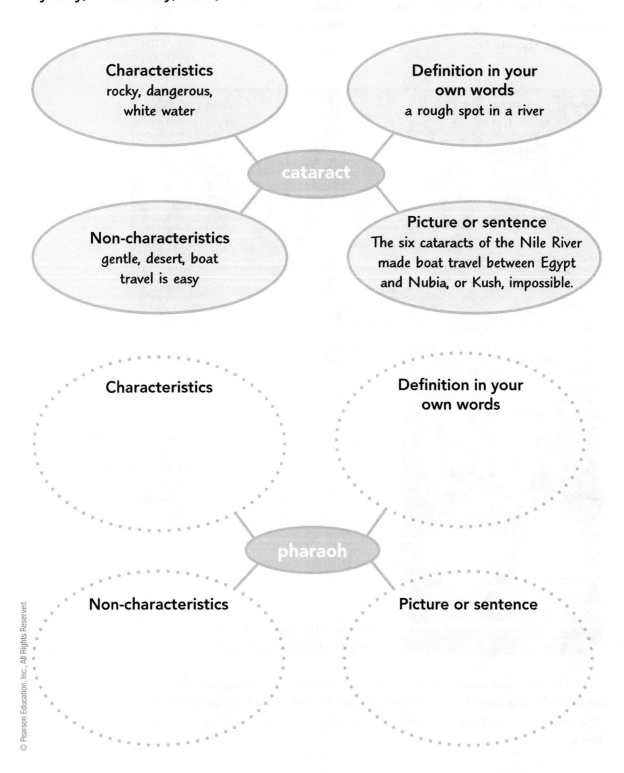

Characteristics
rocky, dangerous, white water

Definition in your own words
a rough spot in a river

cataract

Non-characteristics
gentle, desert, boat travel is easy

Picture or sentence
The six cataracts of the Nile River made boat travel between Egypt and Nubia, or Kush, impossible.

Characteristics

Definition in your own words

pharaoh

Non-characteristics

Picture or sentence

Quick Activity How Did Ancient Egyptians View Their Pharaohs?

Ancient Egypt is famous for the murals and sculptures that honor its pharaohs. In a small group, examine the images below. Think about why elaborate portrayals of Egyptian gods would be painted on the walls of pharaohs' tombs. What do you notice about the sculpture of the pharaoh that signifies his position in Egyptian society?

▲ This mural painting, from the tomb of Ramses I, depicts the pharoah between the gods Horus and Atum.

◀ Pharoah statue outside the Temple of Hatshepsut

Team Challenge! Imagine that you are visiting ancient Egypt. As a group, choose one of the images shown and write a postcard from the past, sharing your thoughts about how the pharaohs are depicted here.

Take Notes

Literacy Skills: Summarize Use what you have read to complete the table. In each space, summarize important ideas that you learned from the section, in your own words. Write your summaries in complete sentences. The first one has been completed for you.

Section	Summary
Writing and Literature	• Ancient Egyptians used hieroglyphics, which are symbols or drawings, to write. • Most Egyptians could not read or write hieroglyphics. Officials, called *scribes*, recorded information. Scribes wrote in ink on papyrus sheets. • Egyptians used hieroglyphics to write poems, stories, songs, histories, religious ideas, and other information.
Art and Architecture	• • •
Science and Mathematics	• • •

INTERACTIVE

For extra help, review the 21st Century Skills Tutorial: **Summarize**.

Practice Vocabulary

Sentence Revision Revise each sentence so that the underlined vocabulary word is used logically. Be sure not to change the vocabulary word. The first sentence is completed for you.

1. Ancient Egyptians used <u>hieroglyphics</u> to represent letters in a word.
   Ancient Egyptians used <u>hieroglyphics</u> to represent words or sounds.

2. Egyptians wrote in ink on a paper-like material called <u>papyrus</u>, made from trees.

3. During the Old Kingdom, large numbers of workers built massive <u>pyramids</u> to serve as palaces for pharaohs.

4. Skilled Egyptian artists made colossal <u>sculptures</u> of royal officials to stand outside their temples.

5. Egyptians learned a great deal about human <u>anatomy</u> from their work with engineers and used this knowledge to become skilled doctors and surgeons.

Quick Activity How Did They Do It?

With a partner or small group, examine this modern-day photo of the Great Pyramid of King Khufu at Giza.

Did you notice the stone blocks that were used to build the Great Pyramid? How did the ancient Egyptians move these massive blocks across the sand to the construction site? No one knows for sure, but the photo includes an important clue.

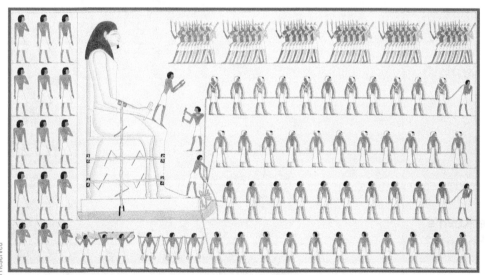

▲ Recreation of a wall painting showing the moving of a statue of a pharoah

Team Challenge! How do you think they did it? Draw or write your theory on a sheet of paper, then post your ideas in your classroom. Take a gallery walk to view everyone's ideas, then compare them to what the experts hypothesize by searching online.

Take Notes

Literacy Skills: Analyze Cause and Effect Use what you have read to complete the table. List appropriate causes from the lesson in the middle column and their effects in the right column. Be sure to record two cause-and-effect relationships for each section. The first one has been completed for you.

Section	Cause	Effect
Why Was Trade Important for Egypt and Kush?	Egypt wanted gold and other luxury items that it did not possess itself.	Egypt began trading its goods to Kush in exchange for gold, ivory, and ebony.
How Did Kush Develop?		
Kush and Egypt		
What Were Kush's Accomplishments?		

👆 **INTERACTIVE**

For extra help, review the 21st Century Skills Tutorial: **Analyze Cause and Effect**.

Practice Vocabulary

Matching Logic Using your knowledge of the underlined vocabulary words, draw a line from each sentence in Column 1 to match it with the sentence in Column 2 to which it logically belongs.

Column 1	Column 2
1. To obtain resources that it did not have, Egypt began engaging in <u>commerce</u> with nearby countries.	Scholars have yet to figure out the language recorded in this alphabet.
2. In addition to gold, Egyptians traded with Kush for <u>ebony</u> and <u>ivory</u>.	New Kingdom pharaohs signed peace treaties with former enemies, such as the Hittites, to promote trade.
3. As a result of increasing trade, Egypt and Kush developed a relationship of <u>interdependence</u>.	Closer economic ties led to an exchange of cultures and ideas.
4. Unlike ancient Egyptians, Kushites developed an alphabetic script called <u>Meroitic script</u>.	In return, Kush came to rely on Egyptian grain.

© Pearson Education, Inc., All Rights Reserved

Writer's Workshop Explanatory Essay

As you read, build a response to this question: **How did geography affect the people of ancient Egypt and Kush?** The prompts below will walk you through the process.

Lesson 1 Writing Task: Develop a Clear Thesis Express in one sentence the most significant effects of the region's geography on ancient Egyptians. This will be your thesis statement for the explanatory essay that you will write at the end of the Topic.

After you read Lessons 2 and 3, re-read your thesis statement. Is it still valid? Does it need any revision to include the information you learned in Lessons 2 and 3? If so, write your revision here:

Lesson 2 Writing Task: Support Thesis With Details Refer to the statement you wrote in Lesson 1. What details from Lessons 1 and 2 support your point? Add details from Lesson 3 after you read the lesson.

Lesson 1	
Lesson 2	
Lesson 3	

Lesson 3 Writing Task: Organize Your Essay Make an outline of your essay. Start with an introduction, followed by three paragraphs that explain the effect of geography on ancient Egypt and Kush, and end with a conclusion. Use the chart below to help you.

Introduction Thesis	
Effect 1 Evidence	
Effect 2 Evidence	
Effect 3 Evidence	
Conclusion	

Writing Task Using the outline you created in Lesson 3, answer the following question in a five-paragraph explanatory essay: **How did geography affect the lives of ancient Egyptians and Nubians?**

As you write, consider using the following cause-and-effect signal words to transition between points: *because, consequently, therefore, for this reason,* and *as a result.*

TOPIC 4

Early Civilizations of India Preview

Essential Question **What makes a culture endure?**

Before you begin this topic, think about the Essential Question by answering the following question.

1. Culture includes art, music, literature, food, and dance. It also includes shared ideas about how to live, what to value, and religious beliefs. What would you like people to know about your own culture? Write three ideas below.

Timeline Skills

As you read, write and/or draw at least three events from the topic. Draw a line from each event to its correct position on the timeline.

3000 BCE	2500 BCE	2000 BCE	1500 BCE

Map Skills

Using the map in your text, label the outline map with the places listed. Then, color the mountains, water, and the Indian subcontinent.

Indian Ocean   Indus River   Hindu Kush

Ganges River   Arabian Sea   Himalayas

Deccan Plateau   Bay of Bengal

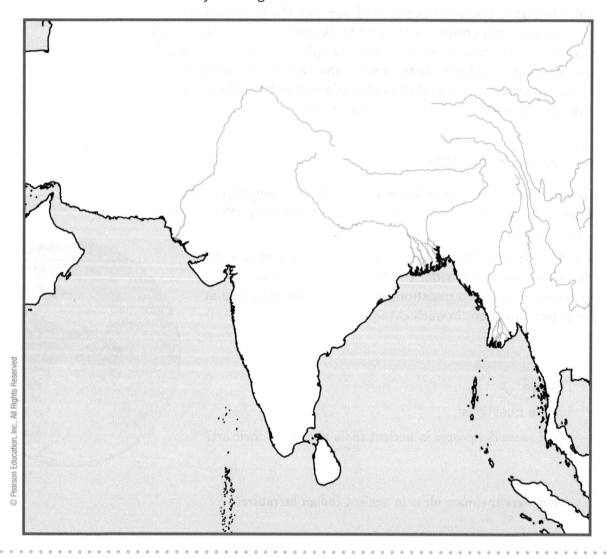

500 BCE	1 CE	500 CE

Quest
Project-Based Learning Inquiry

A Trip Through India

On this Quest, you will need to find out how the influences of ancient India still endure in modern Indian culture. You will examine sources from ancient India and find examples of how they remain a part of modern culture. At the end of the Quest, you will create a travel brochure of some of the culturally and historically important sites that you would want to be sure to visit.

1 Ask Questions

As you begin your Quest, keep in mind the Guiding Question: **Where should you visit?** and the Essential Question: **What makes a culture endure?**

What other questions do you need to ask in order to answer these questions? Consider the following aspects of culture in ancient India. Two questions are filled in for you. Add at least two questions in each category.

Theme Arts and Literature

Sample questions:

What ideas did people in ancient India portray in their art?

What were the main ideas in ancient Indian literature?

Theme Geography

Theme Religion

Theme Rulers and Warfare

Theme Achievements

Theme My Additional Questions

INTERACTIVE

For extra help with Step 1, review the
21st Century Tutorial: **Ask Questions**.

② Investigate

As you read about ancient India, collect five connections from your text to help you answer the Guiding Question. Three connections are already chosen for you.

Connect to the Buddha

Primary Source The Life or Legend of Gaudama
Here's a connection! What did the Buddha learn from his meditation?

Why do you think Buddhism spread to other parts of the world and is still practiced today?

Connect to Asoka

Lesson 6 What Was Asoka's Legacy?

Encouraged by Asoka's conversion to Buddhism, Buddhists spread the teachings of the Buddha to neighboring regions. What could visitors learn about Buddhism by visiting a monastery outside of India?

Based on the photo of the Sri Lankan monastery, how might the practice of Buddhism today be both similar and different from ancient times?

Connect to the Guptas

Lesson 7 What Was Gupta Culture Like?

Here's another connection! Gupta culture was the golden age of India. What kinds of art were created during the Gupta reign?

How do you think this affects the culture of present-day India?

It's Your Turn! Find two more connections. Fill in the title of your connections, then answer the questions. Connections may be images, primary sources, maps, or text.

Your Choice | Connect to

Location

What is the main idea of this connection?

What does this tell you about how culture endures and where you should visit in India?

Your Choice | Connect to

Location

What is the main idea of this connection?

What does this tell you about how culture endures and where you should visit in India?

③ Conduct Research

You will need to conduct research about places to visit and things to do in India. With your group, start by making a list of possible places that you may want to highlight in your brochure. You may continue your list on a separate sheet of paper. Refine your list as you learn more. Assign researchers for each location. Be sure to take good notes as you research and collect photos that you might want to use.

Places to Visit	Assigned to

INTERACTIVE

For extra help with Step 3, review the 21st Century Tutorial: **Work in Teams**.

FINDINGS

④ Create a Travel Brochure

Once you have concluded your research, create a travel brochure that includes historical and cultural things to do and see in India. Your brochure should include specific information about each of the sites you'll visit. Be sure to include why the sites you have chosen are still relevant to the culture of present-day India.

Follow these steps to put together all of the information you have gathered and use it to create your brochure.

1. **Narrow Your Focus** You have collected connections and conducted research about places to visit that are of cultural and historical significance in India. Look through your notes, and decide with your group which places you will include and why.

2. **Write a Draft** Decide who in your group will be assigned to describe which place(s) and decide on the order in which to present the places selected. Then, write a rough draft describing each place and its significance. Assign someone in your group to write an introduction.

3. **Share with a Partner** Exchange your draft with other members of your group. Tell each other what you like about each draft and suggest improvements.

4. **Finalize Your Brochure** Correct any spelling or grammatical errors. Include photos with captions where they are relevant. Use technology to finalize and publish your brochure. Consider a layout and design that will be appealing and useful for your audience.

5. **Reflect on the Quest** Think about your experience completing this topic's Quest. What did you learn about ancient India and how its culture has endured into the present day? What questions do you still have about ancient India? How will you answer them?

Reflections

INTERACTIVE

For extra help with Step 4, review the 21st Century Tutorial: **Publish Your Work**.

Take Notes

Literacy Skills: Identify Main Ideas and Details Use what you have read to complete the table. In each space, write one main idea and two details. The first one has been completed for you.

What Is the Indian Subcontinent?
Main Idea: The Indian subcontinent is set apart from the rest of the continent. **Details:** The Himalayas and the Hindu Kush separate the continent geographically. The climate of the subcontinent is influenced by the mountains to the north and the ocean to the south.

Indus Valley Civilization	What Mysteries Surround the Indus Valley Civilization?
Main Idea: Details:	Main Idea: Details:

INTERACTIVE

For extra help, review the 21st Century Tutorial: **Identify Main Ideas and Details**.

Practice Vocabulary

Use a Word Bank **Choose one word from the word bank to fill in each blank. When you have finished, you will have a short summary of important ideas from the section.**

Word Bank

granary   subcontinent   citadel

river system   monsoon

The Indus Valley Civilization formed on the Indian

_____ around 7000 BCE. Geography was

very important to how the civilization developed. One important

geographic feature was the _____

that included the Indus River. Another was the summer

_____ winds that brought rain, causing the

rivers to flood. This fertile land meant that there was enough food

to save some in a _____, so everyone had

enough to eat. As the cities grew, each one protected itself with a

_____.

Quick Activity Museum Gallery

Examine the artifacts shown. With a partner, select one artifact to focus on.

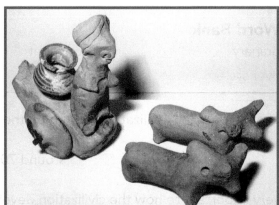

Team Challenge! Imagine that you and your partner are writing the description of your artifact for the museum exhibit. Write a short description of the artifact. Then, write what you think it tells us about life in the Indus Valley.

Take Notes

Literacy Skills: Summarize Use what you have read to complete the table. For each major topic in this section, write down 2–3 of the most important facts. Use your notes to write a summary of the section.

The Indo-Aryans	The Vedas	Caste

Summary:

INTERACTIVE

For extra help, review the 21st Century Tutorial: **Summarize**.

Practice Vocabulary

Sentence Builder **Finish the sentences below with a key term from this section. You may have to change the form of the word(s) to complete the sentences.**

Word Bank

Veda   caste

jati   varna

1. A fixed social class into which a person is born is called a

   ....
   ....

2. One of two social groupings that is based on one's skill is called

   ....
   ....

3. The sacred hymns written by the Indo-Aryans came to be known as

   the ....

4. One of two social groupings that is based on one's occupation is

   called ....

Take Notes

Literacy Skills: Sequencing Use what you have read to complete the sequence. In each space, write one main idea that traces the development of Hinduism in India.

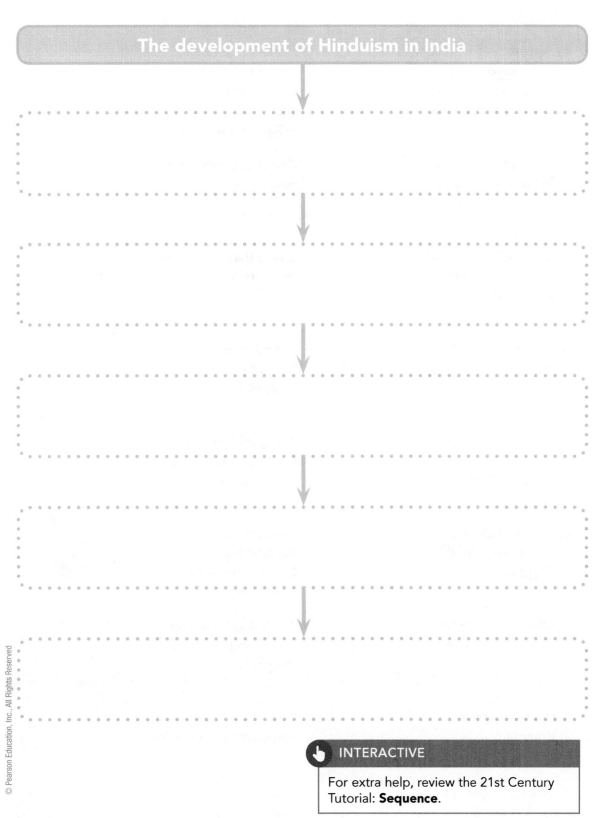

The development of Hinduism in India

INTERACTIVE

For extra help, review the 21st Century Tutorial: **Sequence**.

Practice Vocabulary

Matching Logic Using your knowledge of the underlined vocabulary words, draw a line from each sentence in Column 1 to match it with the sentence in Column 2 to which it logically belongs.

Column 1	Column 2
1. Brahmanism is the name some scholars give to early Hinduism.	These thinkers and teachers wanted to think and talk about religious ideas.
2. You must always follow your dharma.	The soul is reborn in a new body.
3. Gurus often left their homes to go live in the forest.	Living things are never to be harmed.
4. The final goal of Hinduism is moksha.	Hinduism is flexible because all Gods are a form of this.
5. When people die, they will most likely go through reincarnation.	The goal is to live your life so you can return as something better.
6. You must always follow the rule of ahimsa.	When your soul is liberated, you may become one with Brahman.
7. All of your actions affect your karma.	A religion based on rituals and sacrifices to the gods.
8. Hindus worship Brahman.	One of the goals is to always do what is right.

Quick Activity Ancient Indian Poetry

These excerpts from Book XII of the Vedas are part of a hymn praising Prithivī, an ancient Hindu deity of the Earth. Examine the passages with a partner. Pick two and explain them in your own words in the spaces below.

1:   May she, the Queen of all that is and is to be, may Prithivī make ample space and room for us.

7:   May Earth, may Prithivī, always protected with ceaseless care by Gods who never slumber, May she pour out for us delicious nectar, may she bedew us with a flood of splendour.

8:   She who at first was water in the ocean, whom with their wondrous powers the sages [wise men] followed, May she whose heart is in the highest heaven, compassed [circled] about with truth, and everlasting, May she, this Earth, bestow upon us lustre [shininess, splendor], and grant us power in loftiest dominion [control].

18: A vast abode [home] hast thou become, the Mighty. Great stress is on thee, press[ure] and agitation, but with unceasing care great Indra guards thee. So make us shine, O Earth, us with the splendour of gold. Let no man look on us with hatred.

44: May Earth the Goddess, she who bears her treasure stored up in many a place, gold, gems, and riches, Giver of opulence [luxury, wealth], grant great possessions to us bestowing them with love and favour.

1.

2.

Team Challenge! What did the Earth mean to people in ancient India as suggested by this hymn? Write a few words or phrases on a file card or slip of paper. Take turns sharing what you wrote.

Take Notes

Literacy Skills: Compare and Contrast Use what you have read to complete the table.

Siddhartha's Life Before Enlightenment	Siddhartha's Life After Enlightenment

 INTERACTIVE

For extra help, review the 21st Century Tutorial: **Compare and Contrast**.

Practice Vocabulary

Words in Context For each question below, write an answer that shows your understanding of the boldfaced key term.

1. Why is **meditation** an important part of Buddhism?

2. What happened when Buddha achieved **enlightenment**?

3. Why is it important for Buddhists to reach the goal of achieving **nirvana**?

4. Why did Buddhists live in **monasteries**?

5. What is the focus of the Buddhist sect **Theravada Buddhism**?

6. What is the focus of the Buddhist sect **Mahayana Buddhism**?

Take Notes

Literacy Skills: Analyze Cause and Effect Use what you have read to
complete the table. For each cause given, write the effect.

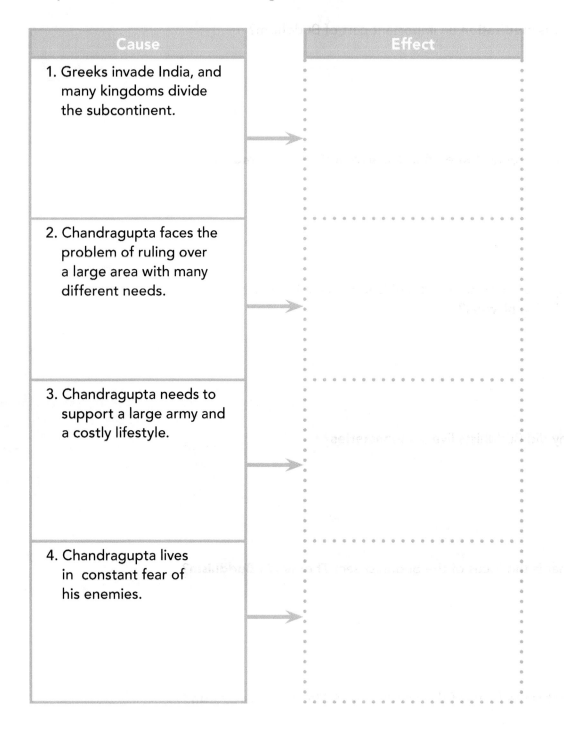

Cause	Effect
1. Greeks invade India, and many kingdoms divide the subcontinent.	
2. Chandragupta faces the problem of ruling over a large area with many different needs.	
3. Chandragupta needs to support a large army and a costly lifestyle.	
4. Chandragupta lives in constant fear of his enemies.	

INTERACTIVE

For extra help, review the 21st Century
Tutorial: **Analyze Cause and Effect**.

Practice Vocabulary

Sentence Revision Revise each sentence so that the underlined vocabulary word is used logically. Be sure not to change the vocabulary word. The first one is done for you.

1. As part of his <u>strategy</u>, Chandragupta attacked regions of India in no particular order.
   As part of his <u>strategy</u>, Chandragupta attacked regions of India from outside to inside.

2. Chandragupta governed each <u>province</u> by himself.

3. Chandragupta set up a <u>bureaucracy</u> so that there would be no rules or regulations.

4. Chandragupta's <u>subjects</u> spied on him.

Lesson 6 Asoka's Rule

Take Notes

Literacy Skills: Sequence Use what you have read to complete the
sequence of events that led to prosperity and peace during Asoka's rule.

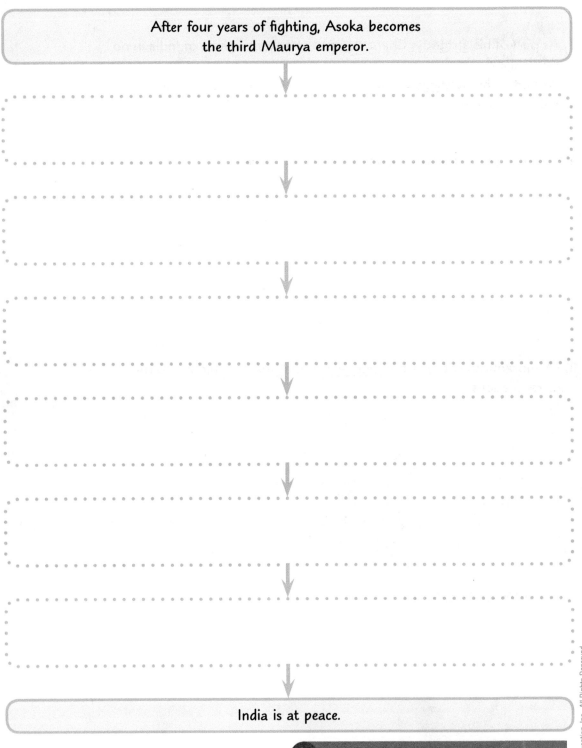

After four years of fighting, Asoka becomes
the third Maurya emperor.

India is at peace.

👆 **INTERACTIVE**

For extra help, review the 21st Century
Tutorial: **Sequence**.

Practice Vocabulary

True or False? Decide whether each statement below is true or false. Circle T or F, and then explain your answer. Be sure to include the underlined vocabulary word in your explanation.

1. **T / F** A <u>stupa</u> is another word for a Buddhist monastery.

2. **T / F** <u>Tolerance</u> is a willingness to respect differences in beliefs and customs.

Take Notes

Literacy Skills: Summarize Use what you have read to complete the table. Fill in notes about government, culture, and achievements under the Gupta empire. Then, use your notes to write a summary of this lesson.

Government	Culture	Achievements

Summary:

INTERACTIVE

For extra help, review the 21st Century Tutorial: **Summarize**.

Practice Vocabulary

Word Map Study the word map for the word *citizenship*.
Characteristics are words or phrases that relate to the word in the
center of the word map. Non-characteristics are words and phrases
not associated with the word. Use the blank word map to explore the
meaning of the word *numeral*. Then make word maps of your own for
these words: *decimal system* and *metallurgy*.

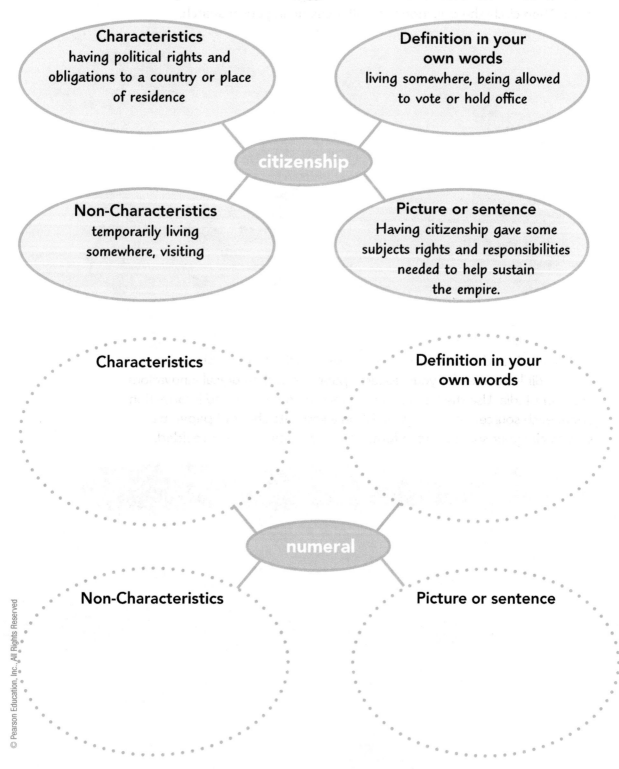

Writing Workshop Research Paper

In this topic, you will write a research paper on the technological innovations of ancient India. The prompts below will help walk you through this process.

Lessons 1 and 2 Writing Task: Generate Questions to Focus Research

Write three to four questions about technological innovations in ancient India. Then circle the question you will focus on in your research.

Lessons 3, 4, and 5 Writing Task: Find, Use, and Cite Credible Sources

Find credible sources for your research paper on technological innovations in ancient India. Use the table below to record your notes and information about each source. Continue your list on a separate sheet of paper. Be sure to cite your sources in the format that your teacher has provided.

Sources	Notes

Lesson 6 Writing Task: Support Ideas with Evidence Think about what you understand so far about technological innovation in ancient India. Use the spaces below to help you organize your ideas and the evidence that supports them to draw conclusions. Then write a thesis statement.

Conclusion:

Evidence:

Evidence:

Evidence:

Thesis:

Lesson 7 Writing Task: Write an Introduction Using your thesis statement and the information you have gathered, write an introductory paragraph for your research paper on a separate sheet of paper. Explain what you concluded from your research and how you are going to show it in the body of the paper.

Writing Task Using the introductory paragraph you wrote, complete your research paper discussing technological innovations in ancient India. Use transition words to clarify your ideas and make good connections between your ideas and supporting evidence found in your sources.

Essential Question How do societies preserve order?

Before you begin this topic, think about the Essential Question by completing the following activity.

1. Order means a state of peace and security, free from chaos, violence, and unruly behavior. Why do you think people in your society would want to preserve order?

2. Preview the topic by skimming lesson titles, headings, and images and captions. On a sheet of paper, list features of ancient Chinese society that you believe helped preserve order.

Timeline Skills

As you read, write and/or draw at least three events from the topic. Draw a line from each event to its correct position on the timeline.

5000 BCE

2000 BCE

Map Skills

Using the map in your text, label the outline map with the places listed. Then color in water, mountains, desert, and fertile river valleys.

Bay of Bengal	Chang River	East China Sea
Gobi Desert	Himalayas	Huang River
Pacific Ocean	South China Sea	Plateau of Tibet
Xi River	Yellow Sea	Shang Civilization
Zhou Civilization	Qin Dynasty	Han Dynasty

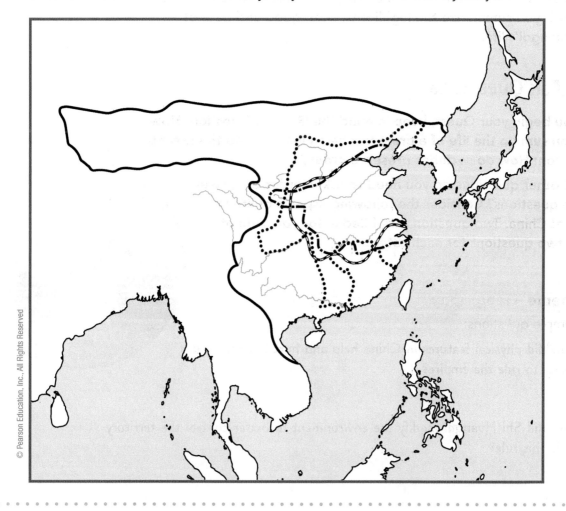

1000 BCE	1 CE

Quest

Document-Based Writing Inquiry

Evaluating a Leader's Legacy

On this Quest, you will explore primary and secondary sources about ancient China under the rule of Shi Huangdi. You will use what you learn to write an obituary, the life story of someone who has died, in which you summarize the highlights, both good and bad, of Shi Huangdi's life.

1 Ask Questions

As you begin your Quest, keep in mind the Guiding Question: **How do you sum up the life of a great but harsh leader?** and the Essential Question: **How do societies preserve order?**

What other questions do you need to ask in order to answer these questions? Consider the following aspects of life in ancient China. Two questions are filled in for you. Add at least two questions for each category.

Theme Geography

Sample questions:

How did physical features in China help and hurt Shi Huangdi's ability to rule the empire?

How did Shi Huangdi modify the environment to better control the territory under his rule?

Theme Government

Theme Social Structure

Theme Economic Activity

Theme Religion and Culture

Theme My Additional Questions

 INTERACTIVE

For extra help with Step 1, review the 21st Century Skills Tutorial: **Ask Questions**.

Quest CONNECTIONS

2 Investigate

As you read about ancient China, collect five connections from your text to help you answer the Guiding Question. Three connections are already chosen for you.

Connect to the Unification of China

Lesson 4 Unity Under the Qin

Here's a connection! Study the infographic. How did Shi Huangdi try to standardize and centralize aspects of Chinese life? How did these methods help unify China under his rule?

What benefits and drawbacks did Shi Huangdi's efforts to create uniform standards have for China?

Connect to Orders to Burn Records

Analysis Skills Draw Sound Conclusions from Sources

Here's another connection! Read the primary source excerpt.
What orders did Shi Huangdi give to try to control history and literature
in Chinese society?

Why do you think Shi Huangdi ordered such harsh methods?

Connect to Confucian Ideals

Primary Source Confucius, *The Analects*

Confucius lived and wrote his ideas before the rise of the Qin dynasty.
Read the primary source excerpt. What virtues does Confucius
suggest would be admirable in a ruler?

How did Shi Huangdi succeed or fail to live up to Confucian ideals of leadership?

Now it's your turn! **Find two more connections on your own. Fill in the title of your connections, then answer the questions. Connections may be images, primary sources, maps, or text.**

Your Choice | Connect to

Location in text

What is the main idea of this connection?

What does it tell you about the legacy of Shi Huangdi as a ruler?

Your Choice | Connect to

Location in text

What is the main idea of this connection?

What does it tell you about the legacy of Shi Huangdi as a ruler?

③ Examine Primary and Secondary Sources

Examine the primary and secondary sources provided online or from your teacher. Fill in the chart to show how these sources provide further information about the legacy of Shi Huangdi. The first one is completed for you.

Source	Shi Huangdi's strengths and weaknesses as a ruler include . . .
Biography of Qin Shihuang	bringing harmony, order, and justice to China; standardizing tools and measurements as well as writing; laying out a clear set of laws; regulating local customs, and making waterways and dividing up the land to support farming.
Wei Liao's Report on Shi Huangdi	
Construction of the Great Wall of China	
Shi Huangdi's Tomb Complex	
The Five Confucian Classics	

👆 **INTERACTIVE**

For extra help with Step 3, review the 21st Century Skills Tutorials: **Analyze Primary and Secondary Sources** and **Analyze Images**.

4 Write an Obituary for Shi Huangdi

Now it's time to put together all of the information you have gathered and use it to write an obituary for the Qin emperor Shi Huangdi.

1. **Prepare to Write** You have collected connections and explored primary and secondary sources that show the legacy of Shi Huangdi. Look through your notes and decide which achievements and shortcomings of his rule you want to include in your obituary. Record them here.

Achievements and Shortcomings of Shi Huangdi's Rule

2. **Organize Your Ideas** On a separate sheet of paper, make an outline for your obituary. List the achievements and shortcomings of Shi Huangdi's rule and put them in the order you want to discuss them. You may wish to organize your ideas in a chronological sequence or by theme, such as his impact on government and his impact on culture.

3. **Write a Draft** Using evidence from the clues you found and the documents you explored, write a draft of your obituary for Shi Huangdi. Be sure to include basic biographical information, such as when he was born and when he died. Then, describe the ways in which he affected Chinese society, good and bad. Be sure to use vivid details from the documents you've studied in this Quest.

4. **Revise Your Draft** Exchange your draft with a partner. Tell your partner what you like about his or her draft and suggest any improvements. Revise your draft based on your partner's feedback. Then, read your draft aloud. Correct any grammatical or spelling errors.

5. **Reflect on the Quest** Think about your experience completing this topic's Quest. What did you learn about ancient China under the rule of Shi Huangdi? What questions do you still have about the Qin dynasty and its society? How will you answer them?

Reflections

Take Notes

Literacy Skills: Summarize Use what you have read to complete the chart. Summarize key ideas about the geography of China and the Shang dynasty. The first one has been completed for you. Then write a summary of the lesson in the space below.

Geography of China

River Systems
China's two main rivers, the Huang and Chang, provide water for farming and movement of goods. The Huang River picks up loess and deposits it on the North China Plain when it overflows its banks. The fertile North China Plain was well-suited for agriculture and became the site of the first large settlements in China.

Isolation

The Shang Dynasty

The Shang Rise

Shang Government

Achievements

My Summary:

 INTERACTIVE

For extra help, review the 21st Century Skills Tutorial: **Summarize**.

Practice Vocabulary

Vocabulary Quiz Show Some quiz shows ask a question and expect the contestant to give the answer. In other shows, the contestant is given an answer and must supply the question. If the blank is in the Question column, write the question that would result in the answer in the Answer column. If the question is supplied, write the answer.

Question	Answer
1. What is a fine, dust-like material that can form soil?	1.
2.	2. dike
3. What are the earliest written records from China?	3.
4.	4. pictographs
5. What type of written character represents a complete word or phrase?	5.

Take Notes

Literacy Skills: Identify Main Idea and Details Use what you have read to complete the table. In each space write one main idea and two details. The first one has been completed for you.

Main Ideas	Supporting Details
The Zhou overthrew the Shang and started a new dynasty.	• Shang kings had become corrupt, and many Shang warriors accepted the Zhou king as their new ruler. • Zhou rulers claimed that their victory against the Shang proved that they had the support of heaven.
	• •
	• •
	• •
	• •

INTERACTIVE

For extra help, review the 21st Century Skills Tutorial: **Identify Main Ideas and Details**.

Practice Vocabulary

Words in Context For each question below, write an answer that shows your understanding of the boldfaced key term.

1. How did Chinese leaders use the idea of the **Mandate of Heaven** to justify the overthrow of a dynasty?

2. How did **warlords** weaken the Zhou dynasty?

3. How did the Warring States period result in **chaos**?

Quick Activity Letter to the People

You are the ruler of the new Zhou dynasty. Officials at your court have warned that the Chinese people are fearful of your power. You need to announce to the people how and why the Zhou are now in charge. Work with a partner or in a small group to complete the letter to the people below, which will be posted throughout the empire.

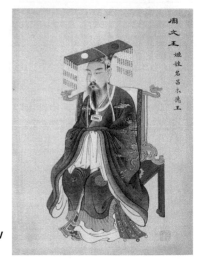

LETTER TO THE PEOPLE

I, the Zhou ruler, hereby establish a new dynasty and a new era! I hold power by right of the Mandate of Heaven.

Explain the Mandate of Heaven:

The Zhou defeated the Shang because the Shang had lost the support of heaven.

Explain which actions of the Shang caused them to lose the Mandate of Heaven:

I and my descendents will hold the Mandate of Heaven for many, many generations because we will rule wisely, and we will achieve great things.

Explain what the Zhou and you, as ruler, intend to do:

Team Challenge! Appoint a group spokesperson to read your letter aloud to the class. Discuss which letters contain the best explanations and use those to create a single class letter to post in the classroom.

Take Notes

Literacy Skills: Compare and Contrast Use what you have read to complete the table. Describe key beliefs and practices of spirit and ancestor veneration, Confucianism, and Daoism. The first one has been completed for you.

Spirit and Ancestor Veneration	Confucianism	Daoism
1. What kinds of spirits did people believe in? *good spirits and bad spirits*	1. Who founded it?	1. Who founded it?
2. Where did different spirits dwell?	2. What were its goals?	2. What were its goals?
3. Why did people honor ancestors?	3. What text contains its beliefs?	3. What text contains its beliefs?
4. How did people honor ancestors?	4. What were its core teachings?	4. What were its core teachings?

INTERACTIVE

For extra help, review the 21st Century Skills Tutorial: **Compare and Contrast**.

Practice Vocabulary

Matching Logic Using your knowledge of the underlined vocabulary words, draw a line from each sentence in Column 1 to match it with the sentence in Column 2 to which it logically belongs.

Column 1	Column 2
1. Confucianism was an important <u>philosophy</u> in ancient China.	Confucius argued that it was "the source of all virtues."
2. Confucius stressed the importance of <u>filial piety</u>.	This view of the world had a lasting impact on Chinese culture.

Quick Activity   How Do Ideas Change Lives?

How did Confucianism and Daoism shape life in China? Read the quotes from Confucius and Laozi below. Work with a partner to explain each in your own words.

"The art of governing is to keep its affairs before the mind without weariness, and to practice them with undeviating consistency."

—*Confucius*

"Those who are born with the possession of knowledge are the highest class of men. Those who learn, and so readily get possession of knowledge, are the next. Those who are dull and stupid, and yet compass the learning, are another class next to these. As to those who are dull and stupid and yet do not learn; they are the lowest of the people."

—*Confucius*

"If any one desires to take the Empire in hand and govern it, I see that he will not succeed. The Empire is a divine utensil which may not be roughly handled."

—*Laozi*

"I have three precious things, which I hold fast and prize. The first is gentleness; the second is frugality; the third is humility, which keeps me from putting myself before others. Be gentle and you can be bold; be frugal, and you can be liberal; avoid putting yourself before others, and you can become a leader among men."

—*Laozi*

Team Challenge! Which philosophy do you think offered more to the ancient Chinese? Form opinion groups with those favoring the views of Confucius on one side of the room and those supporting the views of Laozi on the other. Be ready to defend your choice.

Take Notes

Literacy Skills: Use Evidence Use what you have read to complete the charts. List evidence from the lesson to support each idea. The first one has been completed for you.

Shi Huangdi unified the kingdoms of northern China and established the Qin dynasty.

He united the Warring States.	He defended the empire.	He established uniform standards.	He organized the empire.
King Zheng was skilled and ruthless and brought down rival kingdoms one by one.			

The Qin's strict laws helped forge a single nation from China's diverse regions but led to the downfall of the Qin dynasty.

The Qin government followed Legalism.	The Qin had harsh laws.	The Qin aimed for thought control.	The Qin ultimately fell from power.

INTERACTIVE

For extra help, review the 21st Century Skills Tutorial: **Support Ideas with Evidence**.

Practice Vocabulary

Vocabulary Quiz Show Some quiz shows ask a question and expect the contestant to give the answer. In other shows, the contestant is given an answer and must supply the question. If the blank is in the Question column, write the question that would result in the answer in the Answer column. If the question is supplied, write the answer.

Question	Answer
1.	1. Great Wall
2.	2. standardize
3. What system of governing has strong laws and harsh punishments?	3.
4.	4. censor

Take Notes

Literacy Skills: Analyze Cause and Effect Use what you have read to complete the table. Record one or more effects for each cause listed. The first one has been completed for you.

Causes	Effects
To learn how to govern, Liu Bang consulted with Confucian scholars.	The new Han government followed Confucian teachings. The emperor encouraged learning and ended many harsh rules of the Qin. He lowered taxes, reduced punishments for crimes, and ended censorship.
Han emperors sought to avoid the disunity that the Zhou dynasty faced.	
Emperor Wudi wanted to find talented officials.	
Emperor Wudi needed allies to fight against the nomadic Xiongnu.	
Zhang Qian described exotic lands and horses that sweat blood.	
Han emperors made it illegal to export silk worms from China.	
The Silk Road became a path for the exchange of products and ideas.	

INTERACTIVE

For extra help, review the 21st Century Skills Tutorial: **Analyze Cause and Effect**.

Practice Vocabulary

Sentence Builder Finish the sentences below with a key term from this section. You may have to change the form of the words to complete the sentences.

Word Bank

civil service	cuisine	envoy
official	Silk Road	

1. The network of trade routes connecting China to Central Asia and Southwest Asia was known as the

2. In the Han dynasty, many layers of government existed between the villages at the bottom and the emperor at the top, and these layers included people assigned to their positions, or

3. Various types of food exchanged through trade enriched Chinese

4. Government workers who were selected based on skills and knowledge made up the

5. The Han created trade relations with kingdoms to the east by sending representatives of the emperor, known as

Take Notes

Literacy Skills: Summarize Use what you have read to complete the chart. Record important ideas from each section, and use what you have read to write a summary statement about the lesson. The first one has been completed for you.

Han Society	Economic Life	Han Achievements
The Social Order Scholars had the highest rank, followed by farmers and artisans. Below them were merchants, with slaves at the bottom.	Agriculture	China's Traditional Arts
Family Life	Industry	Advances in Science
The Role of Women	Controlling Prices and Production	Chinese Inventions

Summary Statement

INTERACTIVE

For extra help, review the 21st Century Skills Tutorial: **Summarize**.

Practice Vocabulary

Matching Logic Using your knowledge of the underlined vocabulary words, draw a line from each sentence in Column 1 to match it with the sentence in Column 2 to which it logically belongs.

Column 1	Column 2
1. Wudi turned salt mining and iron production into <u>monopolies</u>.	A metal jar dropped small balls when an earthquake was felt.
2. Among important traditional crafts practiced in the Han empire was <u>calligraphy</u>.	Artists added this hard finish to metal and wood objects.
3. Han inventors developed a <u>seismometer</u>.	The state controlled the production of these goods.
4. The Han excelled at the making of <u>lacquer</u>.	This therapy used needles to cure sickness and stop pain.
5. Han doctors began using <u>acupuncture</u> as a treatment.	Writers expressed emotion in the way that they painted Chinese characters.

Writing Workshop Arguments

As you read, build a response to this question: **Which ancient Chinese values or belief systems helped produce the most effective government in ancient China?** The prompts below will help walk you through the process.

Lesson 1 Writing Task: Introduce Claims List the values that you think made the Shang successful. Then write a sentence claiming that those values made the Shang government effective.

Lesson 2 Writing Task: Support Claims In the table, identify what values you think helped the Shang and the Zhou govern effectively, and what challenges each government faced.

Shang	
Zhou	

Lesson 3 Writing Task: Support Claims Complete the table by describing what values from each philosophy make government more effective and how those values support your claims about the Shang and Zhou.

Confucianism	
Daoism	

Lesson 4 Writing Task: Use Credible Sources On a separate sheet of paper, list primary and secondary sources from the text, as well as appropriate sources from the library and the Internet, that support your claims. Consider the values that made the Qin effective, and find sources that support claims about those values. On note cards, begin taking notes and citing your sources.

Lesson 5 Writing Task: Shape Tone Consider the values or belief systems behind the success of the Han. What claims could you make about those? Now consider your claims and evidence from previous lessons. What values or belief systems were *most* effective in governing China? Draft an argument for this claim. Be sure to include at least three details from the text and from other sources to support your claim. When you finish, share your argument with a partner. Discuss whether your arguments are clear, accurate, organized, and respectful in tone. Revise your argument based on this feedback.

Lesson 6 Writing Task: Write a Conclusion To complete your argument, write one to three sentences summarizing your argument, and explaining why it matters. Write your conclusion on a separate sheet of paper.

Writing Task Using your notes, revise your draft into an argument that answers this question: Which ancient Chinese values or belief systems helped produce the most effective government in ancient China? Reread your argument and correct it for misspellings, other errors, or points of confusion. After revising it, present it to the class.

Essential Question **What is the best form of government?**

Before you begin this topic, think about the Essential Question by answering the following questions.

1. What are some ways in which local, state, or federal government affects your life?

. . . .

2. Preview the topic by skimming lesson titles, headings, and graphics. Then place a check mark next to ancient Greek ideas or practices that you think have had the greatest influence on the modern world.

__monarchy   __democracy

__slavery   __colonization

Timeline Skills

As you read, write and/or draw at least three events from the topic. Draw a line from each event to its correct position on the timeline.

. . . .

800 BCE	**700** BCE	**600** BCE

Map Skills

Using the map in your text, label the outline map with the places listed.
Then color in significant features of the region, such as mountains.

Europe   Asia   Greece   Aegean Sea

Ionian Sea   Mediterranean Sea   Athens   Sparta

Olympia   Troy   Peloponnesian Peninsula   Crete

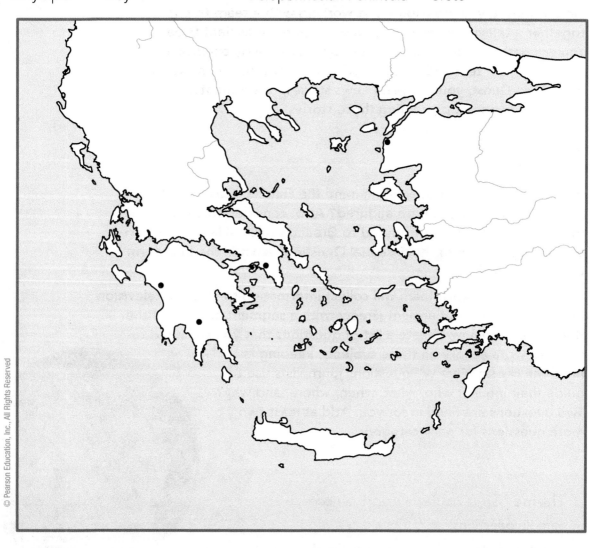

500 BCE	400 BCE	300 BCE

Quest

The Influence of Ancient Greece

On this Quest, you are a journalist working with a team to put together a television news magazine program on ancient Greece. You will gather information about ancient Greece by examining sources in your text and by conducting your own research. At the end of the Quest, you will write news stories, or segments, and perform a newscast presenting those stories.

1 Ask Questions

As you begin your Quest, keep in mind the Guiding Question: **Why has ancient Greece's culture endured?** Also, consider how ancient forms of government contributed to Greece's cultural legacy, as part of your exploration of the Essential Question: **What is the best form of government?**

For your project, each team will collect information to create a television news magazine about ancient Greece with a segment on each of the themes listed below. Create a list of questions that you will need to know to write a story on these subjects, keeping in mind the classic "Five W" questions journalists use to guide their inquiry: who, what, when, where, and why? Two questions are filled in for you. Add at least two more questions for each category.

Theme Government and Politics

Sample questions:

What kinds of government did the Greek city-states set up?

Which form of Greek government influenced many later governments, including the United States?

Theme Arts, including literature, sculpture, and architecture

Theme Science, medicine, or mathematics

Theme Sports and leisure

Theme My Additional Questions

 INTERACTIVE

For extra help with Step 1, review the 21st Century Tutorial: **Ask Questions**.

Quest CONNECTIONS

2 Investigate

As you read about ancient Greece, collect five connections from your text to help you answer the Guiding Question. Three connections are already chosen for you.

Connect to Athenian Democracy

Lesson 2 How did Athenian Democracy Work?

Here's a connection! Look at the diagram on Athenian Democracy. In what ways did Athenian democracy influence the government of the United States?

What does this diagram reveal about the difference between Athenian democracy and democracy in the United States?

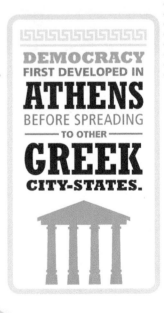

DEMOCRACY FIRST DEVELOPED IN **ATHENS** BEFORE SPREADING — TO OTHER — **GREEK** CITY-STATES.

Connect to Ancient Greek Arts

Lesson 6 Arts in Ancient Greece

Here is another connection! Study the photographs. What elements of order, harmony, and balance do you see in these buildings?

How has ancient Greek architecture endured in the modern age?

Connect to Greek Doctors and Scientists

Lesson 7 Science and Technology

Read the information about Thales and the quote about Aristotle. How did these scientists influence how we study science today?

What role does logic and observation play in modern science?

It's Your Turn! **Find two more connections. Fill in the title of your**
connections, then answer the questions. Connections may be images,
primary sources, maps, or text.

Your Choice | Connect to

Location in text

What is the main idea of this connection?

What does it tell you about how ancient Greek culture has endured?

Your Choice | Connect to

Location in text

What is the main idea of this connection?

What does it tell you about how ancient Greek culture has endured?

③ Conduct Research

Form teams based on your teacher's instructions. Meet to decide who will create each segment. In the chart below, record which team member will perform which task.

You will research further only the segment that you are responsible for. Use the ideas in the connections to further explore the subject you have been assigned. Pick who or what you will report about, and find more sources about that subject.

Be sure to find valid sources and take good notes so you can properly cite your sources. Record key information about your story's subject and brainstorm ways to enhance your points with visuals.

Team member	Segment	Specific Topic of Segment
	Philosophy and religion	
	Government and politics	
	Arts, including literature, sculpture, and architecture	
	Science, medicine, or mathematics	
	Sports and leisure	

INTERACTIVE

For extra help, review the 21st Century Tutorials: **Work in Teams, Search for Information on the Internet,** and **Avoid Plagiarism**.

④ Create Your News Magazine

Now it's time to put together all of the information you have gathered and write your segment.

1. **Prepare to Write** Review the research you've collected, and make sure the information you've gathered really supports the main point of your segment.

The main point of your piece:

Key information to support that point:

Sources to cite:

Possible visual/visuals to support your main point:

2. **Write a Draft** The segment should be about three minutes long, which is about one to one-and-one-half pages of single-spaced typed text. This means you will have to be brief and get straight to the point.

3. **Share with a Partner** Once you have finished your draft, ask one of your team members to read, or listen to you read, your draft and provide comments on the clarity and flow of the information. Revise the segment based on his or her comments, and comment on his or her segment, if possible.

4. Create a Visual Now that you have the text of your segment, find or create a visual to support your key points. This will give your viewers something to look at while you are delivering your segment.

5. Put Together Your News Magazine Once all the team members have written and revised their segments, it's time to put them together. You can do this in a couple of ways: 1) by recording each segment using a phone or video camera and editing them together; or 2) by performing the news magazine for the class live. Your teacher will let you know her/his preference for delivery. Either way, you should rehearse the newscast beforehand, taking care to write smooth transitions from one segment to the next.

6. Perform Your News Magazine Show or perform your news magazine for the class. View the other teams' news magazines, and take notes on the information they shared.

Notes on other news magazines:

7. Reflect After all the presentations, discuss your thoughts on your news magazine and the other news magazines. Reflect on the project, and list what you might do differently next time so the teamwork goes more smoothly.

Reflections

 INTERACTIVE

For extra help, review the 21st Century Tutorial: **Give an Effective Presentation**.

Take Notes

Literacy Skills: Analyze Cause and Effect Use what you have read to complete the organizer. For each event, write the cause in the box to the left and the effect in the box to the right. The first one has been completed for you.

Cause	Event	Effect
The mountains of Greece were too steep and rocky for farming.	People settled in the lowland valleys and plains.	The mountains isolate these lowland settlers, who develop independent communities.
	The Greeks become skillful sailors and merchants.	
	Mycenaean civilization is destroyed.	
	In the 700s BCE, the Greeks develop an alphabet.	

INTERACTIVE

For extra help, review the 21st Century Tutorial: **Analyze Cause and Effect**.

Practice Vocabulary

Vocabulary Quiz Show Some quiz shows ask a question and expect the contestant to give the answer. In other shows, the contestant is given an answer and must supply the question. If the blank is in the Question column, write the question that would result in the answer in the Answer column. If the question is supplied, write the answer.

Question	Answer
1.	1. polis
2.	2. citizens
3. Where were temples and public buildings located in Greek city-states?	3.
4. What did the Greeks call the art and practice of government?	4.
5. What term means "rule by the best people"?	5.

Take Notes

Literacy Skills: Summarize Use what you have read to complete the flowcharts. Write a summary for each set of facts. The first flowchart has been completed for you.

Summary: Great Political Variety Existed Among City-States.

Tyrants came to power in some Greek cities, while oligarchs ruled other cities.

First Athens, and then other Greek cities, developed democracy.

Summary:

The reforms of Solon and Cleisthenes increased the number of citizens who could vote.

Pericles' reforms allowed citizens to be paid for jury service and other civic duties.

Summary:

The population of Athens was small.

Not all the people who lived in Athens were citizens.

INTERACTIVE

For extra help, review the 21st Century Tutorial: **Summarize**.

Practice Vocabulary

Sentence Builder Finish the sentences below with a key term from this section. You may have to change the form of the words to complete the sentences.

Word Bank

oligarchy   phalanx   representative democracy

democracy   citizenship   direct democracy

tyranny

1. Many city-states moved toward rule by the many, a form of government called

2. Membership in a community in which people help make government decisions is called

3. A political system in which citizens elect others to represent them in government is called a(n)

4. Political power is held by a small group of people in a(n)

5. A political system in which citizens participate directly in decision-making is called a(n)

6. A formation of heavily armed foot soldiers who moved together as a unit was called a(n)

7. Government run by a strong ruler is known as

Take Notes

Literacy Skills: Compare and Contrast Use what you have read to complete the graphic organizers. For each category, compare and contrast Sparta and Athens. The first organizer has been done for you.

Government	
Sparta	Athens
A mix of monarchy, oligarchy, and democracy	Democracy

Economy	
Sparta	Athens

Culture and the Arts	
Sparta	Athens

👆 **INTERACTIVE**

For extra help, review the 21st Century Tutorial: **Compare and Contrast**.

© Pearson Education, Inc., All Rights Reserved

Practice Vocabulary

Words in Context For each question below, write an answer that shows your understanding of the boldfaced key term.

1. How did **ephors** give the Spartan assembly an important power?

2. How were **helots** different from slaves?

3. Why did Sparta become a **military state**?

4. Why did Spartan males live in **barracks**?

Quick Activity Contrasting Primary Sources

With a partner or small group, contrast these two primary sources to answer the question: What were the differences in point of view and perspective between Athenians and Spartans?

[Lycurgus, law-maker of the Spartans] believed motherhood to be the most important function of freeborn woman. Therefore, in the first place, he insisted on physical training for the female no less than for the male sex: moreover, he instituted races and trials of strength for women competitors as for men, believing that if both parents are strong they produce more vigorous offspring. . . .

Lycurgus, on the contrary, instead of leaving each father to appoint a slave to act as tutor, gave the duty of controlling the boys to a member of the class from which the highest offices are filled, in fact to the "Warden" as he is called. He gave this person authority to gather the boys together, to take charge of them and to punish them severely in case of misconduct. He also assigned to him a staff of youths provided with whips to chastise them when necessary; and the result is that modesty and obedience are inseparable companions at Sparta.

— From Xenophon's *Constitution of the Lacedaimonians,* translated by E.C. Marchant and G.W. Bowersock, Chapter 1

"If we turn to our [the Athenians'] military policy, there also we differ from our antagonists. We throw open our city to the world, and never by alien acts exclude foreigners from any opportunity of learning and observing, although the eyes of an enemy may occasionally profit by our liberality; trusting less in system and policy than to the native spirit of our citizens; while in education, where our rivals from their very cradles by a painful discipline seek after manliness, at Athens we live exactly as we please, and yet are just as ready to encounter every legitimate danger."

— From Pericles' *Funeral Oration from the Peloponnesian War,* in *The History of the Peloponnesian War,* Thucydides, Book 2

Team Challenge! **For each primary source, write out a statement of the author's perspective on education. Then, find a partner and discuss education in ancient Greece, with one of you taking the Spartan point of view and the other the Athenian point of view.**

Take Notes

Literacy Skills: Use Evidence Use what you have read to complete the table. On each row, provide either evidence or a conclusion, based on your reading of the text. The first row has been done for you.

Evidence	Conclusion
Spartan women could sell property; they were educated and trained in sports.	In contrast to the women of other city-states, Spartan women had more freedom.
	The economy of all the city-states depended on slavery.
Greek colonies spread across the Mediterranean Sea and the Black Sea.	
Most Greek women were expected to remain indoors, managing the home, while men conducted business outside the home.	

INTERACTIVE

For extra help, review the 21st Century Tutorial: **Support Ideas With Evidence**.

Practice Vocabulary

Word Map Study the word map for the word *tenant farmer*. Characteristics are words or phrases that relate to the word in the center of the word map. Non-characteristics are words and phrases not associated with the word. Use the blank word map to explore the meaning of the word *metic*. Then make a word map of your own for the word *slavery*.

Characteristics
poorer than small farmers and aristocrats
paid rent in either money or crops

Definition in your own words
farmers who did not own land but paid rent to grow crops on another person's land

tenant farmer

Non-characteristics
rich, great landowner
raised livestock
produced a food surplus

Picture or sentence
The tenant farmer paid rent to the landowner.

Characteristics

Definition in your own words

metic

Non-characteristics

Picture or sentence

Take Notes

Literacy Skills: Compare and Contrast Use what you have read to complete the tables. For each battle or war, compare and contrast the advantages and/or disadvantages of each side in the conflict. The first table has been done for you.

Battle of Marathon	
Persians	**Athenians**
Outnumbered the Athenians by about two to one	Unlike the Persians, had no archers or cavalry, but won the battle because they relied on surprise

Second Persian War	
Persians	**Greeks**

Peloponnesian War	
Spartans	**Athenians**

INTERACTIVE

For extra help, review the 21st Century Tutorial: **Compare and Contrast**.

Practice Vocabulary

Words in Context For each question below, write an answer that shows your understanding of the boldfaced key term.

1. What happened at the **Battle of Salamis**?

2. What was the **Delian League**, and why was it formed?

3. Who made up the **Peloponnesian League**, and why did its members resent Athens?

4. Why was the **Battle of Marathon** significant?

Take Notes

Literacy Skills: Synthesize Visual Information Use what you have read and the images in the lesson to complete the graphic organizers. For each visual, find a passage in the text that will allow you to combine the visual and the information in the text in order to create a fuller picture, or synthesis. The first graphic organizer has been done for you.

Photograph of the Discus Thrower Found in the Text	Information Found in the Text
The figure looks proud and heroic, like an "ideal." The fact that a sculptor chose an athlete as a subject shows that the Greeks admired athletes.	The text says, "The most famous sports event was the Olympic games, which honored Zeus. These games took place every four years. During the games, all conflicts between city-states ceased."

Synthesis: The Greeks believed that sports were among the most important things in life and even pleased the gods.

Table of Oympian Gods Found in the Text	Information Found in the Text

Synthesis:

INTERACTIVE

For extra help, review the 21st Century Tutorial: **Synthesize**.

Practice Vocabulary

Vocabulary Quiz Show Some quiz shows ask a question and expect the contestant to give the answer. In other shows, the contestant is given an answer and must supply the question. If the blank is in the Question column, write the question that would result in the answer in the Answer column. If the question is supplied, write the answer.

Question	Answer
1. What is the worship of many gods called?	1.
2.	2. mythology
3. Which famous sports event took place every four years and honored Zeus?	3.
4.	4. lyric poetry
5.	5. chorus

Quick Activity Create a Comic Strip

Hundreds of fables from ancient Greece are said to have been written by Aesop, an enslaved person who was given his freedom because of his wisdom and talent. Although Aesop was likely not a real person, the fables said to be written by him have endured for hundreds of years. Read this text from one of Aesop's Fables.

The Fox and the Crow

A crow, having stolen a bit of flesh, perched in a tree and held it in her beak. A Fox, seeing this, longed to possess himself of the flesh, and by a wily stratagem succeeded.

"How handsome is the Crow," he exclaimed, "in the beauty of her shape and in the fairness of her complexion! Oh, if her voice were only equal to her beauty, she would deservedly be considered the Queen of Birds!"

This he said deceitfully; but the Crow, anxious to [respond to the criticism of] her voice, set up a loud caw and dropped the flesh.

The Fox quickly picked it up, and thus addressed the Crow: "My good Crow, your voice is right enough, but your wit is wanting."

— From *Three Hundred Aesop's Fables*, translated by George Fyler Townsend

Team Challenge! **Form teams to create a comic strip that illustrates the story. Use speech bubbles to have the characters talk to one another.**

Take Notes

Literacy Skills: Summarize Use what you have read to complete the flowcharts. Write a summary for each set of facts. The first flowchart has been completed for you.

Summary: The Greeks valued the human power of reason to help people understand their lives and world.

By asking questions, Socrates encouraged people to think more clearly.

Plato wrote about the nature of reality.

Summary:

Thucydides hoped that his history of the Peloponnesian War would help people avoid repeating the mistakes of the past.

The historian Xenophon believed that the study of history could teach people how to live moral lives.

Summary:

Through observation, the Greeks realized that natural laws governed the universe.

The philosopher Aristotle sought knowledge through observation. He was a great collector and classifier of data.

👆 **INTERACTIVE**

For extra help, review the 21st Century Tutorial: **Summarize**.

Practice Vocabulary

Sentence Builder Finish the sentences below with a key term from this section. You may have to change the form of the words to complete the sentences.

Word Bank

Academy   hypothesis

Hippocratic oath   Socratic method

1. A question-and-answer method of teaching is called the

2. Plato's famous school of philosophy was called the

3. After making observations of a natural event, Greek scholars explained their observations by forming a logical guess called a(n)

4. When promising to use their knowledge only in ethical ways, doctors state the

Take Notes

Literacy Skills: Sequence Use what you have read to complete the flowcharts in order to show the sequence of events. The first flowchart has been completed for you.

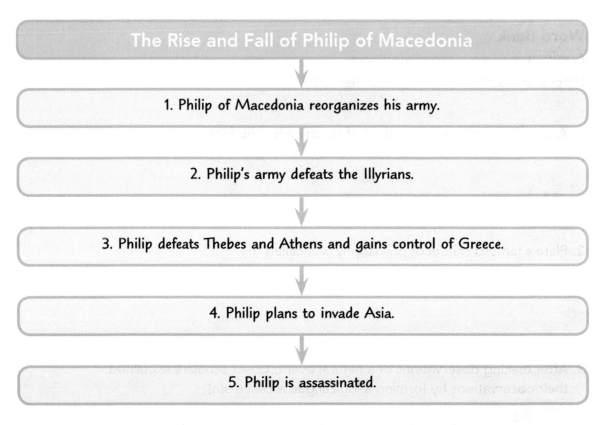

The Rise and Fall of Philip of Macedonia

1. Philip of Macedonia reorganizes his army.

2. Philip's army defeats the Illyrians.

3. Philip defeats Thebes and Athens and gains control of Greece.

4. Philip plans to invade Asia.

5. Philip is assassinated.

The Rise and Fall of Alexander the Great
1. Alexander crushes revolts and burns Thebes.
2.
3.
4. In Egypt, Alexander founds the city of Alexandria.
5.
6.
7. Alexander dies in 323 BCE.

INTERACTIVE

For extra help, review the 21st Century Tutorial: **Sequence**.

Practice Vocabulary

Use a Word Bank Choose one word from the word bank to fill in each blank. When you have finished, you will have a short summary of important ideas from the section.

Word Bank

sarissa   Hellenistic   classical civilization

Philip of Macedonia gained control of Greece with powerful, disciplined

troops, each of whom was armed with a ....

After Philip was assassinated, his son Alexander gained the throne.

Alexander secured control of Greece and then captured cities in Asia and

along the Mediterranean coast. He freed Egypt from the Persians and

founded Alexandria on the Nile delta. After defeating the Persian empire,

Alexander moved east into India. Alexander founded Greek-style cities

from which emerged .... culture.

Alexander's conquests helped spread Greek culture. In time, Greek

and Roman culture would form ....

Writing Workshop Explanatory Essay

As you read, build a response to this question: **Why did the power of the independent Greek city-states rise, peak, and fall?** Use examples from this topic to support your main points. The prompts below will help walk you through the process.

Lesson 1 Writing Task: Consider Your Purpose What is your purpose in writing this essay? Who is your audience?

Lesson 2 Writing Task: Pick an Organizing Strategy Choose an organization strategy that lends itself to the type of explanation you are giving. Sometimes, the phrasing of the writing prompt can provide a clue to what type of organization to choose. In this case, the question in the writing prompt starts with "Why?" Here are some common organizational strategies. Check off the one you think will work best for this writing prompt:

__definition   __classification
__compare/contrast   __cause/effect

Lessons 3 and 5 Writing Task: Develop a Clear Thesis and Update Your Thesis Now, express in one sentence the main point you want to make in your essay. From what you've read so far, why did the power of the independent Greek city-states rise, peak, and fall? Update your thesis as you continue to read through the lessons.

Lessons 4 and 6 Writing Task: Support Thesis with Details Begin to organize your essay with an outline showing the string of causes you are explaining. Record supporting details in this outline as you read.

Introduction Thesis	
Cause(s) of rise Evidence	
Cause(s) of peak Evidence	
Cause(s) of fall Evidence	
Conclusion	

Lesson 7 Writing Task: Draft Your Essay Using the outline you created, answer the following question in a five-paragraph explanatory essay: Why did the power of the independent Greek city-states rise, peak, and fall?

Lesson 8 Writing Task: Revise Your Essay Read your draft. Ask yourself: Have I made my point clearly? Is it supported by enough evidence? Exchange drafts with a partner and use their feedback to revise your essay.

The Roman Republic Preview

Essential Question What is the best form of government?

Before you begin this topic, think about the Essential Question by completing the following activity.

1. List five jobs, or purposes, for government. In a small group, discuss why you think these jobs are important.

2. What forms of government do you think might best fulfill these jobs? Place a check mark next to three of the forms listed. Circle the one that you think is the best form of government.

__democracy	__dictatorship	__republic
__monarchy	__aristocracy	__oligarchy

Timeline Skills

As you read, write and/or draw at least three events from the topic. Draw a line from each event to its correct position on the timeline.

900 BCE	700 BCE	500 BCE

Map Skills

Using the map in your text, label the outline map with the places listed.
Then use different colors for areas ruled by the Roman republic in 44 BCE,
146 BCE, 264 BCE, and 500 BCE. Create a map key to define what each color
symbolizes.

Po River	Mediterranean Sea	Tiber River	Alps
Rome	Carthage	Athens	Italy
Greece	Sicily	Gaul	Byzantium

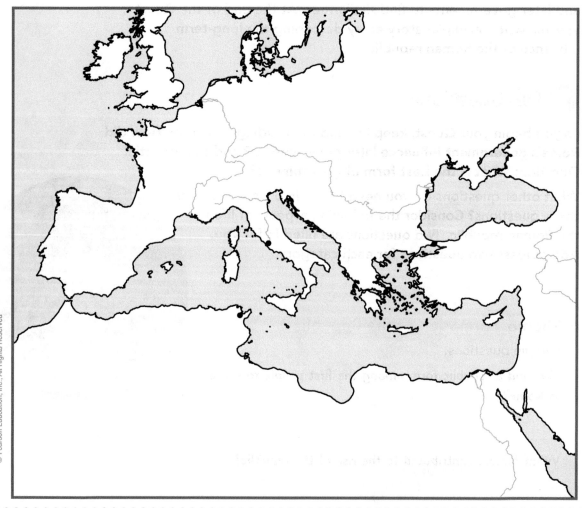

300
BCE

100
BCE

Quest
Document-Based Writing Inquiry
The Roman Influence

On this Quest, you need to find out how Rome influenced later governments. You will examine sources about the Roman republic and later governments to find similarities. At the end of the Quest you will write an explanatory essay describing the long-term influence of the Roman republic.

1 Ask Questions

As you begin your Quest, keep in mind the Guiding Question: **How did Rome's government influence later governments?** and the Essential Question: **What is the best form of government?**

What other questions do you need to ask in order to answer these questions? Consider the following aspects of life in the Roman republic. Two questions are filled in for you. Add at least two questions for each category.

Theme Formation of the Republic

Sample questions:

How did a republic form among the first people to settle in Rome?

What factors contributed to the rise of the republic?

Theme Roman Security, Military Power, and Expansion

Theme Structure, Principles, and Powers of the Roman Republic

Theme Social Hierarchy and Religion under the Roman Republic

Theme Decline and Legacy of the Roman Republic

Theme My Additional Questions

 INTERACTIVE

For extra help with Step 1, review the 21st
Century Skills Tutorial: **Ask Questions**.

Quest CONNECTIONS

2 Investigate

As you read about the Roman republic, collect five connections from your text to help you answer the Guiding Question. Three connections are already chosen for you.

Connect to Founding the Republic

Lesson 1 Rome Becomes a Republic

Here's a connection! What qualities does a republic have? Where did the name *republic* come from?

How did the nature of the Roman republic's government resemble that of the United States today?

Connect to Branches of Government

Lesson 2 Three Branches of Roman Government

Here's another connection! Study the infographic. How did the Roman republic balance power among its three branches of government? How did this structure provide for a separation of powers, and checks and balances?

What influence do you think the branches of government in the Roman republic had on modern democracies?

Connect to Cicero, *The Republic*

Lesson 4 In-text Primary Source *The Republic*

Read the in-text Primary Source excerpt from Marcus Tullius Cicero's *The Republic*. How is what Cicero describes similar to or different from the ways in which people try to influence government in the United States today?

What role did the senate play in Rome's governance? What influence do you think the Roman republic had on modern democracies?

Now it's your turn! **Find two more connections on your own. Fill in the title of your connections, then answer the questions. Connections may be images, primary sources, maps, or text.**

Your Choice | Connect to

Location in the text

What is the main idea of this connection?

What does it tell you about the ways the Roman republic influenced modern democracies, such as that of the United States?

Your Choice | Connect to

Location in the text

What is the main idea of this connection?

What does it tell you about the ways the Roman republic influenced modern democracies, such as that of the United States?

3 Examine Primary and Secondary Sources

Examine the primary and secondary sources provided online or from your teacher. Fill in the chart to show how these sources provide further information about how the Roman republic influenced later governments. The first one is completed for you.

Sources	Ways the Roman Republic Influenced Later Governments
Preamble to the U.S. Constitution	Government should serve the public welfare, establish the rule of law in a constitution, and derive its power from the people.
Law of the Twelve Tables	
Separation of Powers in Practice	
U.S. Capitol Building and Roman Pantheon	
The Founders of the United States' Classical Education	

INTERACTIVE

For extra help with Step 3, review the 21st Century Skills Tutorial: **Analyze Images**.

4 Write Your Explanatory Essay

Now it's time to put together all of the information you have gathered and use it to write your explanatory essay.

1. **Prepare to Write** You have collected connections and explored sources that show how the government of the Roman republic influenced future governments. Look through your notes and decide which lasting influences of the Roman republic you want to highlight in your essay. Record them here.

Lasting Influences

2. **Write a Draft** Using evidence from the connections you found and the documents you explored, write a draft of your explanatory essay. Introduce your thesis in response to the Guiding Question: How did Rome's government influence later governments? Then, in the body of your essay, support your thesis by describing three or more lasting influences of the Roman republic, citing evidence from the documents you've studied in this Quest. Finally, summarize your explanation with memorable insight in the concluding paragraph of your essay.

3. **Share with a Partner** Exchange your draft with a partner. Tell your partner what you like about his or her draft and suggest any improvements.

4. **Finalize Your Essay** Revise your draft based on your partner's feedback. Then, read aloud your essay. Correct any grammatical or spelling errors.

5. **Reflect on the Quest** Think about your experience completing this topic's Quest. What did you learn about the Roman republic and its legacy? What benefits and drawbacks did a republican form of government have for ancient Rome? How has your study of this topic affected your understanding of and opinions about the government of our country today?

Reflections

INTERACTIVE

For extra help with Step 4, review the 21st Century Skills Tutorial: **Write an Essay**.

Take Notes

Literacy Skills: Analyze Cause and Effect Use what you have read to complete the chart. In each space, write ways in which geography and previous cultures affected the Roman republic. The first effect has been started for you.

Cause	Effects
Geography	• Less rugged terrain, including large, flat plains, made it easy for soldiers to travel and unite the country. • • •
Greek Culture	• • • •
Etruscan Culture	• • • •

INTERACTIVE

For extra help, review the 21st Century Skills Tutorial: **Analyze Cause and Effect**.

Practice Vocabulary

Words in Context For each question below, write an answer that shows your understanding of the boldfaced key term.

1. What activities most likely took place in the **forum** of ancient Rome?

2. How did Rome's government change when the **republic** replaced the monarchy?

3. What advantages did a **maniple** give Romans in battle?

4. Approximately how many soldiers made up a **legion**? What kind of soldiers were they?

Take Notes

Literacy Skills: Identify Main Idea and Details Use what you have read to complete the concept web. In each space, write details that support the main idea. The first one has been completed for you.

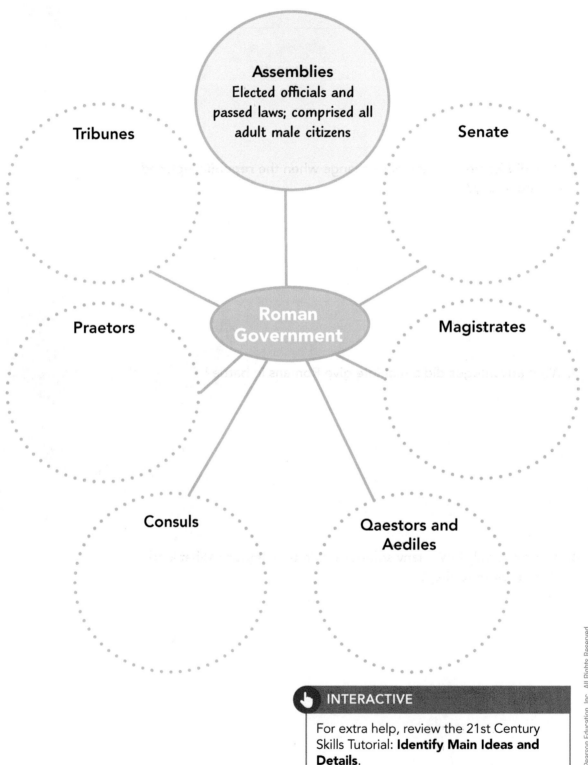

Assemblies
Elected officials and passed laws; comprised all adult male citizens

Tribunes

Senate

Praetors

Roman Government

Magistrates

Consuls

Qaestors and Aediles

Practice Vocabulary

Vocabulary Quiz Show Some quiz shows ask a question and expect the contestant to give the answer. In other shows, the contestant is given an answer and must supply the question. If the blank is in the Question column, write the question that would result in the answer in the Answer column. If the question is supplied, write the answer.

Question

1. What do you call the highest officials in the Roman republic?

2.

3. What power could certain Roman officials use to stop or cancel the actions of other officials?

4.

5. What garment worn by adult male citizens of Rome symbolized their citizenship?

Answer

1.

2. constitution

3.

4. magistrates

5.

Quick Activity Explore Roman Numerals

Between 900 BCE and 800 BCE, Roman numerals appeared. Historians believe that ancient Romans developed their numerals from earlier Etruscan numerals. They used these numerals to track time, goods, money, and even people. Roman numerals appear on many ancient texts and artifacts.

Arabic Numerals	Roman Numerals	Arabic Numerals	Roman Numerals
1	I	9	IX
2	II	10	X
3	III	50	L
4	IV	100	C
5	V	200	CC
6	VI	500	D
7	VII	1000	M
8	VIII		

Roman numbers are based on seven basic numerals combined according to certain rules:

1. Add the total of the numbers shown to determine the amount: XXV = 25 (10 + 10 + 5)

2. Arrange numerals from largest at left to smallest at the right.

3. You may repeat I, X, C, and M in a single number.

4. Do not repeat more than 3 of the same numeral in a row, instead put a I to the left of a larger number: IV = 4; IX = 9; XIX = 19 and so on.

Write these Roman numbers in Arabic numbers. Follow the rules above.

1. XII =

2. LV =

3. CCXXIII =

4. CXLIV =

Team Challenge! Write a few sets of Roman numbers. Switch with a partner to have them write the number in Arabic numerals.

Take Notes

Literacy Skills: Classify and Categorize Use what you have read to complete the chart. In each space, list the people of the Roman republic who belonged to this social group. Then, describe one aspect of life for this social group.

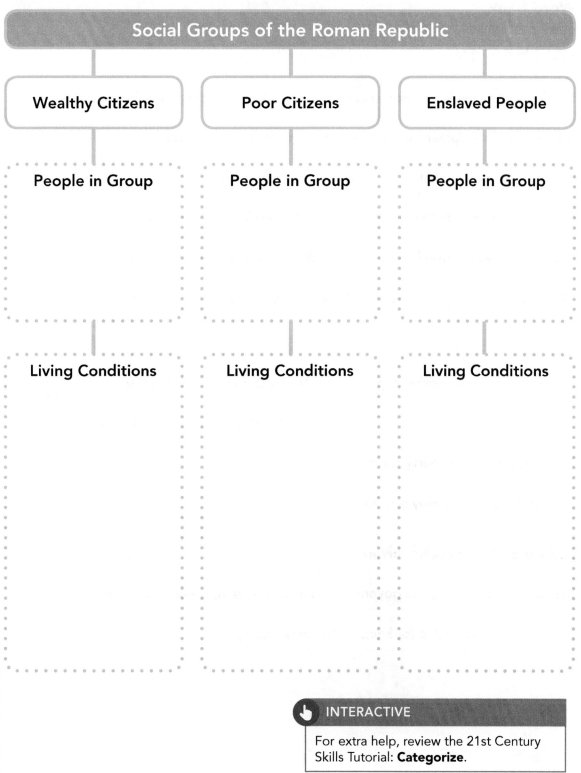

Social Groups of the Roman Republic

Wealthy Citizens	Poor Citizens	Enslaved People
People in Group	People in Group	People in Group
Living Conditions	Living Conditions	Living Conditions

👆 **INTERACTIVE**

For extra help, review the 21st Century Skills Tutorial: **Categorize**.

Practice Vocabulary

Use a Word Bank Choose one word from the word bank to fill in each blank. When you have finished, you will have a short summary of important ideas from the section.

Word Bank

patriarchal society   villas

established religion   paterfamilias

Life for Roman families varied according to the part of society in which

they lived. Most Romans were poor, and many were slaves. These

common people had hard lives filled with hard work and difficult living

conditions. A few Romans were wealthy and lived in great comfort. Their

city homes had beautiful courtyards, gardens, and even running water.

These families sometimes traveled to the countryside to enjoy their

....

Regardless of class, Roman families were led by the oldest man in the

family. A .... had total power over the family.

He owned all the property and made all the decisions. A society that

organizes power this way is called a ....

Romans of all classes also shared an ...., one

that was supported by the government. For this reason, Romans held the

government responsible for keeping the gods happy.

Quick Activity How Does Roman Society Compare?

Ancient civilizations had distinct social systems that, in their own way, preserved order and provided structure. Study the two civilizations shown in the pyramids. What do you notice about their social systems? Discuss your ideas with a partner, and write down three similarities and three differences that you observe.

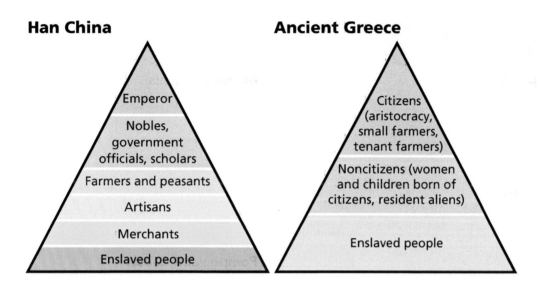

Han China

- Emperor
- Nobles, government officials, scholars
- Farmers and peasants
- Artisans
- Merchants
- Enslaved people

Ancient Greece

- Citizens (aristocracy, small farmers, tenant farmers)
- Noncitizens (women and children born of citizens, resident aliens)
- Enslaved people

Roman Republic

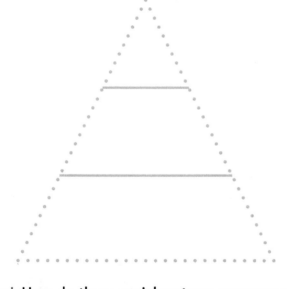

Team Challenge! How do these social systems compare with that of the Roman republic? Use what you have learned to fill in the pyramid for Rome's hierarchy. In small groups, discuss the similarities and differences that you noted between the Han China and Ancient Greece hierarchies. Then, try to think of three similarities and three differences between Roman society and some other societies. Finally, take a class vote: Which two civilizations had the most similar social systems? Which had the most different? Discuss your findings.

Take Notes

Literacy Skills: Summarize Use what you have read to complete the chart. In the box at the left, explain the weaknesses of the Roman republic. In the box at the right, describe the actions of those responsible for the Roman republic's crisis. Then, summarize the effects of those problems during the republic's final crisis.

Weaknesses of the Republic	Actions of Politicians and Military Commanders
Corruption	Marius and Sulla
Urban Poor	
	Pompey and Caesar
Power of the Army	

Final Crisis

INTERACTIVE

For extra help, review the 21st Century Skills Tutorial: **Summarize**.

Practice Vocabulary

Word Map Study the word map for the word *province*. Characteristics are words or phrases that relate to the word in the center of the word map. Non-characteristics are words and phrases not associated with the word. Use the blank word map to explore the meaning of the term *civil war*. Then make word maps of your own for these words: *empire* and *Augustus*.

Characteristics
Controlled by a country or empire; usually located far from main center of government; ruled by magistrates

Definition in your own words
Area or territory inside a country or empire

province

Non-Characteristics
Seat of a country or empire's government; controls own government; controls other territories or areas

Picture or sentence
The government in Rome sent magistrates to govern each province it controlled.

Characteristics

Definition in your own words

civil war

Non-characteristics

Picture or sentence

Writing Workshop Research Paper

As you read, build a response to this question: **How does Rome compare to an earlier or contemporary society in terms of environment, political system, citizenship, or cultural connection?** The prompts below will help walk you through the process.

Lesson 1 Writing Task: Develop a Clear Thesis Express in one sentence the most significant similarities or differences between Rome and one of the following societies that you've already studied in this course: Greek, Hellenistic, Chinese, or Persian. Choose one of the following factors to further focus your comparison on: environment, politics, citizenship, or culture. This will be your thesis statement for the essay that you will write at the end of this topic. Write your thesis on a separate piece of paper. You may revise it throughout the workshop.

Lessons 1, 2, and 3 Writing Task: Support Thesis with Details Gather relevant details from these lessons. Categorize them to form three main ideas. Choose two details from each category that best explain each main idea. If necessary, consult outside sources to find and confirm details. Fill in the table below.

	Key Details (two for each Main Idea)	Supporting outside sources (if needed)
Main Idea 1:		
Main Idea 2:		
Main Idea 3:		

Lesson 3 Writing Task: Draft Your Essay Fill in the outline with key words and phrases to express your plan for your essay. Develop your thesis into an introductory paragraph, and develop your three main ideas and six details into three body paragraphs. Refine your conclusion to reflect any new thoughts and connections that emerge as you write.

I. Introduction:

    A. Thesis:

    B. Main Idea 1:

    C. Main Idea 2:

    D. Main Idea 3:

    E. Introduction Conclusion:

II. Main Idea 1:

    A. Detail:

    B. Detail:

    C. Paragraph Conclusion:

III. Main Idea 2:

    A. Detail:

    B. Detail:

    C. Paragraph Conclusion:

IV. Main Idea 3:

    A. Detail:

    B. Detail:

    C. Paragraph Conclusion:

V. Conclusion Paragraph

Writing Task Exchange essay drafts with a partner. Read and provide feedback on your partner's draft, and invite feedback on your draft. Do your drafts provide a clear thesis statement that answers the question: **How does Rome compare to an earlier or contemporary society in terms of environment, political system, citizenship, or cultural connection?** Do your drafts have appropriate supporting details? Address these questions, and make revisions to your draft as needed.

TOPIC 8

The Roman and Byzantine Empires Preview

Essential Question What forces can cause a society to change?

Before you begin this topic, think about the Essential Question by answering the following question.

1. What are some ways that your community has changed over time? List three ways in which you have seen people, businesses, and other elements of society change.

Timeline Skills

As you read, write and/or draw at least three events from the topic. Draw a line from each event to its correct position on the timeline.

250 BCE	1 CE	250 CE

Map Skills

**Using the maps in your text, label the outline map with the places listed.
Then, color in the territory ruled by the Roman empire.**

Byzantium	Rome	Jerusalem	Mediterranean Sea
Black Sea	Rhine River	Danube River	Anatolia
Egypt	Greece	Gaul	Spain

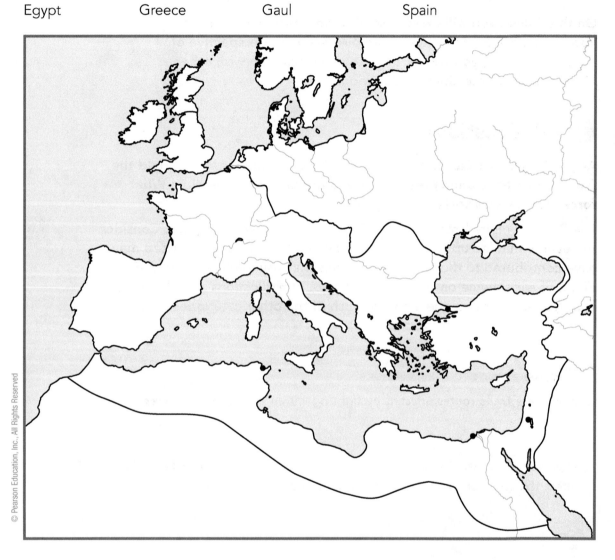

| 500 CE | 1000 CE | 1250 CE | 1500 CE |

Discussion Inquiry

The Fall of Rome

On this Quest, you will explore sources and gather information about the decline of the Roman empire from the perspective of a historian. Then, you will participate in a discussion with other historians about the Guiding Question.

1 Ask Questions

As you begin your Quest, keep in mind the Guiding Question: **Could the fall of Rome have been prevented?** and the Essential Question: **What forces can cause a society to change?**

The Roman empire lasted for about 450 years, but eventually fell. Consider the events that led up to the fall of Rome and how the themes listed may have contributed to the fall. List questions that you might ask about the effect of each theme on the Roman empire. Two questions are filled in for you. Add at least two questions for each of the other categories.

Theme Economic Weakness

How were trade routes affected by fighting within the Roman empire?

If people within the Roman empire could not afford to pay their taxes, how did that affect the emperor's ability to maintain an army?

Theme Political Conflict

Theme Political Corruption

Theme Social Conflict

Theme Invasions from Outside

Theme My Additional Questions

 INTERACTIVE

For extra help with Step 1, review the
21st Century Skills Tutorial: **Ask Questions**.

② Investigate

As you read about the decline of the Roman empire, collect five connections from your text to answer the Guiding Question. Three connections are already chosen for you.

Connect to Augustus

Primary Source Augustus, *The Deeds of the Divine Augustus*

Here's a connection! Consider the list of great deeds that Augustus wrote about himself. What evidence can you find that Augustus was concerned about maintaining the strength of the empire?

Considering he was one of the greatest of Rome's emperors, why do you think Augustus found it necessary to write a long list of the things he had done?

Connect to Satire and Biography

Lesson 4 In-text Primary Source *Juvenal's Satire 10*

What does this connection tell you about what Roman citizens were thinking about during times of trouble?

How do you think the Roman citizenry's attitude toward the government affected the empire's stability?

Connect to Economic Problems Worsen

Lesson 5 What was the Imperial Crisis?

Here's another connection! Read the description of inflation in your text. What does the description tell you about the value of the Roman coins over time?

What does that indicate about what was happening to the Roman economy?

It's Your Turn! **Find two more connections. Fill in the title of your connections, then answer the questions. Connections may be images, primary sources, maps, or text.**

Your Choice | Connect to

Location in text

What is the main idea of this connection?

What does it tell you about the decline of the Roman empire?
Could it have been prevented?

Your Choice | Connect to

Location in text

What is the main idea of this connection?

What does it tell you about the decline of the Roman empire?
Could it have been prevented?

③ Examine Sources

Examine the secondary sources provided online or from your teacher. Fill in the chart to note the viewpoints of four historians on the question of whether Rome's fall could have been prevented. The first one is completed for you.

Could the fall of Rome have been prevented?	
Source	**Yes or No? Why?**
The Decline and Fall of the Roman Empire	NO, because the empire was too big to support.
The Day of the Barbarians	
History of the Later Roman Empire	
The Fall of the Roman Empire	

 INTERACTIVE

For extra help with Step 3, review the 21st Century Skills Tutorial: **Compare Viewpoints**.

 **FINDINGS**

4 Discuss!

Now that you have collected connections and explored documents about the fall of the Roman empire, you are ready to discuss with your fellow historians the Guiding Question: **Could the fall of Rome have been prevented?** Follow the steps below, using the spaces provided to prepare for your discussion.

You will work with a partner in a small group of historians. Try to reach consensus, a situation in which everyone is in agreement, on the question. Can you do it?

1. **Prepare Your Arguments** You will be assigned a position on the question, either YES or NO.

   My position:

   Work with your partner to review your Quest notes from the Quest Connections and Quest Sources.

   • If you were assigned YES, agree with your partner on what you think were the strongest arguments from Bury and Grant.

   • If you were assigned NO, agree on what you think were the strongest arguments from Gibbon and Barbero.

2. **Present Your Position** Those assigned YES will present their arguments and evidence first. As you listen, ask clarifying questions to gain information and understanding.

What is a Clarifying Question?	
These types of questions do not judge the person talking. They are only for the listener to be clear on what he or she is hearing.	
Example: Can you tell me more about that?	Example: You said [x]. Am I getting that right?

 INTERACTIVE

For extra help with Step 4, review the 21st Century Skills Tutorial: **Participate in a Discussion or Debate**.

While the opposite side speaks, take notes on what you hear in the space below.

3. **Switch!** Now NO and YES will switch sides. If you argued YES before, now you will argue NO. Work with your same partner and use your notes. Add any arguments and evidence from the clues and sources. Those *now* arguing YES go first.

When both sides have finished, answer the following:

Before I started this discussion with my fellow historians, my opinion was that	*After* I started this discussion with my fellow historians, my opinion was that
_____the fall of Rome could have been prevented. _____the fall of Rome could not have been prevented.	_____the fall of Rome could have been prevented. _____the fall of Rome could not have been prevented.

4. **Point of View** Do you all agree on the answer to the Guiding Question?

_____ Yes

_____ No

If not, on what points do you all agree?

Take Notes

Literacy Skills: Analyze Cause and Effect Use what you have read to complete the table. Factors that helped the Roman empire grow appear in the left column. Record ways that those factors contributed to the empire's growth in the right column. One has been completed for you.

Causes	Effects
Rule by emperors	ended civil wars; brought peace; made the empire more stable for a time; began the Pax Romana
Pax Romana	
Rome's practical achievements	
Roman military	
Roman trade and economic activity	

INTERACTIVE

For extra help, review the 21st Century Skills Tutorial: **Analyze Cause and Effect**.

Practice Vocabulary

Sentence Builder Finish the sentences below with a vocabulary term from this section. You may have to change the form of the words to complete the sentences.

Word Bank

aqueduct   concrete

deify   Pax Romana

1. Emperors who are officially declared to be gods have been

2. Romans experienced a long period of peace and prosperity during the

3. Mixing stone and sand with limestone, clay, and water produces a useful building material called

4. Roman cities grew rapidly, partly because engineers brought water great distances through

Quick Activity Where Do They Go Next?

The Roman empire reached its greatest territorial extent under Emperor Trajan who ruled from 98 CE to 117 CE. With a partner, study the map of the Roman empire and what surrounded its borders in 117 CE.

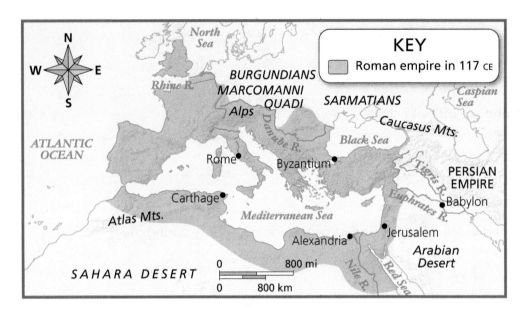

Team Challenge! You probably noticed that the Roman empire expanded across a large area of southern Europe, North Africa, and parts of southwestern Asia. What lands were left to conquer? Where could the Romans go next? What physical features, peoples, or empires lie at the empire's northern, southern, eastern, and western borders? Form a group with three other students. In your group, answer the question: Why did the Roman empire fail to expand after 117 CE? Write your responses on sticky notes, and add them to the class board.

Take Notes

Literacy Skills: Sequence Use what you have read to complete the timeline. Record what happened on each of the dates listed. Then connect each box to the timeline at the appropriate spot. One has been completed for you.

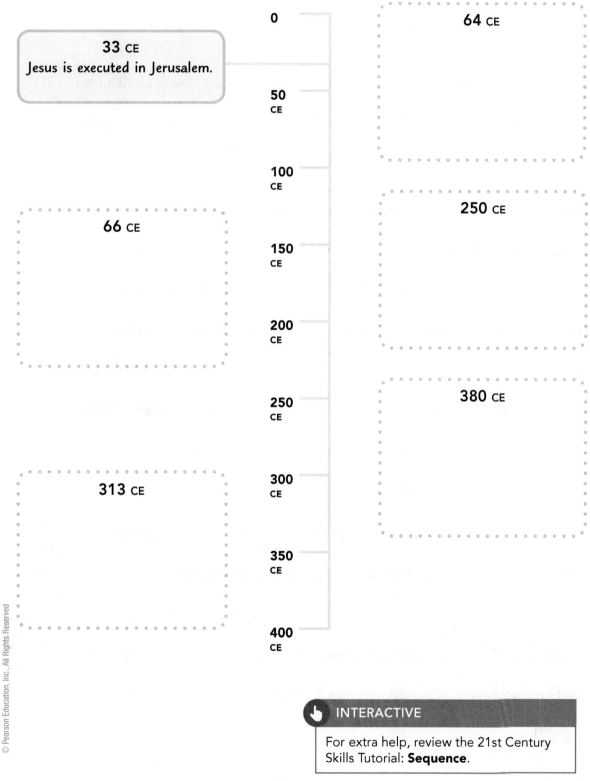

33 CE
Jesus is executed in Jerusalem.

64 CE

66 CE

250 CE

313 CE

380 CE

0
50 CE
100 CE
150 CE
200 CE
250 CE
300 CE
350 CE
400 CE

INTERACTIVE

For extra help, review the 21st Century Skills Tutorial: **Sequence**.

Practice Vocabulary

Word Bank Choose one word from the word bank to fill in each blank. When you have finished, you will have a short summary of important ideas from the section.

Word Bank

baptism   conversion   crucifixion

martyr   resurrection

Christianity began in Judea, then part of the Roman empire. The Jews of Judea practiced many religious traditions, including a ritual plunging into water, which was later adopted by Christianity as the rite of _____.

According to Christian tradition, Jesus of Nazareth preached ideas from the Hebrew Bible and added other ideas about how to live a good life. Many people began to believe that Jesus was the Messiah. As more and more people followed Jesus, the Roman government saw Jesus as a threat and had him executed by _____. Some of Jesus' followers said that they saw him again after his death. These believers helped form a new religion called Christianity. They believed that Jesus' _____ was proof that he was the Messiah.

After Jesus' death, some of his followers worked to spread his teachings. One was Paul, who opposed Christianity until he experienced a _____ that changed his views. As Christianity spread, many Roman emperors responded with persecution. Many Christians died for their beliefs. A person who dies for his or her beliefs is called a _____.

Take Notes

Literacy Skills: Analyze Text Structure Use what you have read to complete the outline. The items listed below reflect the headings and subheadings in the lesson. Record key details beneath the headings. The first one has been completed for you.

I. The Christian Bible
    A. The Old and New Testaments
        1. The Old Testament comprises the scriptures of the Hebrew Bible.
        2. The New Testament comprises 27 documents, called *books*, added by Christians.
    B. What Are the Gospels?

    C. Teachings in Other Books

II. What Do Christians Believe About God?
    A. The Son of God

    B. The Soul and Salvation

    C. The Trinity

III. Practicing Christianity
    A. Following Jesus' Teachings

    B. Christianity Today

    C. Christian Rituals and Holidays

IV. What Is the Judeo-Christian tradition?

 INTERACTIVE

For extra help, review the 21st Century Skills Tutorial: **Organize Your Ideas**.

Practice Vocabulary

Vocabulary Quiz Show **Some quiz shows ask a question and expect the contestant to give the answer. In other shows, the contestant is given an answer and must supply the question. If the blank is in the Question column, write the question that would result in the answer in the Answer column. If the question is supplied, write the answer.**

Question	Answer
1. What text makes up the second part of the Christian Bible, and is not part of the Hebrew Bible?	1.
2.	2. epistles
3.	3. Trinity
4. What stories did Jesus often use to teach important lessons?	4.
5. What are large groups within Christianity that share certain beliefs and rituals, but disagree on others?	5.
6.	6. Gospel
7. What subject deals with issues of right and wrong and the best way to treat people?	7.

Take Notes

Literacy Skills: Identify Main Ideas and Details Use what you have read to complete the concept web. Record details about each aspect of Roman culture under the empire. The first one has been completed for you.

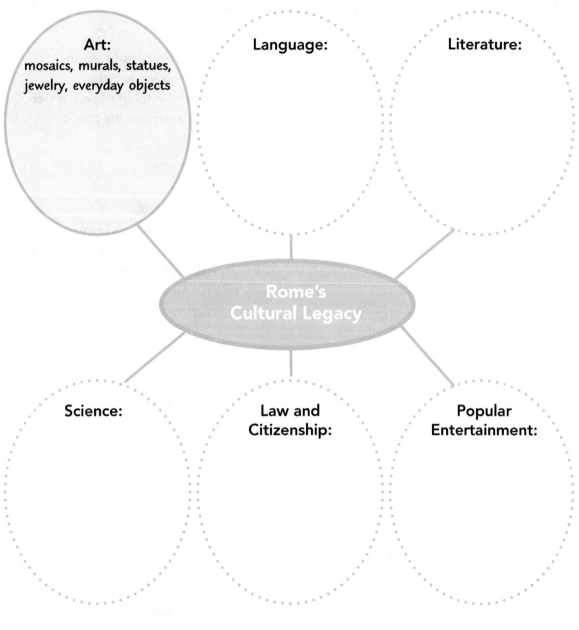

Art:
mosaics, murals, statues, jewelry, everyday objects

Language:

Literature:

Rome's Cultural Legacy

Science:

Law and Citizenship:

Popular Entertainment:

INTERACTIVE

For extra help, review the 21st Century Skills Tutorial: **Identify Main Ideas and Details**.

Practice Vocabulary

Word Map Study the word map for the word *gladiator*. Characteristics are words or phrases that relate to the word in the center of the word map. Non-characteristics are words and phrases not associated with the word. Use the blank word map to explore the meaning of the word *oratory*. Then make word maps of your own for these words: *site of encounter, mosaic, Romance languages, Greco-Roman,* and *satire.*

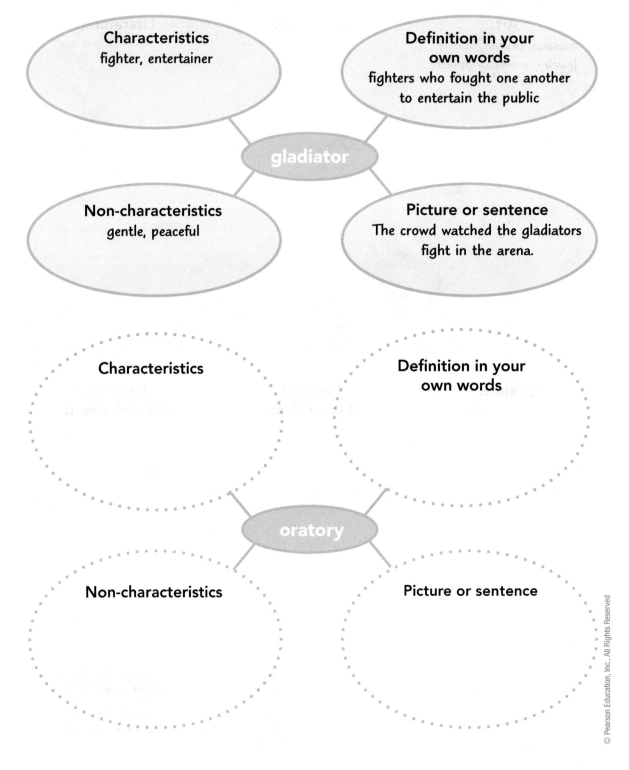

Characteristics
fighter, entertainer

Definition in your own words
fighters who fought one another to entertain the public

gladiator

Non-characteristics
gentle, peaceful

Picture or sentence
The crowd watched the gladiators fight in the arena.

Characteristics

Definition in your own words

oratory

Non-characteristics

Picture or sentence

Lesson 5 The Decline of the Roman Empire

Take Notes

Literacy Skills: Analyze Cause and Effect Use what you have read to complete the chart. Record specific events and their effects that contributed to the decline of the Roman empire.

Cause	Event	Effect
Marcus Aurelius dies.		Pax Romana ends.
Civil wars erupt.	Inflation grows. Trade networks are disrupted. Foreign invasions advance.	
Diocletian tries to stabilize Rome.		Military leaders fight for power.
Theodosius dies.		Rome falls.

INTERACTIVE

For extra help, review the 21st Century Skills Tutorial: **Analyze Cause and Effect**.

Practice Vocabulary

Words in Context For each question below, write an answer that shows your understanding of the **boldfaced** key term.

1. What are problems that people might have in a time of **inflation**?

2. According to the Romans, why were the Germans **barbarians**?

3. How did Emperor Theodosius show his support for Christian **orthodoxy**?

4. What role did **mercenaries** play in the Roman empire's fight to survive?

Quick Activity Did the Roman Empire Fall?

Read the excerpt below. Discuss with a partner what the excerpt suggests about the "fall" of the western Roman empire.

> "Nations innumerable and most savage have invaded all Gaul. The Whole region between the Alps and the Pyrenees, the ocean and the Rhine, has been devastated … Oh wretched Empire! … Who could believe that Rome, built upon the conquest of the whole world, would fall to the ground?"
>
> —*St. Jerome on the Germanic Invasions, 409* C.E.

In 476 CE, Germanic invaders overthrew the last Roman emperor in the western empire, Romulus. The city of Rome fell. Meanwhile, to the east, the Byzantine empire continued and even thrived. Not until 1453 did the Ottoman Turks capture the Byzantine capital of Constantinople. Historians often refer to the end of the western Roman empire as the "fall" of the Roman empire. Some argue that the empire did not fall, however. They maintain that the empire broke down slowly, over a long period of time, and that Roman civilization continued in the east as the Byzantine empire, up until 1453. Use what you have learned in the lessons to discuss, in a small group, the causes of the decline of the western Roman empire as well as the ways in which Roman civilization continued.

Team Challenge! Take a Thumb Vote in response to the question **Did the Roman empire fall?** Organize into groups based on your votes. With your new group, write a paragraph that answers the question and provides at least two pieces of evidence to support your position. If you answer "yes," explain why *fall* is an appropriate description, despite suggestions that Roman civilization continued beyond 476 CE. If you answer "no," explain why *fall* is wrong and suggest an alternative word or phrase as a more appropriate description.

Take Notes

Literacy Skills: Use Evidence Use what you have read to complete the table. Record the main idea for each heading in the lesson. Then, list evidence to support the main idea. The first one has been completed for you.

Main Idea	Evidence
What Was the New Rome? The Eastern Roman, or Byzantine, empire grew around a new political and economic center.	• Constantine established the capital of the Eastern Roman empire at Constantinople, on the site of Byzantium. • Located on the Bosporous Strait, Constantinople became a center for trade and was easier to defend than Rome.
Who Were Justinian and Theodora?	• •
The Shrinking Empire	• •
The Empire's Influence	• •
Early Russia	• •

Practice Vocabulary

Sentence Revision Revise each sentence so that the underlined vocabulary word is used logically. Be sure not to change the vocabulary word. The first one is done for you.

1. The <u>Byzantine</u> empire was named after Emperor Constantine.

   The <u>Byzantine</u> empire was so named because its capital, Constantinople, was built at a place once called Byzantium.

2. A <u>strait</u> is a wide body of water surrounding an island.

3. The <u>moat</u> was a trench filled with stones.

4. <u>Greek fire</u> was a liquid that quickly stopped flames from spreading.

5. A <u>missionary</u> generally lacked the confidence to promote his religion.

6. The <u>Cyrillic alphabet</u> was used by the Romans.

Take Notes

Literacy Skills: Compare and Contrast Use what you have read to complete the chart. List features that the Roman Catholic Church and the Eastern Orthodox Church share, as well as features that make each church unique. One has been completed for you.

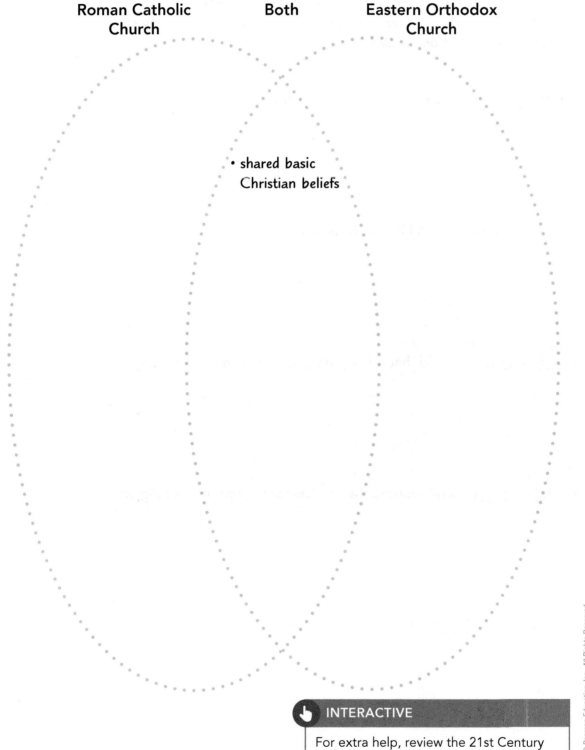

Roman Catholic Church   Both   Eastern Orthodox Church

• shared basic Christian beliefs

INTERACTIVE

For extra help, review the 21st Century Skills Tutorial: **Compare and Contrast**.

Practice Vocabulary

Sentence Builder Finish the sentences below with a key term from this section. You may have to change the form of the words to complete the sentences.

Word Bank

creed	Great Schism	icon
iconoclast	Justinian's Code	pope

1. Church leadership was the most important issue between Eastern Orthodox and Roman Catholic churches in the

2. The leader of the Roman Catholic Church was the

3. Many Christians believed it was wrong to worship holy images called

4. The Byzantine empire and its emperor benefited from the unified body of law organized under

5. In 325, Church officials prepared a clear statement of beliefs, or

6. Byzantines who destroyed holy images in churches were called

Writing Workshop Arguments

As you read, build a response to this question: Which civilization was greater, the Greek city-states or the Roman empire? The prompts below will help walk you through the process.

Lessons 1 and 2 Writing Tasks: Introduce Claims and Gather Details
In this topic, you will write an argument based on the question: Which was greater, the Greek city-states or the Roman empire? Consider the following factors: size, longevity, economic power, cultural achievements, and influence. Add facts about each civilization to this chart.

Factor	Greece	Rome	Advantage? (G/R)
Size			
Longevity			
Economic Power			
Cultural Achievements			

Lesson 3 Writing Task: Use Credible Sources On a separate sheet of paper, list at least three print or digital sources, other than your text, that you will use to check your conclusions.

Lesson 4 Writing Task: Introduce a Claim Look at your chart and mark which civilization had the advantage in each area in your opinion. From this exercise, can you choose which civilization you think was greater? If you can't support choosing one, argue that they both have claims to greatness. Form your conclusion into a one-sentence statement and write it in the outline.

Lessons 5 and 6 Writing Tasks: Support a Claim and Distinguish Claims from Opposing Claims Make an outline of your essay. List your best examples of why one society might be greater than the other. Make sure to include an opposing claim.

Claim statement	
2nd best example	
3rd best example	
Opposing claim	
Best example	

Lesson 7 Writing Task: Shape Tone As you write, use phrases such as "clearly" or "in fact" to emphasize your points, and phrases such as "on the other hand" or "in contrast" to introduce an opposing claim.

Writing Task Using the outline you created, answer the following question in a five-paragraph argument: Which was greater, the Greek city-states or the Roman empire?

 INTERACTIVE

For extra help, review the 21st Century Skills Tutorials: **Support Ideas with Evidence** and **Consider and Counter Opposing Arguments**.

Essential Question **How did societies preserve order?**

Before you begin this topic, think about the Essential Question by answering the following question.

1. What are some ways that people and institutions keep order and prevent conflict in your community? Work with a partner to brainstorm five ideas. List them below. Circle the two that you think are the most important or effective.

Timeline Skills

As you read, write and/or draw at least three events from the topic. Draw a line from each event to its correct position on the timeline.

500 CE	750 CE

Map Skills

Using the map in your text, label the outline map with the places listed. Then color in bodies of water, mountain ranges, and plains.

Alps	Atlantic Ocean	Balkan Peninsula
Black Sea	Caspian Sea	Iberian Peninsula
Italian Peninsula	Mediterranean Sea	North European Plain
North Sea	Scandinavian Peninsula	Ural Mountains

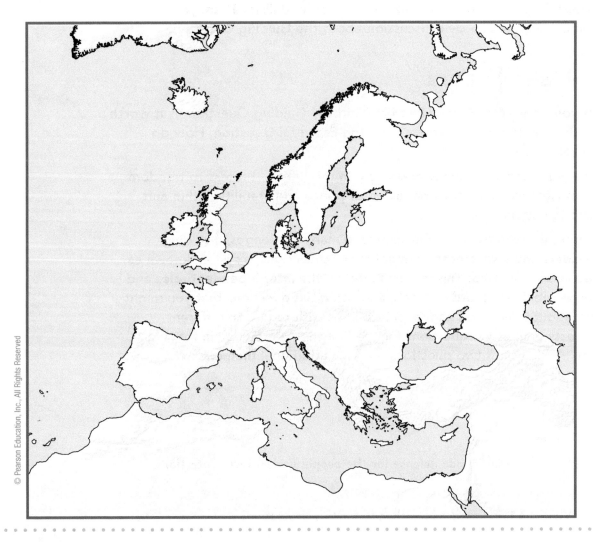

1000 CE   1250 CE

Quest
Discussion Inquiry

Freedom vs. Security?

On this Quest, you will explore sources and gather information about the relationships that existed under feudalism. Then, you will participate in a civic discussion about the Guiding Question.

1 Ask Questions

As you begin your Quest, keep in mind the Guiding Question: **Is it worth trading freedom for security?** and the Essential Question: **How do societies preserve order?**

The word *order* has many meanings. In this sense, it refers to freedom from violence and unruly behavior, or peace and stability within and among communities.

During the Middle Ages, Europe faced many challenges, including invaders and lawlessness. To meet these challenges, a system known as feudalism emerged. This system relied on the interdependent roles and responsibilities of lords, vassals, and serfs. List questions that you might ask about these roles and responsibilities with regard to different aspects of life. Two questions for the first theme are filled in for you. Add at least two questions for each additional theme.

Theme Defense and Security

Sample questions:

How did lords provide defense for the people under their protection?

What did lords expect in exchange for this protection?

Theme Economic Activity

Theme Government and Law

Theme Social Relations

Theme Religion and Culture

Theme My Additional Questions

INTERACTIVE

For extra help with Step 1, review the
21st Century Tutorial: **Ask Questions**.

② Investigate

As you read about medieval Europe, collect five connections
from your text to help you answer the Guiding Question.
Three connections are already chosen for you.

Connect to Charlemagne

Primary Source Einhard, *The Life of Charlemagne*

Here's a connection! Read the description of Charlemagne, King of the
Franks. What does the text describe the king doing? What does it show
about life in medieval Europe, and the responsibilities of kings? How did
medieval knights help provide security for lords and peasants?

What trade-offs do people at different levels of society make for security?

Connect to Feudalism

Lesson 3 Feudalism in Medieval Europe

Here's another connection! Look at the diagram of feudalism and social relationships in your text. The king is at the top. What roles do the people on the other levels fulfill? How do they support the king and what do they get in exchange? How do these relationships preserve order in feudal society?

What trade-offs do people at different levels of society make for security?

Connect to the Medieval Manor

Lesson 3 How Did Medieval Manors Work?

What does this diagram show you about the social structure that existed on medieval manors? How does this structure illustrate the relationship between serfs and their feudal lords?

What trade-offs do people at different levels of society make for security?

It's Your Turn! **Find two more connections. Fill in the title of your connections, then answer the questions. Connections may be images, primary sources, maps, or text.**

Your Choice | Connect to

Location in text

What is the main idea of this connection?

What does it tell you about how feudal roles and relationships provided for security in medieval Europe?

Your Choice | Connect to

Location in text

What is the main idea of this connection?

What does it tell you about how feudal roles and relationships provided for security in medieval Europe?

③ Examine Sources

Examine the primary and secondary sources provided online or from your teacher. Fill in the chart to show what these sources suggest about the trade-off of freedom for security in today's world. The first one is completed for you.

Is It Worth Trading Freedom for Security?	
Source	**Yes or No? Why?**
"Theresa May's Speech on Terrorism and Extremism"	YES, because there are certain responsibilities one has in a free society, such as respect for British laws.
"Hollande Seeks to Extend State of Emergency Despite Critics"	
"UN Rights Experts Urge France to Protect Fundamental Freedoms While Countering Terrorism"	

 INTERACTIVE

For extra help with Step 3, review the 21st Century Tutorials: **Compare Viewpoints** and **Analyze Primary and Secondary Sources**.

 **FINDINGS**

4 Discuss

You have collected clues about life in medieval Europe and the relationships that existed under feudalism and explored documents about freedom and security in today's world. Now, you are ready to discuss with your classmates the Guiding Question: **Is it worth trading freedom for security?**

You will work with a partner in a small group. Try to reach consensus, a situation where everyone is in agreement, on the question.

1. **Prepare Your Arguments** You will be assigned a position on the question, either YES or NO.

   My position: ....

   Work with your partner to review your Quest notes from the Quest Connections and Quest Sources.

   • If you were assigned YES, agree with your partner on what you think were the strongest arguments from May and Jacinto.

   • If you were assigned NO, agree on what you think were the strongest arguments from the UN Rights Experts.

2. **Present Your Position** Those assigned YES will present their arguments and evidence first. As you listen, ask clarifying questions to gain information and understanding.

What is a Clarifying Question?	
These types of questions do not judge the person talking. They are only for the listener to be clear on what he or she is hearing.	
Example: Can you tell me more about that?	Example: You said [x]. Am I getting that right?

 INTERACTIVE

For extra help with Step 4, review the 21st Century Tutorial: **Participate in a Discussion or Debate**.

While the opposite side speaks, take notes on what you hear in the space below.

3. **Switch!** Now NO and YES will switch sides. If you argued YES before, now you will argue NO. Work with your same partner and use your notes. Add any arguments and evidence from the clues and sources. Those *now* arguing YES go first.

When both sides have finished, answer the following:

Before I started this discussion with my classmates, my opinion was that	After I started this discussion with my classmates, my opinion was that
____ it is worth trading freedom for security. ____ it is not worth trading freedom for security.	____ it is worth trading freedom for security. ____ it is not worth trading freedom for security.

4. **Point of View** Do you all agree on the answer to the Guiding Question?

• __ Yes

• __ No

If not, on what points do you all agree?

Take Notes

Literacy Skills: Sequence Use what you have read to complete the timeline. Draw a line from each event to its correct space on the timeline. Then, write a brief description of each event. The first one has been completed for you.

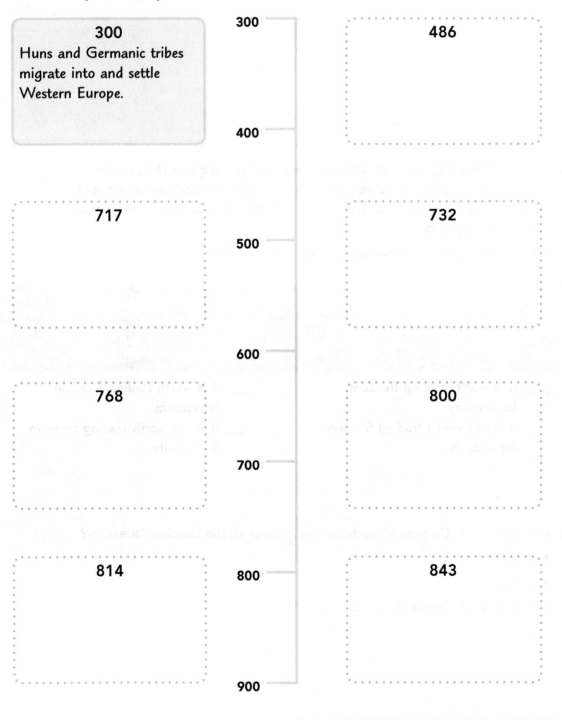

300
Huns and Germanic tribes migrate into and settle Western Europe.

486

300

400

717

732

500

600

768

800

700

814

800

843

900

INTERACTIVE

For extra help, review the 21st Century Tutorial: **Sequence**.

Practice Vocabulary

True or False? Decide whether each statement below is true or false. Circle T or F, and then explain your answer. Be sure to include the underlined vocabulary word in your explanation. The first one is done for you.

1. **T / F** The <u>Middle Ages</u> in Europe began with the rise of the western Roman empire.
False; The <u>Middle Ages</u> in Europe began with the fall of the western Roman empire.

2. **T / F** Under Charlemagne, much of <u>medieval</u> civilization in Europe adopted Christianity.

3. **T / F** Pope Leo III strengthened the role of the Church and the <u>clergy</u> in Europe when he crowned Charlemagne emperor of the Romans.

4. **T / F** Europe has a generally flat and open <u>topography</u> that has left the continent vulnerable to invasion.

 Life in Medieval Christendom

Quick Activity Traveling the Rhine

Study the map of the Rhine River and its major tributaries, or branch rivers, below. What do you notice about the river? How do you think the river encouraged the growth of medieval civilization in Western Europe? Discuss your ideas with a partner.

Did you know?

Estimates of the length of the Rhine River vary from 765 to 820 miles.

Several tributaries, including the Neckar and the Main, extend the reach of the Rhine by several hundred miles.

The Rhine River flows generally in a northwesterly direction.

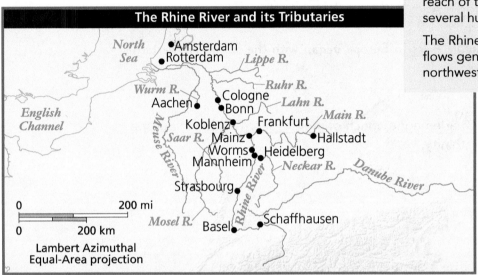

The Rhine River and its Tributaries

Team Challenge! In the classroom, the hallway, or another appropriate space, use masking tape to make a large model of the Rhine River and its major tributaries. Divide the class into a Towns group and a Directions group. Write the names of medieval towns on labels, and affix the labels to the backs of Towns students. Have the Directions students take turns guiding Towns students to the correct location on the map by answering questions, such as "Am I located downstream (in the direction the river flows) or upstream (in the opposite direction)? Am I on the Rhine or a tributary? Near what other town am I located?"

Take Notes

Literacy Skills: Summarize Use what you have read to complete the chart. The column headings correspond to the headings in the text. Summarize information for each section in the text as you read. The first one has been completed for you.

How Did Europe Become Christian?	The Role of Monasteries and Convents	The Medieval Church
Patrick Converts Ireland In the 4th century, Patrick, a man sold into slavery went on to become a missionary who founded the first Catholic Church in Ireland and helped spread Christianity throughout the British Isles. For his work, the Church named him a saint.	The Benedictine Rule	Catholic Teachings
Missionaries Arrive in Britain	Everyday Life in Monasteries	The Power of the Medieval Church
Christianity Spreads Through Europe	Primary Source	What Was Christendom?

INTERACTIVE

For extra help, review the 21st Century Tutorial: **Summarize**.

Practice Vocabulary

Matching Logic Using your knowledge of the underlined vocabulary words, draw a line from each sentence in Column 1 to match it with the sentence in Column 2 to which it logically belongs.

Column 1	Column 2
1. In the Early Middle Ages, many people across Europe remained <u>pagans</u>.	They converted many people and their rulers to Christianity.
2. Catholics believed that they must follow God's laws as the Church taught them and practice the <u>sacraments</u>.	Men followed a strict rule of life that balanced prayer and work.
3. The monk Benedict founded the first European <u>monastery</u> in 529.	They believed in many gods and goddesses.
4. Over the course of the Middle Ages, most of Europe came to view themselves as part of a wider <u>Christendom</u>.	He was believed to be especially holy because he founded the first Catholic Church in Ireland.
5. The Catholic Church recognized the work of a formerly enslaved man named Patrick by naming him a <u>saint</u>.	This large community of Christians extends beyond Europe to places all across the world.
6. Medieval popes sent <u>missionaries</u> to kingdoms and lands across Europe.	They joined the Church through baptism and consumed bread and wine that they believed became the body and blood of Christ through communion.
7. Some medieval women chose to devote themselves to the Catholic Church by entering <u>convents</u>.	They took vows similar to those of monks to seclude themselves in worship.

Take Notes

Literacy Skills: Identify Main Idea and Details Use what you have read to complete the table. In each column, write one main idea and three supporting details from each section of the text. The first one has been completed for you.

A Violent Time	How Did Feudal Society Provide Protection?	How Did Medieval Manors Work?
Main Idea: Between 800 and 1000, waves of invasions changed life in Western Europe.	Main Idea:	Main Idea:
Supporting Detail: Vikings invaded from the north, Muslims from the south, and Magyars from the south and east.	Supporting Detail:	Supporting Detail:
Supporting Detail:	Supporting Detail:	Supporting Detail:
Supporting Detail:	Supporting Detail:	Supporting Detail:

👆 INTERACTIVE

For extra help, review the 21st Century Tutorial: **Identify Main Ideas and Details.**

Practice Vocabulary

Words in Context For each question below, write an answer that shows your understanding of the boldfaced key term.

1. In exchange for land, what did a **vassal** pledge to a more powerful lord?

2. What is the significance of a **fief** in the feudal system?

3. How did a young man become a **knight**?

4. What did **chivalry** require of a knight?

5. Why was the **manor** considered the heart of the medieval economy?

6. What standing did a **serf** have in medieval society?

Take Notes

Literacy Skills: Summarize Use what you have read to complete the table. Record important details from each section of the lesson to summarize change that took place during the Middle Ages. The first one has been completed for you.

New Ways of Farming	Trade and Industry	Growth of Towns
Plows with iron blades pulled by horses replace wooden plows pulled by oxen, so thicker soils of northern Europe could be worked faster.		

INTERACTIVE

For extra help, review the 21st Century Tutorial: **Summarize**.

Practice Vocabulary

Sentence Builder Finish the sentences below with a key term from this section. You may have to change the form of the words to complete the sentences.

Word Bank

crop rotation   fallow

three-field system   guild

1. Farmers planted spring crops, winter crops, and no crops in the

2. To allow the soil to recover some of its natural fertility, farmers every year left one field

3. The practice of changing the use of fields over time is known as

4. Workers who practiced the same craft joined together to protect their economic interests in a

Take Notes

Literacy Skills: Analyze Text Structure Use what you have read to complete the outline. List important details from each section, as well as text features like primary sources and infographics, in the lesson beneath the headings and subheadings. The first one has been completed for you.

Forms of Devotion	How Did Religion Affect Medieval Culture?	Why Did Learning Grow?
Religious Orders At first, monks and nuns prayed and meditated in remote monasteries. Later, monasteries became centers of agricultural production and were located in towns. Mendicant orders were founded to fight heresy and to preach to ordinary people in cities.	Revival of Drama	Medieval Universities
Francis and Clare	New Architecture	Thomas Aquinas
	The Church Shapes Chivalry	An Age of Confidence

INTERACTIVE

For extra help, review the 21st Century Tutorial: **Summarize**.

Practice Vocabulary

Words in Context **For each question below, write an answer that shows your understanding of the boldfaced key term.**

1. How did **mendicant orders** help the people of the growing towns?

2. How did the Church influence the growth of **universities**?

3. How did Thomas Aquinas use **natural law** to explain that both faith and reason come from God?

Quick Activity Illuminating the Middle Ages

With a partner, examine these photos of medieval illuminated texts.

Did you notice the elaborate design and handwritten script of the two pages? During the Middle Ages skilled monks and others copied manuscripts by hand. These manuscripts were often illuminated, or illustrated, with pictures or designs. Most illuminations had religious themes. However, some depicted scenes of everyday life.

Team Challenge! Read the excerpts from Geoffrey Chaucer's The Canterbury Tales below. With your partner, select one of the passages and create your own illuminated text. Be sure to pick a design that fits the content of the excerpt.

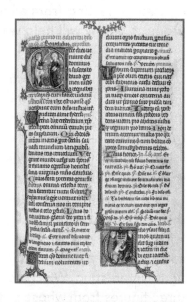

The Knight

> A knight there was, and he a worthy man,
>
> Who, from the moment that he first began
>
> To ride about the world, loved chivalry,
>
> Truth, honour, freedom and all courtesy.
>
> Full worthy was he in his liege-lord's war,
>
> And therein had he ridden (none more far)
>
> As well in Christendom as heathenesse,
>
> And honoured everywhere for worthiness.

The Prioress

> There was also a nun, a prioress, . . .
>
> She was so charitable and piteous
>
> That she would weep if she but saw a mouse
>
> Caught in a trap, though it were dead or bled.
>
> She had some little dogs, too, that she fed
>
> On roasted flesh, or milk and fine white bread.
>
> But sore she'd weep if one of them were dead,
>
> Or if men smote it with a rod to smart:
>
> For pity ruled her, and her tender heart.
>
> — *Prologue from The Canterbury Tales, by Geoffrey Chaucer*

Writing Workshop Narrative

As you read, brainstorm ideas, gather information, and prepare to write diary entries from the perspective of three medieval figures—selecting from a knight, a serf, a monk, or a nun. The prompts below will help walk you through the process.

Lesson 1 Writing Task: Use Credible Sources Consider the historical figures from whose perspective you can write. On a separate sheet of paper, list five sources other than the textbook that you could use to learn about the lives of these figures. Keep in mind that you can list primary and secondary sources. These can be text, visual, video, or audio.

Lesson 2 Writing Task: Identify Main Ideas In the chart, write two things that you think you know about each of the historical figures—knight, serf, monk, and nun—in the first column. Then, in the second column, write a main idea that describes why you find each historical figure interesting. Which do you consider most interesting? Circle the three figures from whose perspective you will write.

	What Do I Know About This Person?	I Find Them Interesting Because . . .
knight		
serf		
monk		
nun		

Lesson 3 Writing Task: Use Narrative Techniques As you prepare to write, consider the tone and style of language each of the figures might use. Think about the types of figurative language, such as metaphors and similes, as well as the level of detail, formality, and emotion with which the figures might write. Pick one figure and write your thoughts on his or her tone and style of language on a separate sheet of paper.

Lesson 4 Writing Task: Identify Supporting Details Consider what you have learned about the three figures from whose perspective you will write. List three details about each figure to support the main ideas you wrote in the second column of the chart on the previous page.

Figure 1:	Figure 2:	Figure 3:
Details:	**Details:**	**Details:**

Lesson 5 Writing Task: Draw Conclusions Review the details you have collected to draw a conclusion about each medieval figure from whose perspective you will write: What was life like for this person? What role did this person play in society? Why did this person matter? Record your conclusions in the space below.

Writing Task Use the main ideas, details, and conclusions you wrote to write a diary entry for each of the three medieval figures you chose. Be sure to use a distinct voice for each diary entry. Each diary entry should reflect the experiences of these figures in their daily lives, their roles in medieval society, and their interests, hopes, and concerns.

Struggle in Medieval Europe Preview

Essential Question What forces can cause a society to change?

Before you begin this topic, think about the Essential Question by completing the following activity.

1. List three things that might happen that can disrupt the way a family or community functions.

2. Preview the topic by skimming lesson titles, headings, and graphics. Then, place a check mark next to the events that you think may have caused struggle in the Middle Ages.

__war	__religion	__music and art
__famine	__rulers' claim to throne	__floods
__different opinions	__peace	__plague

Timeline Skills

As you read, write and/or draw at least three events from the topic. Draw a line from each event to its correct position on the timeline.

900	1000	1100

Map Skills

Label the following locations on your map. Then, color England, Iberian Peninsula, and the area of Holy Roman Empire one color, and the Mediterranean Sea a different color.

Iberian Peninsula	Balkan Peninsula	North European Plain
The Alps	England	Italian Peninsula
Mediterranean Sea	Black Sea	North Sea
France	Holy Roman Empire	

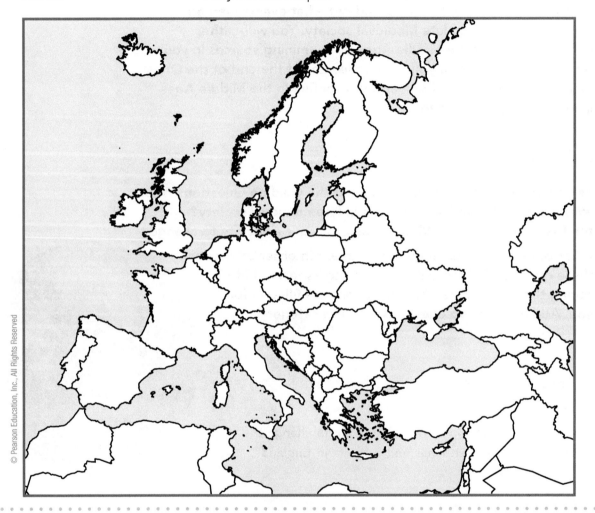

1200	1300	1400	1500

Quest
Project-Based Learning Inquiry

Medieval Monarchs Face Conflicts

On this Quest, you will need to find out what events marked significant changes in late Medieval society. You will gather information about the Middle Ages by examining sources in your text and by conducting your own research. At the end of the Quest, you will design a comic book about a conflict in the Middle Ages involving a king or emperor.

1 Ask Questions

As you begin your Quest, keep in mind the Guiding Question: **What events marked significant changes in late medieval society?** and the Essential Question: **What forces can cause a society to change?**

What other questions do you need to ask in order to answer these questions? Consider the following aspects of life during the Middle Ages. Two questions are filled in for you. Add at least two questions for each category.

Theme Government and the People

Sample questions:

How did the signing of the Magna Carta change the relationship between kings and subjects in England?

What causes contributed to the end of feudalism?

Theme Religion and the Church

Theme Trade and Warfare

Theme Science and Medicine

Theme My Additional Questions

 INTERACTIVE

For extra help with Step 1, review the 21st Century Tutorial: **Ask Questions**.

2 Investigate

As you read about Europe in the Middle Ages, collect five connections from your text to help you answer the Guiding Question. Three are already chosen for you.

Connect to the Magna Carta

Primary Source The Magna Carta

Here's a connection! What does this Primary Source tell you about the Magna Carta? What is the significance of the Magna Carta?

How might different kings or emperors of the Middle Ages have felt about the Magna Carta?

Connect to the Crusades

Lesson 3 What Were the Effects of the Crusades?

Here's another connection! Examine the effects of the Crusades on the crusaders. How will this change the medieval society of Europe?

How do you think the effects of the Crusades influenced the decisions of rulers?

Connect to the Black Death

Primary Source Giovanni Boccaccio, *The Decameron*

What does this connection tell you about the kind of social changes the plague caused in medieval society? Why do you think the plague caused these changes?

How do you think the plague affected the rule of kings and emperors?

It's Your Turn! **Find two more connections. Fill in the title of your connections, then answer the questions. Connections may be images, primary sources, maps, or text.**

Your Choice | Connect to

Location in text

What is the main idea of this connection?

What does it tell you about a conflict involving a king or emperor during the Middle Ages?

Your Choice | Connect to

Location in text

What is the main idea of this connection?

What does it tell you about a conflict involving a king or emperor during the Middle Ages?

③ Conduct Research

Begin your research by finding additional primary and secondary sources of valid information on your own. Fill in the chart to show how these sources provide further information about conflicts involving kings and emperors during the Middle Ages. Use your research to help your team select a specific topic for your comic.

Source	Information About Conflicts

INTERACTIVE

For extra help, review the 21st Century Tutorials: **Work in Teams, Search for Information on the Internet,** and **Avoid Plagiarism**.

4 Create Your Comic Book

You will now work together as a team to fully research, write, illustrate and summarize a comic book about a specific conflict covered in this topic.

1. **Prepare to Write** Decide, as a group, what conflict you would like to focus on and what the title of your comic book will be. Record your decisions below.

Title of Comic Book:

Conflict:

Team Member Assignments

Use the chart below to help your team assign responsibility for each part of your project. You may have more than one teammate working on a given section, or one team member may need to be responsible for more than one section.

Responsibility	Teammate(s) Responsible
Additional Research	
Write Cover	
Illustrate Cover	
Write Illustrated Page	
Draw Illustrated Page	
Write Summary	

2. **Write a Draft** Using your research, outline the pieces of the project according to your responsibilities. Make sure that all of your facts are correct and consistent with your sources.

3. **Share with Your Team** Share your draft with your team. Tell your team what you like about their pieces and suggest any improvements. Use positive and professional language as you critique each others' work.

4. **Finalize Your Project** Correct any grammatical, spelling, or factual errors. Be sure to complete an illustrated cover page, an illustrated page, and a well-written summary of your comic.

5. **Reflect** Think about your experience in completing this topic's Quest. What did you learn about Europe in the Middle Ages and the conflicts involving its rulers? What questions do you still have? How will you answer them?

Reflections

Take Notes

Literacy Skill: Compare and Contrast Use what you have read to complete the diagram. Identify the objectives of the German emperors and the popes. What was different? What was the same?

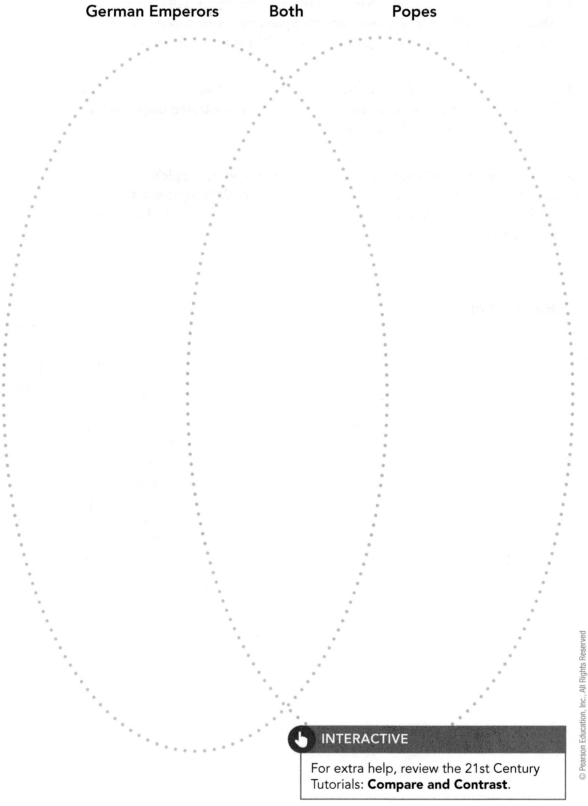

German Emperors   Both   Popes

INTERACTIVE

For extra help, review the 21st Century Tutorials: **Compare and Contrast**.

Practice Vocabulary

Word Map Study the word map for the word *excommunicate*. Characteristics are words or phrases that relate to the word in the center of the word map. Non-characteristics are words or phrases not associated with the word. Use the blank word map to explore the meaning of the word *secular*.

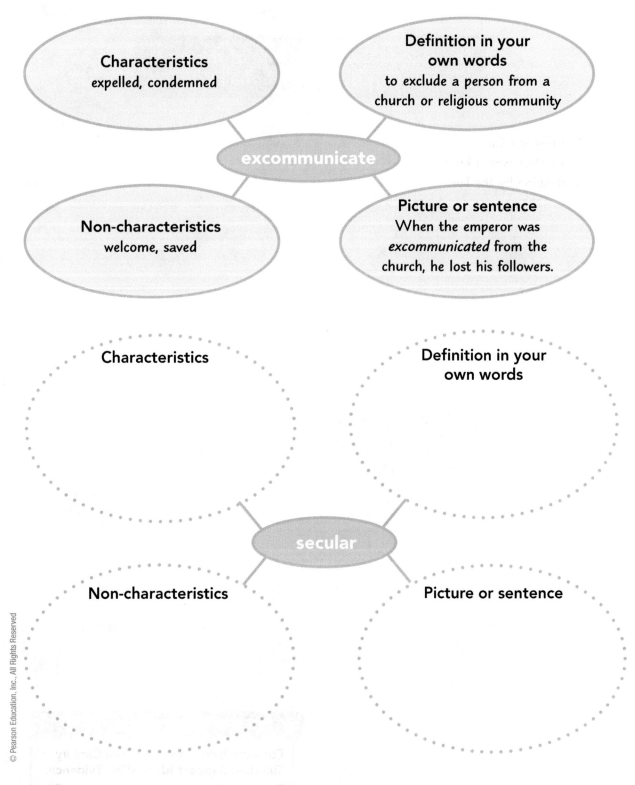

Characteristics
expelled, condemned

Definition in your own words
to exclude a person from a church or religious community

excommunicate

Non-characteristics
welcome, saved

Picture or sentence
When the emperor was *excommunicated* from the church, he lost his followers.

Characteristics

Definition in your own words

secular

Non-characteristics

Picture or sentence

Take Notes

Literacy Skills: Cite Evidence For each statement, cite evidence from the text that supports the idea. One example has been provided for you. Complete the chart with supporting evidence. For the second chart, draw your own conclusion from the text and use evidence to support your claim.

The Magna Carta was one of the most important documents of all time.

The Magna Carta stated that even a king must abide by the law.

The Norman Conquest transformed English history and culture.

INTERACTIVE

For extra help, review the 21st Century Tutorials: **Support Ideas With Evidence**.

Practice Vocabulary

Words in Context For each question below, write an answer that shows your understanding of the boldfaced key term.

1. Why is a **pilgrimage** significant for religious people?

2. What is the significance of the **Magna Carta**?

3. What is **common law**?

4. What is **habeas corpus**, and what is its significance?

5. What is another way of saying a **writ**?

6. What is a **parliament** and why is it important?

7. How was the **judiciary** system first formed in England?

Take Notes

Literacy Skills: Sequence Use what you have read to complete the table. Use the flowchart to sequence the events of the Crusades. In each box, draw or write about important details associated with the event. The first one has been partially filled in for you.

Before the Crusades

- Peter the Hermit rallied thousands of people to join his fight to free Jerusalem.

First Crusade

Second and Third Crusades

Fourth Crusade

Final Crusades

Inquisition

INTERACTIVE

For extra help, review the 21st Century Tutorials: **Sequence**.

Practice Vocabulary

Matching Logic Using your knowledge of the underlined vocabulary words, draw a line from each sentence in Column 1 to match it with the sentence in Column 2 to which it logically belongs.

Column 1	Column 2
1. A lot of people were killed or tortured during the Inquisition.	They were a series of campaigns to establish Christian control in the Holy Land.
2. Many people were excommunicated, exiled, or killed for heresy.	These courts targeted people who did not agree with the church.
3. The Crusades involved peasants, soldiers and kings from across Europe.	The Church did not tolerate differences in religious beliefs.

Quick Activity Crusade Diary

Imagine that you are living at the time of the Crusades. Choose a point of view, and write a short diary entry from that perspective. Consider including details such as: What do you see? How does it make you feel? Why did this crusade take place? Why did people join this crusade? What happened during this crusade? What were some of the results of this crusade? Here are some possible points of view you could choose.

• You are a knight who has joined the First Crusade.

• You are a member of one of the later crusades.

• You live in Constantinople when the Fourth Crusade comes through your city.

Take Notes

Literacy Skills: Summarize Use what you have read to complete the table. Write two details for each main idea, and use them to write a summary of the chapter below. One detail has been provided for you.

Spain Under the Moors	The Reconquista	Spain After the Reconquista
• There was a blend of cultures.	•	•
•	•	•

Summary

👆 INTERACTIVE

For extra help, review the 21st Century Tutorials: **Summarize**.

Practice Vocabulary

True or False? Decide whether each statement below is true or false.
Circle T or F, and then explain your answer. Be sure to include the
underlined vocabulary word in your explanation. The first one has been
completed for you.

1. **T / F** The <u>Iberian Peninsula</u> contains present-day Italy.
   False. The <u>Iberian Peninsula</u> contains present-day Spain and Portugal.

2. **T / F** The <u>Moors</u> ruled a diverse society that made advances in art and medicine.

3. **T / F** The <u>Reconquista</u> was the Christian reclaiming of the Holy Land.

Take Notes

Literacy Skills: Identify Cause and Effect Use what you have read to complete the table. For each event, identify three causes that led to the event. One example has been completed for you.

Effect: The population of Europe decreased dramatically in the 1300s.

Cause:
Famine—bad weather ruined crops and killed livestock, leading to a food shortage

Cause:

Cause:

Effect: The end of the Middle Ages brought the end of feudalism.

Cause:

Cause:

Cause:

👆 **INTERACTIVE**

For extra help, review the 21st Century Tutorials: **Analyze Cause and Effect**.

Practice Vocabulary

Use a Word Bank Choose one word from the following word bank to fill in each blank. When you have finished, you will have a short summary of important ideas from this section.

Word Bank

bubonic plague	Peasants' Revolt	famine
Black Death	Hundred Years' War	

In the 1300s, a series of events caused the decline of medieval society.

Heavy rainfall over two years ruined many crops, leading to widespread

_____ across northern Europe. Following

that, a new kind of war, a war between nations, broke out between

England and France. Lasting from 1337–1453, it became known as

the _____. After about ten years of war,

the _____ spread throughout Asia and

Europe. The population decreased so much that the epidemic became

known as the _____. As economic and social

tensions about feudalism increased, English peasants mounted the

_____. The end of the Middle Ages was the

beginning of the modern era in Europe.

Quick Activity Dark Times Skit

With a partner or small group, develop a short skit about one of the terrible disasters of the late Middle Ages.

Setting	Character	Plot
Where does your skit take place?	Create at least two characters and describe their names, ages, occupations, and history.	What is the conflict? What events unfold?

Team Challenge First, choose the disaster that your team will focus on. Next, brainstorm its effects on the lives, feelings, and outlook of ordinary people. Use the chart above to outline your skit. Then, write your script on a separate piece of paper.

Which disaster will your skit cover?

____ Famine ____ Plague ____ Hundred Years' War

Writing Workshop: Write a Research Paper

Do research and write a brief account of some aspect of Jewish life in medieval Europe, such as the impact of the Crusades or the Plague on Jewish populations, Jewish life in Spain before or after the Reconquista, or Jewish migration. The prompts below will help guide you through the process.

Lesson 1 Writing Task: Generate Questions to Focus Your Research
What do you know about Jewish life in Medieval Europe? Consider ideas, such as the impact of the Crusades or the Plague on Jewish populations, Jewish life in Spain before or after the Reconquista, or Jewish migration during the Middle Ages. Use the box below to formulate two to four questions and then select one question on which to focus.

Lesson 2 Writing Task: Find and Use Credible Sources Look for reliable sources that provide credible and accurate information about Jewish life in Medieval Europe. Take notes on information that you may use in your paper. Record web addresses and other source information so you can find them again, and so you can cite accurately.

Source (Title and Author or Web Address)	Notes

Lesson 3 Writing Task: Support Ideas with Evidence Examine your credible sources for evidence that supports what you have learned about Jewish life in Medieval Europe. Use a separate piece of paper to write a brief outline of your ideas, with supporting details from the text. Be sure to indicate from which source you got your information.

Lesson 4 Writing Task: Cite Sources Review the sources that you noted. Write full citations for all of your sources, following the format provided by your teacher. Include the name of the article or text, the author, the publisher, the date of publication, and the web address (if applicable). This information should be included at the end of your research paper.

Source (Title and Author or Web Address)	Correct Citation

Lesson 5 Writing Task: Use Technology to Produce and Publish Using your outline and the information you have gathered, write a brief account of some aspect of Jewish life in medieval Europe. Make use of appropriate technology to create and distribute your research paper. Consider your audience as you decide in what form(s) to publish your work.

The Islamic World and South Asia Preview

Essential Question **How do ideas grow and spread?**

Before you begin this topic, think about the Essential Question by completing the following activity.

1. What people, places, experiences, or things have influenced or changed your personal values and ideas?

2. Preview the topic by skimming lesson titles, headlines, and graphics. Then place a check mark next to the items below that you predict will influence how ideas grow and spread.

__traveling   __conquering other lands   __staying home by yourself

__technological advances   __art, architecture, literature __making carpets

__being curious   __talking with people

Timeline Skills

As you read, write and/or draw at least three events from the topic. Draw a line from each event to its correct position on the timeline.

500	700	900

Map Skills

Using the map in your text, label the outline map with the places listed.
Then, color the land showing the extent of the Muslim world in the
year 1000.

Sasanian Persian empire	Arabia	Europe	Morocco
Egypt	Spain	Asia	Mecca
Medina	Cairo	Baghdad	Jerusalem

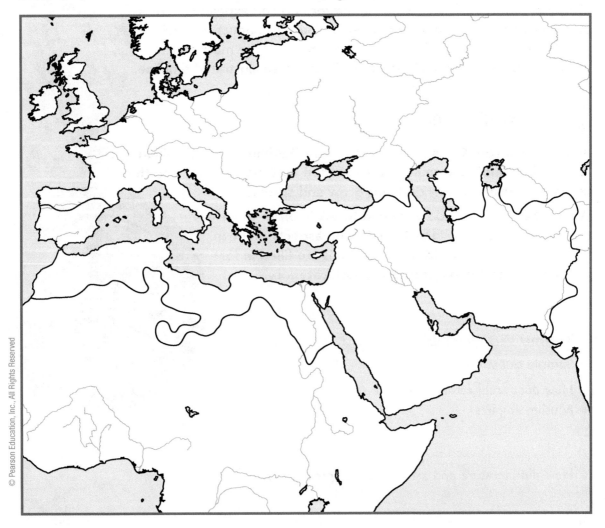

1100	1300	1500	1700

Quest
Project -Based Learning Inquiry

Growth of Muslim Empires

On this Quest, you need to find out which key events best show the history of different Muslim empires that formed and expanded across Southwest Asia, South Asia, and beyond. You will conduct research about the expansion of Islam and find examples of the most critical events. At the end of the Quest, you will create an illustrated timeline.

1 Ask Questions

As you begin your Quest, keep in mind the Guiding Question: **What key Muslim empires formed and expanded during this time?** and the Essential Question: **How do ideas grow and spread?**

What other questions do you need to ask in order to answer these questions? Consider the following aspects of life in the ancient Muslim world. Two questions are filled in for you. Add at least two questions in each category.

Theme Art, Architecture, and Literature
Sample questions:

How does architecture reveal the spread and influence of Muslim empires?

How did literature and art reflect the spread of Islam and other ideas?

Theme Trade

Theme Warfare and Conquest

Theme Religion and Cultural Life

Theme Science, Mathematics, and Medicine

Theme My Additional Questions

 INTERACTIVE

For help with Step 1, review the
21st Century Skills Tutorial: **Ask Questions.**

② Investigate

As you read about the growth and expansion of Muslim empires, collect five connections from your text to help you answer the Guiding Question. Three connections are already chosen for you.

Connect to the Spread of Islam

Lesson 3 The Caliphs

Here's a connection! Examine the how cultures change. What cultural changes did the spread of Islam during the time of the caliphs bring within empires? How did these changes affect society?

How did those changes affect the expansion of Muslim empires?

Connect to Timelines

Analysis Skills Construct a Timeline

Here's another connection! What other events do you think would help show what key Muslim empires formed and expanded? Where do they fall on the timeline?

What changes did they inspire?

Connect to the Arrival of Islam in India

Lesson 5 Islam Arrives in India

What does this connection tell you about the specific events that brought Islam to India?

What new ideas came from that meeting of cultures?

It's Your Turn! **Find two more connections. Fill in the title of your connections, then answer the questions. Connections may be images, primary sources, maps, or text.**

Your Choice | Connect to

Location

What is the main idea of this connection?

What does it tell you about how ideas grow and spread?

Your Choice | Connect to

What is the main idea of this connection?

What does it tell you about how ideas grow and spread?

③ Conduct Research

Begin your research by finding out more about the various empires and dynasties of the Islamic world from the 600s to the 1600s. Fill in the chart below with key events and dates to help you organize your information. Circle the dates since they will become the key to designing and organizing your timeline.

Empire or Dynasty	Important Events and Dates

 INTERACTIVE

For extra help with Step 3, review the 21st Century Skills Tutorial: **Sequence**.

4 Make Your Illustrated Timeline

Now it's time to put together all of the information you have gathered and use it to create your illustrated timeline.

1. **Prepare to Write** Begin by looking through your information above and choosing the events that you think are most important to the expansion of key empires in the Muslim world. Then use the flowchart below to put your events in chronological order.

2. **Write a Draft** Create a rough draft listing the events you want to include on your timeline. Decide on the start and end dates and how long the time intervals will be. Include notes on the design. For example, you might want to include color-coded bars showing the length of time for each empire and how they overlapped. Choose or draw illustrations to go with your events.

3. **Share with a Partner** Exchange your draft with a partner. Tell your partner what you like about his or her draft and suggest any improvements.

4. **Finalize Your Timeline** Correct any spelling or grammatical errors. Use technology to finalize and publish your timeline.

5. **Reflect on the Quest** Think about your experience completing this topic's Quest. What did you learn about Muslim empires and how they expanded? What questions do you still have about the Muslim empires? How will you answer them?

Reflections

The Islamic World and South Asia

Take Notes

Literacy Skills: Identify Main Ideas and Details Use what you have read
to complete the table. In each space, write one main idea and two
details. The first column is completed for you.

The Arabian Setting	The Rise of Islam
Main Idea: The environment significantly influenced life in Arabia.	**Main Idea:**
Details: The harsh environment helped keep foreign invaders out. In dry regions, people depend on oases for water, because there is very little water otherwise.	**Details:**

Preaching a New Message	The Hijra
Main Idea:	**Main Idea:**
Details:	**Details:**

👆 **INTERACTIVE**

For extra help, review the 21st Century Skills
Tutorial: **Identify Main Ideas and Detail.**

Practice Vocabulary

True or False? Decide whether each statement below is true or false. Circle T or F, and then explain your answer. Be sure to include the underlined vocabulary word in your explanation. The first one is done for you.

1. **T / F** An <u>oasis</u> is a place in the desert where only sand can be found.
   False; An <u>oasis</u> is a place in the desert where water can be found.

2. **T / F** Muhammad said that <u>revelations</u> he received in the cave were messages from God.

3. **T / F** <u>Nomads</u> are people who live in one place for their entire lives.

4. **T / F** The <u>Hijra</u> is another name for Muhammad's journey back to Mecca.

5. **T / F** A <u>prophet</u> is a person believed to bring messages to the people from God.

Quick Activity Caption This!

With a partner, analyze the following three images.

Team Challenge! With your partner, write a short caption for each image that explains how geography affects an aspect of life in Arabia. Post your captions to the class board.

Take Notes

Literacy Skills: Summarize Use what you have read to complete
the chart. Then write a summary of the section in the box below.

Sources of Islamic Teaching	Islamic Beliefs about God	Five Pillars of Islam

Summary

INTERACTIVE

For extra help, review the 21st Century
Skills Tutorial: **Summarize**.

Practice Vocabulary

Sentence Builder Finish the sentences below with a key term from this section. You may have to change the form of the words to complete the sentences.

Word Bank

Quran   Sunnah   hajj

mosque   Sharia

1. A Muslim house of worship is called a

2. Guidelines for living a proper Muslim life are provided by the

3. The Islamic code of law is known as the

4. The pilgrimage to Mecca is called the

5. The holy book of Islam is called the

Take Notes

Literacy Skills: Sequence Use what you have read to complete the timeline. Sequence the events that marked the expansion of the Muslim world. For each date, write or draw in the box about a significant event that occurred at that time. The first one is completed for you.

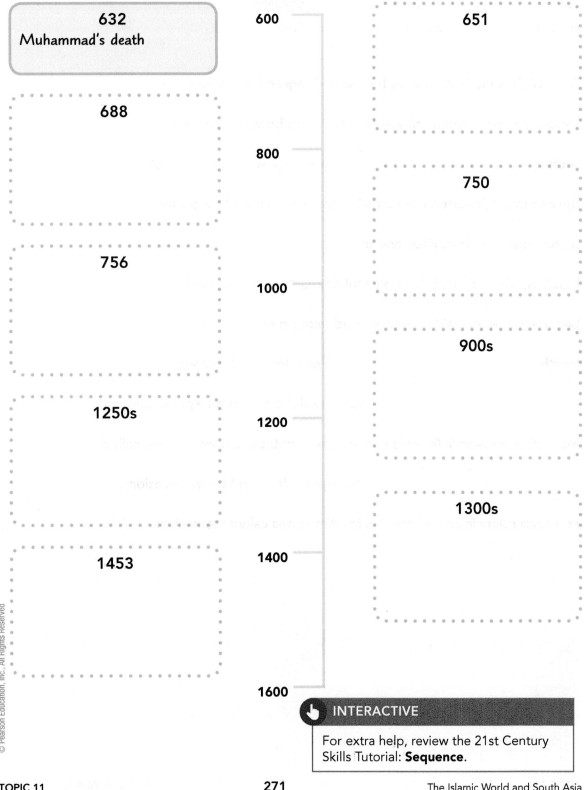

632
Muhammad's death

688

756

1250s

1453

600

800

1000

1200

1400

1600

651

750

900s

1300s

INTERACTIVE

For extra help, review the 21st Century Skills Tutorial: **Sequence**.

Practice Vocabulary

Use a Word Bank Choose one word from the word bank to fill in each blank. When you have finished, you will have a short summary of important ideas from the section.

Word Bank

Sufism	Shia	dynasty
sultans	caliph	Sunni

After Muhammad's death, his followers disagreed about who should lead their community. It lead to a split between the two sects: _____ Muslims, who believed that the community needed a leader with political skills and supported Muhammad's main advisor, and the _____ Muslims, who believed that only Muhammad's relatives should become the leader. When Muhammad's cousin became the fourth _____, or ruler, the Umayyad _____ was established. As Islam spread and expanded, an Islamic lifestyle that stresses controlling ones desires, called _____, emerged. After the Mongol invasions, non-Arab rulers in some surviving Muslim states called themselves _____.

Take Notes

Literacy Skills: Identify Cause and Effect Use what you have read to complete the table. Write the effects of each event or idea below. The first one is completed for you.

> **The Muslim world was at the crossroads of many trade routes.**

- Goods and luxury items came from far-away places, like silk from China.

> **The Muslim world made significant advances in the arts, literature, math, and science.**

INTERACTIVE

For extra help, review the 21st Century Skills Tutorial: **Analyze Cause and Effect**.

Practice Vocabulary

Matching Logic Using your knowledge of the underlined vocabulary words, draw a line from each sentence in Column 1 to match it with the sentence in Column 2 to which it logically belongs.

Column 1	Column 2
1. Advances in mathematics led to the refinement of <u>Arabic numerals</u>.	Persian rugs remain a luxury item in modern times.
2. The Muslim world became well known for its <u>textile</u> work.	Islam prohibits the depiction of humans and animals in religious art, so Muhammad is often represented by his name.
3. <u>Calligraphy</u> is a merging of art and writing.	Much of the modern world continues to write numbers in this style.

Quick Activity

Fun with Words! Many words in the English language originally come from another language. Some common English words are derived from Arabic. Examine the Arabic words below.

Arabic Word	English Definition	English Word
Sukkar	a natural fiber that many clothing products are made from	
Qutn	a caffeinated beverage that many people drink in the morning	
Al-jabr	a comfortable piece of furniture	
Qahwa	a method of mathematics useful for solving problems	
Suffa	a sweetener	

Team Challenge! Working with a partner, draw a line from each Arabic word to its English definition. Then write the modern English word that derives from the Arabic word in the box next to its definition.

Take Notes

Literacy Skills: Cite Evidence Use what you have read to complete the table. Cite three pieces of evidence from the text that support each main idea below. The first one has been completed for you.

> **Trade and expansion affected the development of Hinduism and Buddhism.**

Maritime and overland trade allowed people to exchange ideas with members of other faiths.

> **The arrival of Islam changed the political, cultural, and religious landscape in much of India.**

INTERACTIVE

For extra help, review the 21st Century Skills Tutorial: **Support Ideas With Evidence**.

Practice Vocabulary

Word Map Study the word map for the word *maritime*. Characteristics are words or phrases that relate to the word in the center of the word map. Non-characteristics are words and phrases not associated with the word. Use the blank word map to explore the meaning of the word *Bhakti*. Then make your own word map for the word *bodhisattva*.

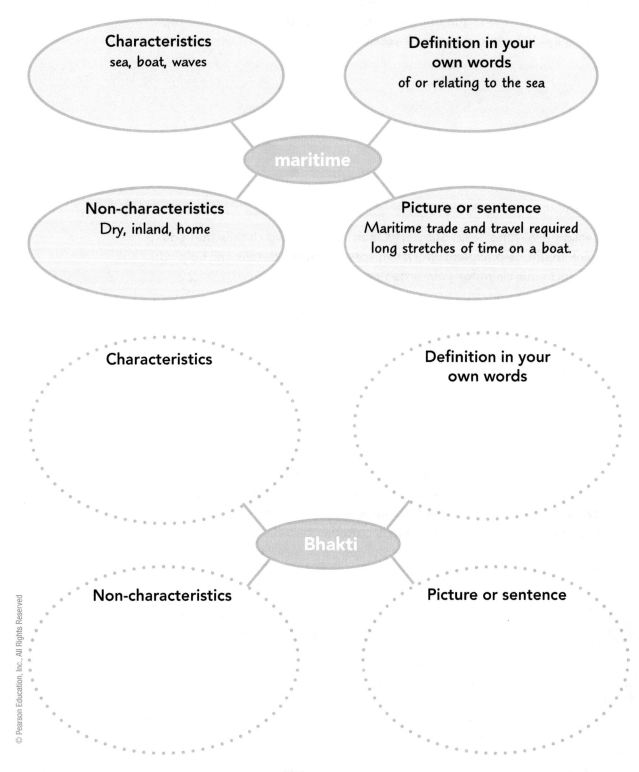

Characteristics
sea, boat, waves

Definition in your own words
of or relating to the sea

maritime

Non-characteristics
Dry, inland, home

Picture or sentence
Maritime trade and travel required long stretches of time on a boat.

Characteristics

Definition in your own words

Bhakti

Non-characteristics

Picture or sentence

Writing Workshop Arguments

As you read, develop a claim in response to this question: **Was conquest or trade the key factor in the growth of Islamic empires?** The prompts below will help walk you through the process.

Lesson 1 Writing Task: Introduce Claim Write one sentence that states your claim about whether you think conquest or trade was the key factor in the growth of Islamic empires. This will be your thesis statement for the argument that you will write at the end of the topic. You may change your thesis as you learn more.

Lesson 2 Writing Task: Support Claim Identify two details that you think might help explain why Islam spread. These details will help you support your claim for your argument.

Lesson 3 Writing Task: Use Credible Sources Choose one source of information that you will use to research your argument about the expansion of Islam. Write a paragraph that identifies the source and explain why you think the source is credible, or believable.

Lesson 4 Writing Task: Distinguish Claims from Opposing Claims
Imagine arguments for and against your main ideas about whether conquest or trade was a key factor in the growth of Islamic empires.

Your Claims	Opposing Claims

Lesson 5 Writing Task: Write an Introduction and a Conclusion
Revise your thesis sentence and write a draft of an introductory paragraph for your essay, introducing your main ideas. Draft a conclusion paragraph, revisiting the thesis from a different angle and formulating how you will leave a lasting impression.

Writing Task Using all of the components that you have created, write an argument about whether conquest or trade was the key factor in the growth of Islamic empires. As you write, consider using signal words to help you transition between making your claims and addressing counterclaims.

Essential Question **How Do Ideas Grow and Spread?**

Before you begin this topic, think about the Essential Question by answering the following question.

1. Think about the language that you speak and write, traditions that you celebrate, food that you know how to grow or prepare, beliefs that you have, skills that you possess, and stories and songs that you know. How did you learn about these things? Write your answers below.

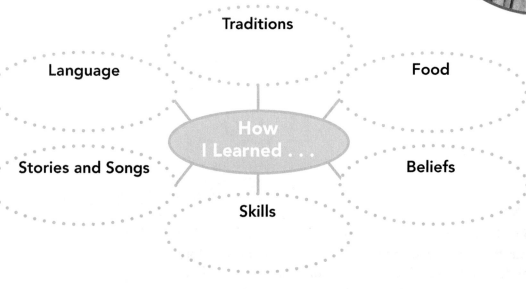

Timeline Skills

As you read, write and/or draw at least three events from the topic. Draw a line from each event to its correct position on the timeline.

400	600	800

Map Skills

**Using the map in your text, label the outline map with the places listed.
Then color in water, desert, plains, plateau, and mountains.**

China   Japan   Korean Peninsula

Pacific Ocean   Sea of Japan (East Sea)   Yellow Sea

Huang River   Chang River   Mekong River

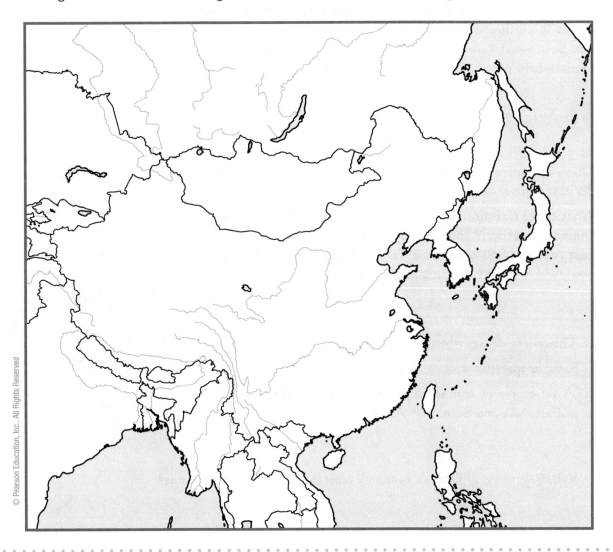

1000   1200   1400

Quest

Document-Based Writing Inquiry

A Strong Influence

On this Quest, you will explore primary and secondary sources about the influence of ancient China on other cultures in East Asia and Southeast Asia. At the end of the Quest you will write an explanatory essay about China's influence.

1 Ask Questions

As you begin your Quest, keep in mind the Guiding Question: **How did China influence the cultures around it?** and the Essential Question: **How do ideas grow and spread?**

What other questions do you need to ask in order to answer the Guiding Question? Think about the following aspects of life in East Asia and Southeast Asia. Two questions are filled in for you. Add at least two questions for each category.

Theme Economic Activity

Sample questions:

What economic contact did China have with other cultures in East Asia and Southeast Asia?

What elements of China's economy appeared in neighboring lands?

Theme Government and Society

Theme Technology and Innovation

Theme Religion and Philosophy

Theme Arts and Literature

Theme My Additional Questions

 INTERACTIVE

For extra help with Step 1, review
the 21st Century Skills Tutorial:
Ask Questions.

2 Investigate

As you read about ancient China and other cultures in East Asia and Southeast Asia, collect five connections from your text to help you answer the Guiding Question. Three connections are already chosen for you.

Connect to the Spread of Buddhism

Lesson 3 Chinese Belief Systems

Here's a connection! Study the map. Where did Buddhism originate? Where did it spread?

How does this source demonstrate the spread of ideas?

Connect to the Constitution of Seventeen Articles

Lesson 4 How Did Shotoku Strengthen Japan?

Here's another connection! Read the quote from the Constitution of Seventeen Articles. How does the quote reflect Chinese influence?

How does this source demonstrate the spread of ideas?

Connect to Chinese and Japanese Architecture

Lesson 6 Japan's Golden Age

Study the images of temple structures found in China and Japan. Compare the styles of architecture. How are they similar and different? What purpose do the structures share?

How does this source demonstrate the spread of ideas?

It's your turn! **Find two more connections on your own. Fill in the title of your connections, then answer the questions. Connections may be images, primary sources, maps, or text.**

Your Choice | Connect to

Location in text

What is the main idea of this connection?

What does this source demonstrate about the spread of ideas in East Asia and Southeast Asia?

Your Choice | Connect to

Location in text

What is the main idea of this connection?

What does this source demonstrate about the spread of ideas in East Asia and Southeast Asia?

③ Examine Primary and Secondary Sources

Examine the primary and secondary sources provided online or from your teacher. Fill in the chart to show how these sources provide further information about the spread of ideas from China to other parts of East Asia and Southeast Asia. The first one is done for you.

Source	How Source Demonstrates the Spread of Ideas from China
Song for the Peace of the People	Shows the spread of Chinese characters as well as Buddhist and Confucian belief systems to Korea
Van Hanh Zen Temple in Vietnam	
Regional Court Examination in Vietnam	
The Spread of Chinese Civilization to Japan	
Chinese, Korean, and Japanese Writing Systems	

👆 **INTERACTIVE**

For extra help with Step 3, review the 21st Century Skills Tutorials: **Analyze Primary and Secondary Sources** and **Analyze Images.**

Quest FINDINGS

4 Write Your Explanatory Essay

Now it's time to put together all of the information you have gathered and use it to write your explanatory essay.

1. **Prepare to Write** You have collected connections and explored documents that show the spread and influence of Chinese culture to neighboring lands and peoples. Look through your notes and decide what evidence of this influence on Korea, Japan, and Southeast Asia you want to discuss in your essay. Summarize your evidence here.

Evidence

2. **Write a Thesis Statement** Your explanatory essay should answer the Guiding Question: **How did China influence the cultures around it?** Use the information you gathered to write a thesis statement in response to the question.

3. **Write a Draft** Your essay should build on your thesis statement by providing evidence to explain that China influenced the cultures around it. Review the evidence you recorded. Plan your essay by numbering each piece of evidence in the order you want to present the information in your essay. Then, write a draft of your explanatory essay. Remember to include an introductory paragraph that includes your thesis statement, as well as a concluding paragraph to restate the thesis. The body of your essay should comprise three to five paragraphs that present and explain evidence from the Quest Connections and Quest Source documents.

4. **Share with a Partner** Exchange drafts with a partner. Read and provide feedback on the drafts. Be sure to consider whether each draft adequately and clearly answers the Guiding Question and provides sufficient evidence to support the thesis statement.

5. **Finalize Your Essay** Revise your essay. Correct any grammatical or spelling errrors.

6. **Reflect on the Quest** Think about your experience completing this topic's Quest. What did you learn about the influence of ancient China on neighboring cultures in Korea, Japan, and Southeast Asia? What questions do you still have about these distinct cultures? How will you answer them?

Reflections

 INTERACTIVE

For extra help with Step 4, review the 21st Century Skills Tutorial: **Write an Essay**.

Take Notes

Literacy Skills: Identify Main Ideas and Details Use what you have read to complete the concept web. Record main ideas from the lesson. The first one has been completed for you.

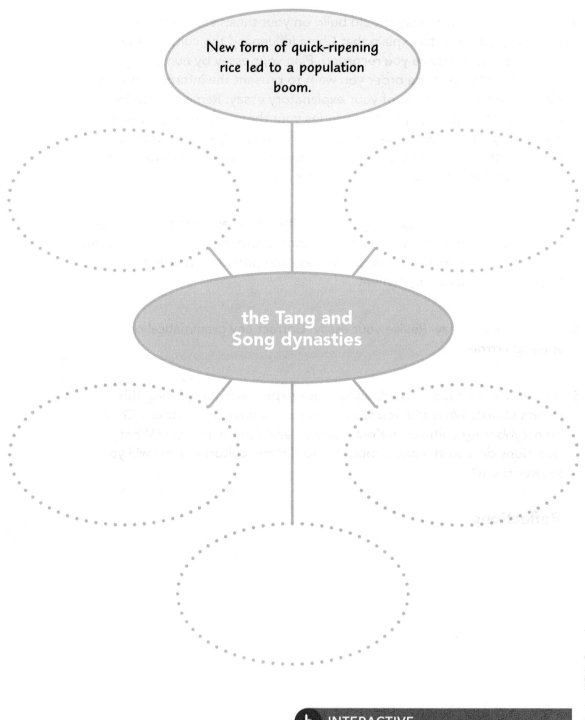

New form of quick-ripening rice led to a population boom.

the Tang and Song dynasties

INTERACTIVE

For extra help, review the 21st Century Skills Tutorial: **Identify Main Ideas and Details**.

Practice Vocabulary

Vocabulary Quiz Show Some quiz shows ask a question and expect the contestant to give the answer. In other shows, the contestant is given an answer and must supply the question. If the blank is in the Question column, write the question that would result in the answer in the Answer column. If the question is supplied, write the answer.

Question	Answer
1. What method of promotion rewards skills and talent?	1.
2.	2. porcelain
3. What system of exchange uses currency, rather than bartering?	3.
4.	4. urbanization
5. What were civil servants in China called?	5.
6.	6. bureaucracy

Take Notes

Literacy Skills: Sequence Use what you have read to complete the timeline. Record important events about the Mongol horde, as well as about the Yuan and Ming dynasties in China. The first one has been completed for you.

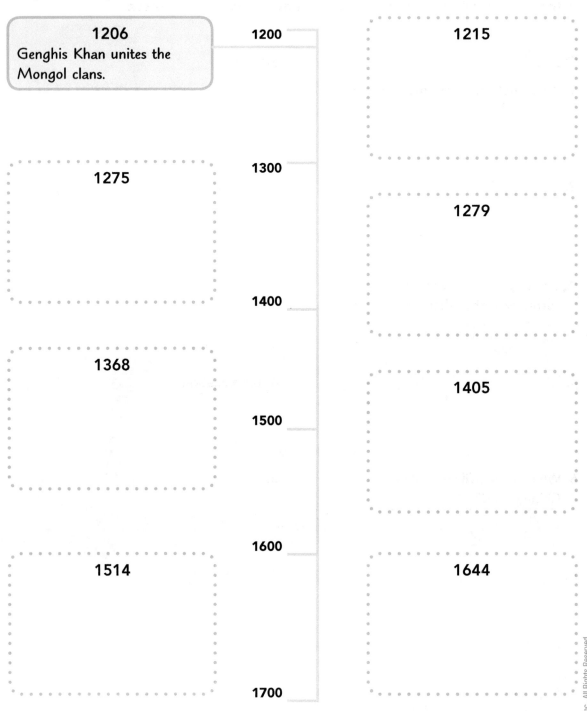

1206
Genghis Khan unites the Mongol clans.

1200

1215

1275

1300

1279

1400

1368

1405

1500

1514

1600

1644

1700

INTERACTIVE

For extra help, review the 21st Century Skills Tutorial: **Sequence**.

Practice Vocabulary

Sentence Builder Finish the sentences below with a vocabulary term from this section. You may have to change the form of the words to complete the sentences.

Word Bank

despot	khan	nomad
smuggler	steppe	tribute

1. The terms *large*, *dry*, and *grass-covered* describe a

2. A cruel tyrant or dictator is also called a

3. Someone who moves from place to place according to the seasons is called a

4. To show their leadership, Genghis and Kublai took the title

5. Ming China forced several foreign countries to make payments called

6. People who trade illegally are called

Take Notes

Literacy Skills: Identify Main Idea and Details Use what you have read to complete the chart. In each column, write a main idea and then support it with details from the text.

Technology	Arts	Belief Systems	Influence

INTERACTIVE

For extra help, review the 21st Century Skills Tutorial: **Identify Main Ideas and Details**.

Practice Vocabulary

Words in Context For each question below, write an answer that shows your understanding of the boldfaced vocabulary term.

1. What steps does **block printing** involve?

2. What advantage did the **compass** provide?

3. What does **Daoism** teach?

4. What are the basic values of **Confucianism**?

5. Why did **Buddhism** appeal to the Chinese during troubled times?

Quick Activity Ways of Thinking and Believing

Read the primary source excerpts below. Identify each quote as reflecting the beliefs of Buddhism, Confucianism, or Daoism.

> They are few who, being filial and fraternal, are fond of offending against their superiors. There have been none, who, not liking to offend against their superiors, have been fond of stirring up confusion. The superior man bends his attention to what is radical. That being established, all practical courses naturally grow up. Filial piety and fraternal submission—are they not the root of all benevolent actions?

> NOT exalting worth keeps the people from rivalry. Not prizing what is hard to procure keeps the people from theft. Not to show them what they may covet is the way to keep their minds from disorder. Therefore the Sage, when he governs, empties their minds and fills their bellies, weakens their inclinations and strengthens their bones.... He practises inaction, and nothing remains ungoverned.

> Moved by their selfish desires, people seek after fame and glory. But when they have acquired it, they are already stricken in years. If you hanker after worldly fame and practise not the Way, your labors are wrongfully applied and your energy is wasted. It is like unto burning an incense stick. However much its pleasing odor be admired, the fire that consumes is steadily burning up the stick.

Team Challenge! Choose one of the belief systems described in Lesson 3: Buddhism, Daoism, or Confucianism. In the space below, write an explanation of the core beliefs of the belief system you chose. Then, circulate around the class room. With your classmates, take turns sharing your explanation and identifying the belief system.

Take Notes

Literacy Skills: Sequence Use what you have read to complete the timeline. In each space write the event that occurred on that date. The first one has been completed for you.

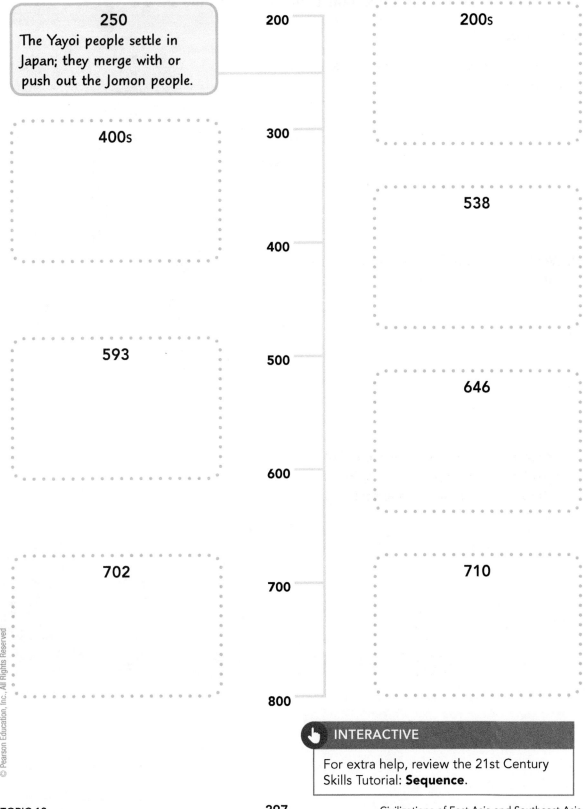

250
The Yayoi people settle in Japan; they merge with or push out the Jomon people.

200

200s

400s

300

538

400

593

500

646

600

702

700

710

800

INTERACTIVE

For extra help, review the 21st Century Skills Tutorial: **Sequence**.

Practice Vocabulary

Vocabulary Quiz Show Some quiz shows ask a question and expect the contestant to give the answer. In other shows, the contestant is given an answer and must supply the question. If the blank is in the Question column, write the question that would result in the answer in the Answer column. If the question is supplied, write the answer.

Question	Answer
1. What is an area that forms part of a continent?	1.
2.	2. archipelago
3. What is the name for a group of people with a common ancestor?	3.
4.	4. regent
5. According to ancient Japanese belief, what holy being represents a spirit of nature, a sacred place, an ancestor, or a clan?	5.

Quick Activity Guiding Principles

In 604, Prince Shotoku of Japan authored the Constitution of Seventeen Articles. The Articles provided guidelines to strengthen the central government against the power of competing warlords and clans. Read the excerpts from the Articles below. As you read, underline the part of each article that suggests why that guideline should be followed. Then, explain what the guideline means, in your own words, and explain whether you agree or disagree with the guideline and why.

1. Deal [fairly] with the legal complaints which are submitted to you. If the man who is to decide suits at law makes gain his motive, and hears cases with a view to receiving bribes, then the suits of the rich man will be like a stone flung into water, meeting no resistance, while the complaints of the poor will be like water thrown upon a stone. In these circumstances the poor man will not know where to go, nor will he behave as he should.

2. Know the difference between merit [good behavior] and demerit [bad behavior], and deal out to each its reward and punishment. In these days, reward does not always follow merit, or punishment follow crime. You high officials who have charge of public affairs, make it your business to give clear rewards and punishments.

Team Challenge! Share your explanations and ideas in a small group. Together, on a separate sheet of paper, write three to five guiding principles that your group thinks would make any government better.

Take Notes

Literacy Skills: Analyze Cause and Effect Use what you have read
to complete the chart. In the left box, list the causes of feudalism.
In the right box, list the effects of feudalism. The first cause has been
completed for you.

Causes of Feudalism	Effects of Feudalism
• Widespread violence and lawlessness	•
•	•
•	•

INTERACTIVE

For extra help, review the 21st Century
Skills Tutorial: **Analyze Cause and Effect**.

Practice Vocabulary

Word Bank Choose one word from the word bank to fill in each blank. When you have finished, you will have a short summary of important ideas from the section.

Word Bank

bushido	daimyo	feudalism
figurehead	samurai	shogun

A series of emperors ruled Japan. They gave nobles powerful positions within their courts. One family, the Fujiwara, gained more and more power. Eventually, the Fujiwara became more powerful than the emperor. Although he remained on the throne, the emperor became a _____ who ruled in name only.

Other clans arose and fought for power. A member of the Minamoto clan gained the title of _____, or supreme military commander. He became so powerful that he ruled Japan. Nevertheless, lawlessness and violence were widespread. This led to the development of a new social system. Based on social, economic, and political relationships, this system was called _____. Land-owning lords became responsible for protecting the people. In return for their protection, the _____ received labor from the peasants. Warriors called _____ also served the lords. These warriors followed the code of _____. Each warrior took great care with his personal appearance and practiced extreme loyalty to his lord.

Take Notes

Literacy Skills: Identify Main Idea and Details Use what you have read to complete the chart. In each space write one main idea and two details.

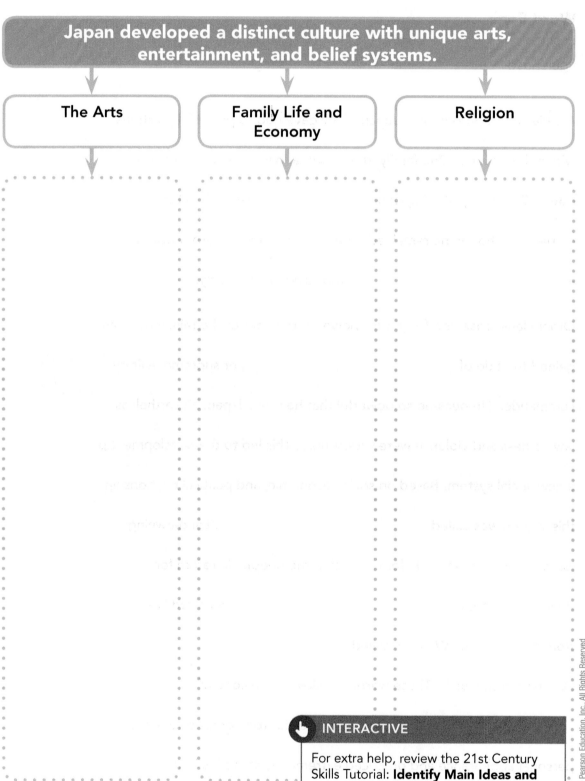

Japan developed a distinct culture with unique arts, entertainment, and belief systems.

| The Arts | Family Life and Economy | Religion |

INTERACTIVE

For extra help, review the 21st Century Skills Tutorial: **Identify Main Ideas and Details**.

Practice Vocabulary

Words in Context For each question below, write an answer that shows your understanding of the boldfaced vocabulary term.

1. Which classes in Japanese society were most likely to enjoy **Noh**?

2. What groups of people did **Kabuki** aim to entertain?

3. Why did Confucianism encourage people to seek **consensus**?

4. How is **Shinto** different from most other religions?

5. Where do the Japanese build **shrines**?

6. How does one use a **mantra**?

Take Notes

Literacy Skills: Analyze Text Structure Use what you have read to complete the charts. As you move through the lesson, record key details about the subjects listed. The first one has been completed for you.

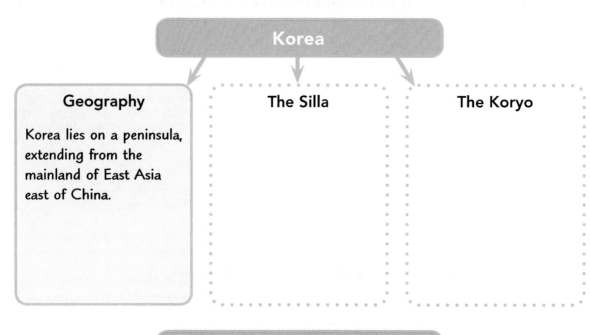

Korea

Geography

Korea lies on a peninsula, extending from the mainland of East Asia east of China.

The Silla

The Koryo

Southeast Asia

Geography

Indian and Chinese Influence

Kingdoms and Empires

Explain how the headings in the lesson organize the text both thematically (by region) and chronologically.

 INTERACTIVE

For extra help, review the 21st Century Skills Tutorial: **Summarize**.

Practice Vocabulary

Decide whether each statement below is true or false. Circle T or F, and then explain your answer. Be sure to include the underlined vocabulary word in your explanation.

1. **T / F** The development of <u>Hangul</u> helped the spread of Buddhism in Korea.
   True; At first, Koreans used Chinese characters to print Buddhist texts, but in time, they developed their own writing system, known as <u>Hangul</u>.

2. **T / F** Koreans learned to make <u>celadon</u> from the Chinese.

3. **T / F** Southeast Asia includes several <u>archipelagos</u>, including those of Indonesia and the Philippines.

4. **T / F** Merchant ships tended to dock in port cities in Southeast Asia during <u>monsoons</u>.

5. **T / F** The construction of <u>stupas</u> demonstrated the strong influence of Japan on Southeast Asia.

Writing Workshop Research Paper

As you read, build a response to this question: **How did new technology and innovations affect China, Japan, Korea, and Southeast Asia?** The prompts below will help walk you through the process.

Lesson 1 Writing Task: Generate Questions to Focus Research

List questions that you have about technologies and innovations in this region. You will use these questions to guide your research and writing.

Lessons 2 and 3 Writing Task: Support Ideas With Evidence and Develop a Clear Thesis

Your research paper will address the effects of technology and innovation in East and Southeast Asia during the medieval time period. Begin to write the first part of your thesis by answering the following question: What affect did technology have on China? Collect evidence from the first three lessons to support your response. As you move through the rest of the lessons, revise your response to include Japan, Korea, and Southeast Asia.

Lesson 4 Writing Task: Find and Use Credible Sources You will need to conduct independent research to complete this paper. To find answers to your questions about technology and innovation in this region, you will need to find historical sources in the library, on the Internet, and in academic periodicals. Online, you should search for information on specific topics, such as technology and farming in Yamato, Japan. Look for sources on websites ending in .edu and .gov. These tend to be more reliable. Avoid using blogs, discussion boards, and other social media sources. Below, list one print source and one digital source that you will use. On a separate sheet of paper, write complete source citations for your sources according to the directions given by your teacher.

Lesson 5 Writing Task: Cite Sources Begin taking notes from additional sources on the impact of Chinese and Japanese technology and innovation. You should record your notes on note cards that you can easily organize according to topic and source. As you take notes, be sure to keep track of your sources.

Lesson 6 Writing Task: Organize Your Essay Revise the thesis statement that you began to write in Lesson 3 as needed. Then, review your notes. Decide how you will organize your essay. For example, you may wish to organize your essay according to country, according to types of technologies and innovations, or chronologically. Plan your paper by completing an outline on a separate sheet of paper.

Lesson 7 Writing Task: Draft Your Essay You are ready to begin writing! Use your thesis, your notes, and your outline to write a draft of your research paper. Remember to include appropriate citations for the information that you include. When you have finished, exchange drafts with a partner and provide feedback. Revise your draft based on your partner's feedback.

Writing Task Be sure that your revised draft answers the following question: How did new technology and innovations affect China, Japan, Korea, and Southeast Asia?

Essential Question **How much does geography shape people's lives?**

Before you begin this topic, think about the Essential Question by answering the following questions.

What geographical features are important to your community? Why are they important?

Timeline Skills

As you read, write and/or draw at least three events from the topic. Draw a line from each event to its correct position on the timeline.

1200 BCE	1000 BCE	800 BCE	1000 CE

Map Skills

**Using the map in your text, label the outline map with the places listed.
Then, color in the areas occupied by the Olmecs, Maya, Aztecs, and Inca.**

North America	South America	Tikal	Cuzco
Tenochtitlan	Gulf of Mexico	Lake Texcoco	Lake Titicaca
Amazon River	Caribbean Sea	Atlantic Ocean	Pacific Ocean

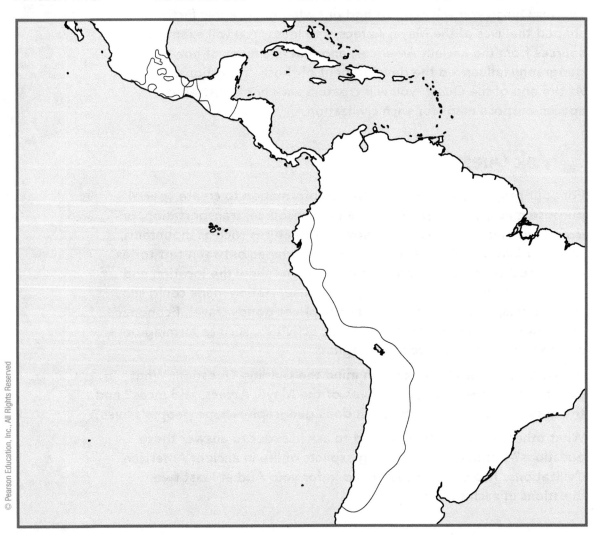

1200 CE	1400 CE	1600 CE

Quest
Project-Based Learning Inquiry

Be a Map-Maker

On this Quest, you will need to find out what geographic factors shaped the lives of the Maya, Aztecs, and Incas. You will examine sources from the ancient Americas, and find examples of how geography influenced the development of those civilizations. At the end of the Quest, you will create a variety of illustrated special-purpose maps for each civilization.

1 Ask Questions

For your project, your team will collect information to create special purpose maps, such as physical, political, resource, transportation, or economic maps. Physical maps show land features such as mountains, rivers, or lakes. Political maps indicate boundaries between territories, or the location of towns/cities. Resource maps show the location and types of natural resources in a region. Transportation maps could show trade routes, roads, or other routes people or goods travel. Economic maps might show the type of economic activities, such as farming or livestock grazing, that occur in a region.

As you begin your Quest, keep in mind the Guiding Question: **What geographic factors shaped the lives of the Maya, Aztecs, and Incas?** and the Essential Question: **How much does geography shape people's lives?**

What other questions do you need to ask in order to answer these questions? Consider the following aspects of life in ancient American civilizations. Two questions are filled in for you. Add at least two questions in each category.

Theme Structure of the Society

Sample questions:

How did the geography of the region influence the organization of the society?

What effect did geography have on achievements in architecture and engineering?

 INTERACTIVE

For extra help with Step 1, review the 21st Century Tutorial: **Read Special Purpose Maps**.

Theme Agriculture and Food

Theme Economy and Trade

Theme Homes and Dwellings

Theme My Additional Questions

 INTERACTIVE

For extra help with Step 1, review the
21st Century Tutorial: **Ask Questions**.

2 Investigate

As you read about the ancient Americas, collect five connections from your text to help you answer the Guiding Question. Three connections are already chosen for you.

Connect to the Mayan Civilization

Lesson 1 Settlement and Geography of the Americas

Here's a connection! The terrain occupied by the Maya varied greatly. What were some of the different environments they lived in?

How do you think geography affected trade across Central America?

Connect to the Aztec Empire

Lesson 2 Where Did the Aztecs Live?

Here's another connection! Examine the development of the Aztec empire. Why were the Aztecs so successful in building such a large empire?

How do you think geography helped them maintain their position?

Connect to Early American Migration

Lesson 3 How Did the Geography of the Andes Shape Life?

What does this connection tell you about how early Americans migrated on foot to find their new homes? What kind of obstacles would they have faced in what is now South America?

What influence do you think these obstacles had on where they ultimately settled and why?

It's Your Turn! **Find two more connections. Fill in the title of your connections, then answer the questions. Connections may be images, primary sources, maps, or text.**

Your Choice | Connect to

Location in text

What is the main idea of this connection?

What does it tell you about how geography shaped the lives of the Maya, Aztecs, and Incas?

Your Choice | Connect to

Location in text

What is the main idea of this connection?

What does it tell you about how geography shaped the lives of the Maya, Aztecs, and Incas?

③ Conduct Research

Your team will be assigned a region in either Mesoamerica or South America. Once your region is assigned, decide as a team on three types of maps that you will create. Circle them in the chart below. Then, record which team member(s) will be responsible for each type of map.

You will do research only about the segment assigned to you. Use the ideas in the connections to further explore the type of map you have been assigned. Pick what your map will show, and find more sources about that subject. Remember, you will also need to illustrate your map, so find images that can help you create that type of map. Be sure to find valid sources and take good notes so you can properly cite your sources.

Type of Map	Team Member(s)	What Information Will the Map Show?
Physical		
Political		
Resource		
Transportation		
Economic		

🔽 INTERACTIVE

For extra help, review the 21st Century Tutorials: **Work in Teams** and **Search for Information on the Internet**.

 **FINDINGS**

4 Create Your Atlas

Now it's time to put together all of the information you have gathered to create your three maps.

1. **Prepare to Make Your Map** Review the research you've collected, and make sure the information you've gathered really supports the main purpose of the map you will create. In the space below, write the specific locations, routes, regions, etc. that you will show on your map.

2. **Draw a Draft** Using the illustrations you found in your research, draw or use technology to create a first draft of your map. Make sure that your map includes important map features, such as a title, key, relevant labels, etc.

3. **Share with a Partner** Once you have finished your draft, ask one of your team members to look it over. Revise your map based on your team member's comments, and comment on his or her map, if possible.

4. **Create Your Atlas** Once all the team members have revised their maps, it's time to put them together. You can do this in a couple of ways:
   1) by using technology to create a single document or presentation; or
   2) by binding your three printed or drawn maps together.
   Your teacher will let you know his or her preference for delivery.

5. **Reflect on the Quest** Think about your experience completing this topic's Quest. What did you learn about how geography shaped and affected the lives and development of early American civilizations? What questions do you still have about these civilizations or the geography that influenced them? How will you answer your questions?

Reflections

 INTERACTIVE

For extra help with Step 1, review the 21st Century Tutorial: **Create Charts and Maps**.

Take Notes

Literacy Skill: Sequence Use what you have read to complete the chart.
In each space, write or draw in sequence the events that led to the rise
and fall of the Maya. Be sure to include an important detail about each
event. The first one has been completed for you.

• The first people
settled in the
Americas between
40,000 and
15,000 years ago.
They may have walked
over the Bering Land
Bridge or come by
boat.

INTERACTIVE

For extra help, review the 21st Century
Tutorials: **Sequence**.

Practice Vocabulary

Words in Context For each question below, write an answer that shows your understanding of the boldfaced key term.

1. How did **slash-and-burn** both help and hurt the populations who used it?

2. What effect did **drought** have on the Mayan civilization?

3. What is a **hieroglyphic**, and why was it important to ancient American civilizations?

4. What is an **observatory**, and why was it an important feature in Mayan cities?

Quick Activity Human Monument Game

With your group, examine some of the major aspects of Mayan civilization. Consider important achievements, such as building remarkable structures in their cities, the Mayan sacred ball game, slash-and-burn agriculture, hieroglyphic writing, and astronomy.

Team Challenge! You have ten minutes to plan your group statue. Decide with your group which of these, or another important feature of Mayan civilization, you would like to showcase. Your group will represent the idea by "freezing" into a statue or scene that represents the aspect of Mayan society or culture you have chosen. Be sure that your idea is recognizable so that other groups can identify what your statue represents!

Take Notes

Literacy Skills: Summarize Use what you have read to complete the table. In each space, write three details about the aspect of Aztec life. One example has been provided. Then, use your notes to summarize the lesson.

Environment	Warfare and Rulers	Society and Achievements
1. Building their capital city, Tenochtitlan, on an island in Lake Texcoco, made it easy to defend.	1.	1.
2.	2.	2.
3.	3.	3.

Summary:

INTERACTIVE

For extra help, review the 21st Century Tutorials: **Summarize**.

Practice Vocabulary

Vocabulary Quiz Show Some quiz shows ask a question and expect the contestant to give the answer. In other shows, the contestant is given an answer and must supply the question. If the blank is in the Question column, write the question that would result in the answer in the Answer column. If the question is supplied, write the answer.

Question	Answer
1. What is the name of the engineering structure used to carry water from one place to another?	1.
2.	2. chinampa
3. What is a system of government in which one person from a ruling family has unlimited power?	3.
4.	4. dike
5. What is the term for a bowl-shaped geographic area?	5.

Take Notes

Literacy Skills: Analyze Text Structure Use what you have read to complete the table. Use the main headings in your text to organize information, and add details to analyze the information offered in each section. Include at least two details under each heading. The first one has been started for you.

Heading	Details
Geography	• The Incas adapted to difficult geography by developing terraces to allow them to farm on the sides of mountains. •

INTERACTIVE

For extra help, review the 21st Century Tutorials: **Take Effective Notes**.

Practice Vocabulary

True or False? Decide whether each statement below is true or false. Circle T or F, and then explain your answer. Be sure to include the underlined vocabulary word in your explanation. The first one is done for you.

1. **T / F** A <u>terrace</u> was where children of the Incas went to play on the swings.
   False. A <u>terrace</u> is a strip of level land cut out of a mountainside for farming.

2. **T / F** A <u>quipu</u> was a device used by the Incas to keep records.

3. **T / F** A <u>hierarchy</u> is a way to carry water up the mountainside.

4. **T / F** An <u>ayllu</u> is the name of an animal similar to a llama or alpaca.

5. **T / F** The Incas paid taxes through the <u>mita system</u>.

Quick Activity Write a Song

Write a song praising the achievements of the Incas.

With a partner, talk about some of your favorite songs. What do they have in common? For example, your favorite songs may have things, such as rhyming, rhythm, and melody, in common.

Team Challenge! Write a short song praising some of the achievements of the Incas. You can use the rhythm or melody of your favorite song, or make up your own.

Use the space provided to make notes and write your song. (Your teacher may ask for volunteers to perform their songs.)

Take Notes

Literacy Skills: Compare and Contrast Use what you have read to complete the table. In each space, write 2-3 facts about how geography affected each broad population. What were the similarities? What were the differences? The first one has been completed for you.

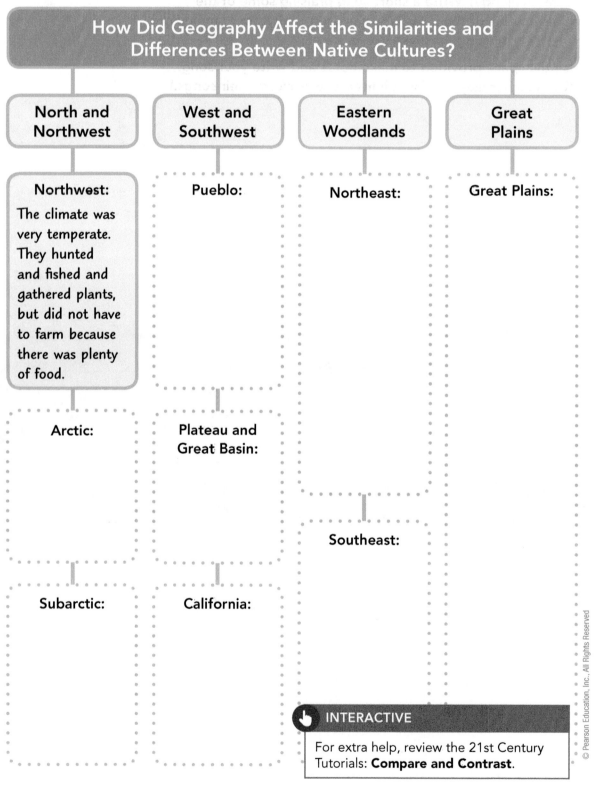

How Did Geography Affect the Similarities and Differences Between Native Cultures?

North and Northwest

West and Southwest

Eastern Woodlands

Great Plains

Northwest:
The climate was very temperate. They hunted and fished and gathered plants, but did not have to farm because there was plenty of food.

Pueblo:

Northeast:

Great Plains:

Arctic:

Plateau and Great Basin:

Southeast:

Subarctic:

California:

👆 INTERACTIVE

For extra help, review the 21st Century Tutorials: **Compare and Contrast**.

Practice Vocabulary

Matching Logic Using your knowledge of the underlined vocabulary words, draw a line from each sentence in Column 1 to match it with the sentence in Column 2 to which it logically belongs.

Column 1	Column 2
1. Native peoples left behind numerous <u>artifacts</u>.	This type of round home was made of tree trunks.
2. Wealthy families hosted <u>potlatches</u> to celebrate important events.	Jewelry, tools, and pottery help us understand what their lives were like.
3. Many native peoples were faced with <u>drought</u>.	These homes were portable and made moving around easier.
4. Some Eastern Woodlands peoples lived in a <u>wigwam</u>.	These were rectangular homes made of tree trunks and covered with bark.
5. Arctic people sometimes lived in <u>igloos</u> during the winter.	These homes made of snow bricks were surprisingly warm.
6. Some native people lived in <u>tepees</u>.	These were also times to share stories about family history and pass down heritage.
7. The Iroquois people lived in <u>longhouses</u>.	Some geographical places get little rain and sometimes none at all.

Writing Workshop Explanatory Essay

As you read, build a response to this topic: **Compare the impact of geography on Mayan, Aztec, and Incan agriculture.** The prompts below will help walk you through the process.

Lesson 1 Writing Task: Develop a Clear Thesis Express in one sentence how you can compare and contrast the impact of geography on Mayan, Aztec, and Incan agriculture. This will be your thesis statement for the explanatory essay you will write at the end of the topic.

Lesson 2 Writing Task: Support Ideas with Evidence Gather evidence from your text, and use the chart below to record information about the agricultural practices of these cultures so that you can identify differences and similarities.

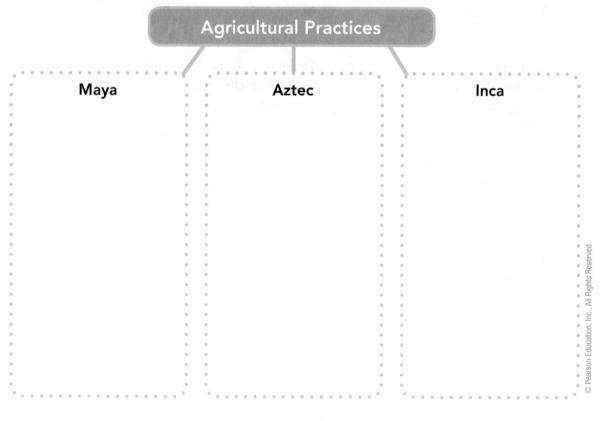

Agricultural Practices

Maya   Aztec   Inca

Lesson 3 Writing Task: Support Thesis with Details Revisit your
evidence chart from Lesson 2. Add any additional details that are
important to your thesis statement.

Thesis	
Impact, Evidence, Details	
Impact, Evidence, Details	
Impact, Evidence, Details	
Conclusion	

Lesson 4 Writing Task: Clarify Relationships with Transition Words
Reread the thesis statement and your supporting details. Clarify
your writing, using words and phrases to create smooth transitions
between different ideas. Use appropriate words to describe
similarities and differences.

Writing Task: Using the outline you created, respond to the following
statement in a five paragraph explanatory essay: **Compare the
impact of geography on Mayan, Aztec, and Incan agriculture**. As
you write, pay close attention to your signal and transition words to
help you compare and contrast effectively.

Essential Question What makes cultures endure?

Before you begin this topic, think about the Essential Question by completing the following activity.

1. List five elements of culture that you have experienced in your family or in your community. Next to each element, write how you learned about or first experienced it.

2. Preview the topic by skimming the images and captions in the lessons. Then place a check mark next to the elements of culture that are physical things made by people.

__architecture   __holidays   __masks   __songs

__religious ritual   __celebrations   __musical instruments   __traditional dress

Timeline Skills

As you read, write and/or draw at least three events from the topic. Draw a line from each event to its correct position on the timeline.

500	**750**
CE	CE

Map Skills

Using the map in your text, label the outline map with the places listed. Then color in significant physical features, such as desert, mountain ranges, savannah, and rainforest. Add the colors and their meanings to a map key.

Axum   Koumbi Saleh   Benin   Meroe

Mediterranean Sea   Red Sea   Timbuktu   Nile River

Atlantic Ocean   Sahara   Indian Ocean

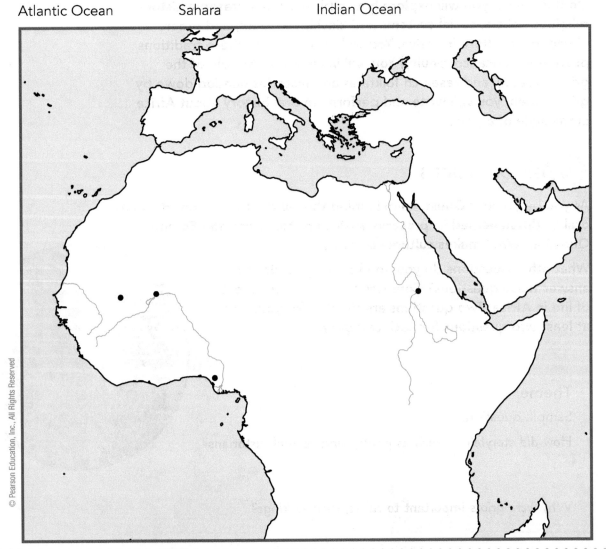

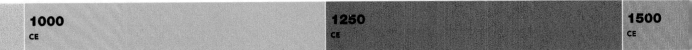

1000	1250	1500
CE	CE	CE

Quest
Project-Based Learning

Create an Oral History

On this Quest, you will explore how oral traditions preserve history, religious beliefs, social customs and kinship, wisdom, and other elements of culture in Africa. You will describe how these traditions provide historical continuity. You will investigate the role of the griot (greeoh), and research folktales and histories handed down by griots. Then, you will write and perform an oral history about Africa in the style of a griot.

① Ask Questions

As you begin your Quest, keep in mind the Guiding Question: **How has oral tradition helped to preserve African history?** and the Essential Question: **What makes cultures endure?**

What other questions do you need to ask in order to answer these questions? Consider the following aspects of life in Africa. Two questions are filled in for you. Add at least two questions for each category.

Theme History

Sample questions:

How did storytellers, such as griots, serve as oral historians?

Why were griots important to rulers, such as kings?

Theme Religion

Theme Society and Economy

Theme Culture

Theme My Additional Questions

 INTERACTIVE

For extra help with Step 1, review the
21st Century Tutorial: **Ask Questions**.

② Investigate

As you read about civilizations in Africa, collect five connections from your text to help you answer the Guiding Question. Three connections are already chosen for you.

Connect to Al-Bakri's Story

Lesson 1 The Growth of the Ghana Empire

Here's a connection! Read the excerpt from a story by Al-Bakri, a historian and geographer who recorded information about the kingdom of Ghana in the 1000s. About whom does Al-Bakri write? What does his story suggest about the ruling class of Ghana? What insights into Ghana's culture does the excerpt offer?

How do accounts like this help preserve African history and culture?

Connect to the Story About Ananse

Lesson 4 What are Key Features of Africa's Cultural Legacy?

Here's another connection! Ananse is a popular trickster character in African folklore. Griots often tell stories like this one. What does the story suggest about how people obtain wisdom? What does the story reveal about African values?

How do stories like this one help preserve African history and culture?

Connect to the Griot's Story Tale Sundiata

Primary Sources Djibril Tamsir Niane, Sundiata: An Epic of Old Mali

What does this connection tell about Sundiata, the first king of Mali in the 1200s? How does the story describe Sundiata as a child? What does this tale reflect about the kingship of Mali? What ideas about life does the story reveal?

How does oral tradition like this griot's tale help preserve African history and culture?

It's Your Turn! Find two more connections. Fill in the titles of your connections, then answer the questions. Connections may be images, primary sources, maps, or text.

Your Choice | Connect to

Location in text

What is the main idea of this connection?

What does it tell you about how African history and culture have been preserved?

Your Choice | Connect to

Location in text

What is the main idea of this connection?

What does it tell you about how African history and culture have been preserved?

③ Conduct Research

As a group, decide whether to research either folktales or an historical event.

- For folktales, research the background and nature of the type of folktales, including the geographic area in which such tales originated or were commonly told. Read at least three examples of this type of folktale. Summarize each in the chart below, including its origin, message, and how dialogue, tone, plot, and setting help get across the meaning.

- For history, research the major historical events of the selected civilization. Choose one notable event or period to further investigate. Record information about the event in the chart below.

Folk Tales	Historical Event
Summary of Folktale 1	What happened in the event you've chosen?
Summary of Folktale 2	Who played an important role in this event?
Summary of Folktale 3	Why is it important to remember this event?

INTERACTIVE

For extra help with Step 3, review the 21st Century Tutorial: **Analyze Primary and Secondary Sources**.

Quest FINDINGS

4 Present Your Oral History

Now it's time to put together all of the information you have gathered and perform your oral history.

1. **Prepare to Write** You have collected connections that show how oral history traditions help preserve African history and culture. You have also researched a specific type of folktale or specific event in African history. Look through your notes and work with your group to decide on the elements to include in your oral history presentation. Record the elements you want to include here.

Outline of Elements

2. Write a Draft Using the primary sources that you read as models, write a draft of the oral history. For a folktale-based project, highlight important elements of culture. Recall how the folktales that you read centered on specific characters and used dialogue, tone, plot, and setting to convey meaning. Incorporate these things into your story. For a history-based project, focus on the most important people and actions, and emphasize how your piece of history fits into the broader story of Africa.

3. Share and Edit the Draft Have the writers combine and share their drafts with the editors. Editors should check the draft against the groups' element notes to be sure that the oral history includes all the relevant information. They should also ask themselves broad questions about the drafts, such as "What will the audience learn from this oral history? What does this oral history say about African history or culture?" Editors should advise revisions, if needed, based on these considerations. They should tell the writers what they like about the draft as well as what parts need improvement. Be sure that editors read aloud the draft to hear how the oral history flows. After all, the final draft will be performed!

4. Finalize and Present Your Oral History Have editors and writers work together to revise the draft. Then, have the presenters practice reading aloud the oral history to the rest of the group. Group members who are not presenting should provide feedback on the presentation. Presenters should speak clearly, at a moderate pace. Consider adding a musical background. Finally, have presenters perform their oral history for the class.

5. Reflect on the Quest Think about your experience completing this topic's Quest and watching other groups' presentations. What did you learn about the oral history traditions of African civilizations?

Reflections

Take Notes

Literacy Skills: Summarize Use what you have read to complete the concept webs. Summarize what you learned, in one to two sentences, for each section in the webs. The first one has been started for you.

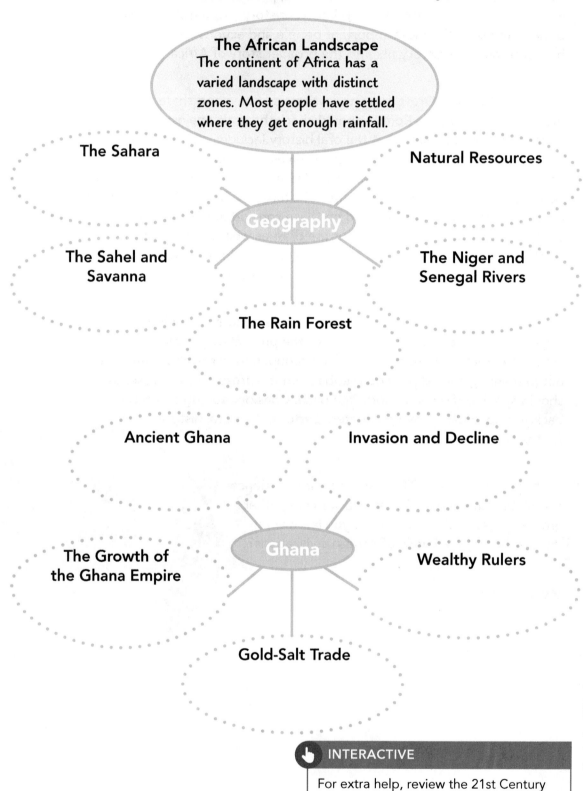

The African Landscape
The continent of Africa has a varied landscape with distinct zones. Most people have settled where they get enough rainfall.

The Sahara

Natural Resources

Geography

The Sahel and Savanna

The Niger and Senegal Rivers

The Rain Forest

Ancient Ghana

Invasion and Decline

The Growth of the Ghana Empire

Ghana

Wealthy Rulers

Gold-Salt Trade

👆 **INTERACTIVE**

For extra help, review the 21st Century Tutorial: **Summarize**.

Practice Vocabulary

Vocabulary Quiz Show Some quiz shows ask a question and expect the contestant to give the answer. In other shows, the contestant is given an answer and must supply the question. If the blank is in the Question column, write the question that would result in the answer in the Answer column. If the question is supplied, write the answer.

Question

1. What do you call the raised area of largely flat land that makes up much of Africa's interior?

2.

3. What are land, trees, and minerals called when they are used by people to meet their needs?

4.

5. What do you call the trade in gold and salt that took place between North African peoples and West African peoples?

6.

Answer

1.

2. This vast region of tropical grassland covers much of Sub-Saharan Africa.

3.

4. This happens when people become experts in specific skills or jobs, like farming, government service, mining, or crafts.

5.

6. Beginning in the 900s, Arab and Berber merchants traversed the Sahara in these camel-mounted groups.

Quick Activity Packing for the Caravan

With a partner, study the map. Consider what the journey from one city to the next would have been like. Use the scale to determine the distance between several urban centers. If a camel caravan, loaded with goods, averages about 20 miles a day, how long would it take to travel between each pair of cities? Compare your findings with those of another pair of students.

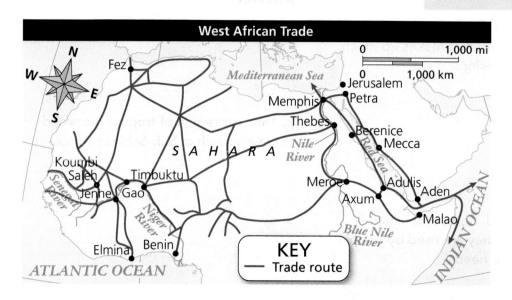

West African Trade

KEY
— Trade route

INTERACTIVE

For extra help, review the 21st Century Tutorial: **Use Parts of a Map**.

Team Challenge! What would you pack to travel with a caravan from Timbuktu to Fez? With your group, brainstorm a checklist, or manifest, of what you would take. Remember that you are traveling in a trading caravan, so you will need goods for trading as well as supplies. Display completed lists on large sheets of paper around the class. Study each list, and point out potential problems or make suggestions.

Take Notes

Literacy Skills: Sequence Use what you have read to complete the timeline. In the spaces provided, write key events in the development of the Mali and Songhai empires. The first one has been completed for you.

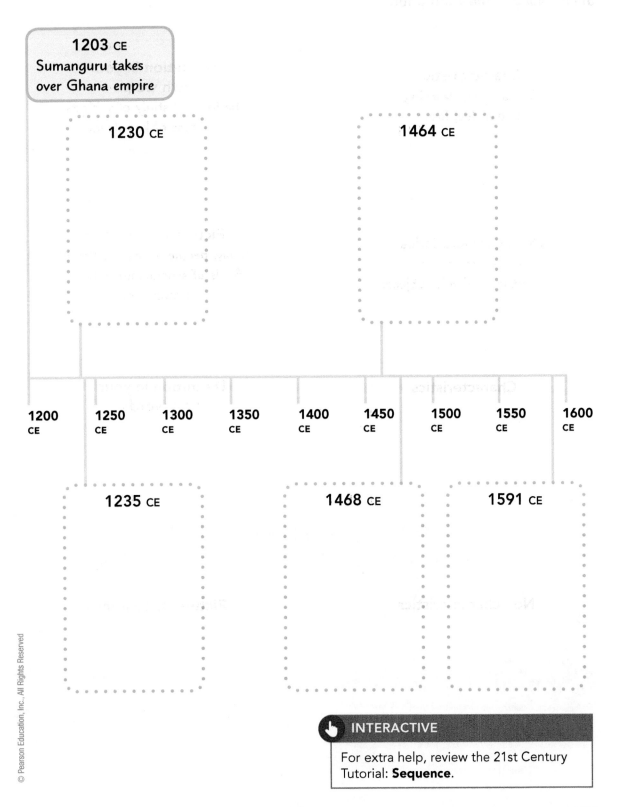

1203 CE
Sumanguru takes over Ghana empire

1230 CE

1464 CE

1200 CE 1250 CE 1300 CE 1350 CE 1400 CE 1450 CE 1500 CE 1550 CE 1600 CE

1235 CE

1468 CE

1591 CE

👆 **INTERACTIVE**

For extra help, review the 21st Century Tutorial: **Sequence**.

Practice Vocabulary

Word Map Study the word map for the word *scholarship*. Characteristics are words or phrases that relate to the word in the center of the word map. Non-characteristics are words and phrases not associated with the word. Use the blank word map to explore the meaning of the word *griot*.

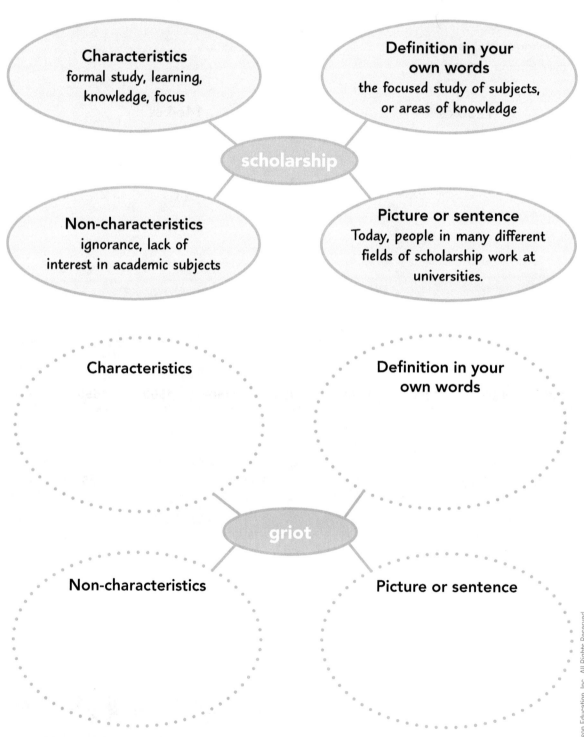

Characteristics
formal study, learning, knowledge, focus

Definition in your own words
the focused study of subjects, or areas of knowledge

scholarship

Non-characteristics
ignorance, lack of interest in academic subjects

Picture or sentence
Today, people in many different fields of scholarship work at universities.

Characteristics

Definition in your own words

griot

Non-characteristics

Picture or sentence

African Civilizations

Quick Activity Perspectives on West African Kingdoms

When you read primary sources, it is important to keep in mind the perspective from which a source is written. Perspective refers to the way in which a person sees and understands a subject. Think about a recent disagreement you had. Your perspective on the issue probably differs from the perspective of the person with whom you disagreed. An author's perspective influences what the author writes. In a small group, take turns reading aloud the primary sources below. Make a chart or web in which you record the main ideas of each excerpt. Consider these questions as you take notes: How does each author write about West Africa? What feelings, or bias, does each author show? What overall impression does each author give of West African kingdoms?

> "In their new-found peace the villages knew prosperity again, for with Sundiata happiness had come into everyone's home. Vast fields of millet, rice, cotton, indigo and fonio surrounded the villages. Whoever worked always had something to live on. Each year long caravans carried the taxes in kind to Niani. You could go from village to village without fearing brigands. A thief would have his right hand chopped off and if he stole again he would be put to the sword."
>
> —from *The Epic of Sundiata*, as handed down by West African griots and told by their descendent, Djibril Tamsir Niane
>
> "A traveller in this country carries nothing but pieces of salt and glass ornaments, which the people call beads, and some sweet-smelling goods. When he comes to a village the womenfolk . . . bring out millet, milk, chickens, pulped lotus fruit, rice, and pounded haricot beans. The traveller buys what he wants of these."
>
> —from the writings of the fourteenth century Moroccan scholar Ibn Battuta
>
> "This king is the greatest of the Muslim kings of the Sahel. He rules the most extensive territory, has the most numerous army, is the bravest, the richest, the most fortunate, the most victorious over his enemies, and the best able to distribute benefits."
>
> —from the fourteenth century Syrian Arab historian al-Umari

Team Challenge! Compare and contrast the perspectives of the three authors. How might the authors' backgrounds affect their perspective of West African kings and kingdoms? Write down your ideas and share with your group.

 INTERACTIVE

For extra help, review the 21st Century Tutorials: **Compare Viewpoints** and **Identify Bias**.

Take Notes

Literacy Skills: Identify Cause and Effect Use what you have read to complete the cause-event-effect charts. For each chart, record the cause(s) and effect(s) of the listed events. The first one has been completed for you.

Cause(s)	King Ezana of Axum took over Kush.
Event	After many generations, the rule of Kushite kings weakened.
Effect(s)	Axum gained control of trade routes to Roman Egypt, southern Arabia, and Asia, and grew prosperous.

Cause(s)	
Event	Christianity spread in East Africa.
Effect(s)	

Cause(s)	
Event	Swahili culture spreads down the east coast of Africa.
Effect(s)	

INTERACTIVE

For extra help, review the 21st Century Tutorial: **Analyze Cause and Effect**.

Practice Vocabulary

True or False? Decide whether each statement below is true or false. Circle T or F, and then explain your answer. Be sure to include the underlined vocabulary word in your explanation. The first one is done for you.

1. **T / F** <u>Monks</u> prevented the adoption of Christianity by people in Axum and other African kingdoms.
   False; <u>Monks</u> helped spread Christianity to people in Axum and other African kingdoms.

2. **T / F** Monumental <u>stele</u> marked the burial places of Axum's rulers.

3. **T / F** The people of Axum benefited from trade with <u>Greco-Roman</u> outposts along the Red Sea and the Mediterranean Sea.

4. **T / F** Ruling <u>dynasties</u> in Ethiopia ensured that no one family came to dominate the rule of the kingdom.

5. **T / F** Swahili <u>stonetowns</u> in East Africa remained largely isolated from non-African cultures.

Take Notes

Literacy Skills: Integrate Visual Information Use what you have read and studied in the lesson's visual aids to complete the charts. In each space provided, record important details about the topics of each section. Be sure to include information gained from the infographic and photographs in your charts. The first one has been completed for you.

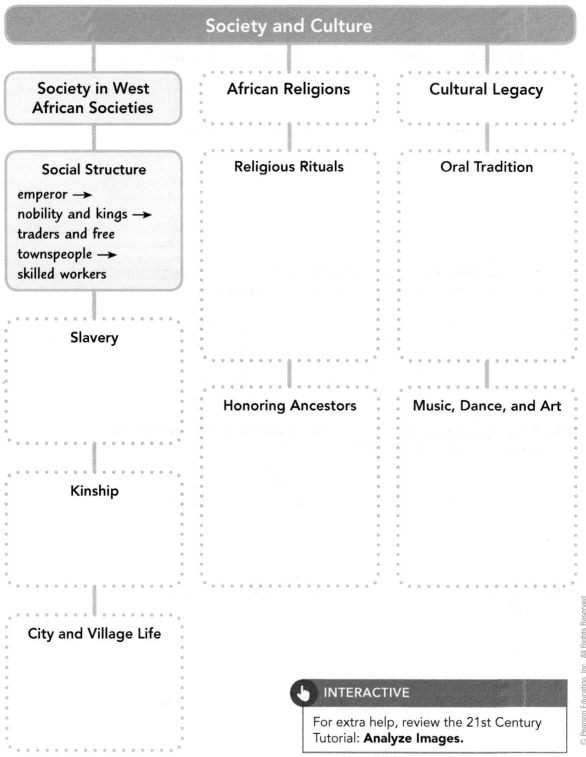

Society and Culture

Society in West African Societies

Social Structure
emperor →
nobility and kings →
traders and free
townspeople →
skilled workers

Slavery

Kinship

City and Village Life

African Religions

Religious Rituals

Honoring Ancestors

Cultural Legacy

Oral Tradition

Music, Dance, and Art

INTERACTIVE

For extra help, review the 21st Century Tutorial: **Analyze Images.**

Practice Vocabulary

Words in Context For each question below, write an answer that shows your understanding of the **boldfaced** key term.

1. What role did **caste** play in West African empires?

2. How were **kinship** and **lineage** related in West African society?

3. What characteristics defined **ethnic groups** within West African empires?

4. Why is **oral tradition** an important source of information about West African cultures?

5. Why did West African griots learn and share **proverbs**?

6. How does **polyrhythmic drumming** affect performers who dance to the music?

Writing Workshop Explanatory Essay

As you read, build a response to this question: **How did the environment affect the development of African empires and the trade networks that connected them to other lands, including Europe and Asia?** The prompts below will help walk you through the process.

Lesson 1 Writing Task: Develop a Clear Thesis Express in one sentence how environmental conditions affected the empire of Ghana and the development of trading networks in the region. This will be your thesis statement for the explanatory essay you will write at the end of the topic. Re-read your thesis statement after you read Lessons 2 and 3 and make any revisions needed to include the new information.

Lesson 2 Writing Task: Support Thesis with Details Now add details from Lessons 1 and 2 to support your thesis statement. Update your chart after you read Lessons 3 and 4 as well.

Lesson 1	
Lesson 2	
Lesson 3	
Lesson 4	

Lesson 3 Writing Task: Pick an Organizing Strategy Think about what type of organization suits your essay. Sometimes the phrasing of the writing prompt can provide a clue. In this writing prompt, the word *affect* is used. Your essay should tell the effects of geography on Ghana and Mali, so an organization in which you explain multiple effects would be a good way to go. Make an outline of your essay. Start with an introduction, followed by three paragraphs that explain key effects and end with a conclusion. Use the chart below to help you.

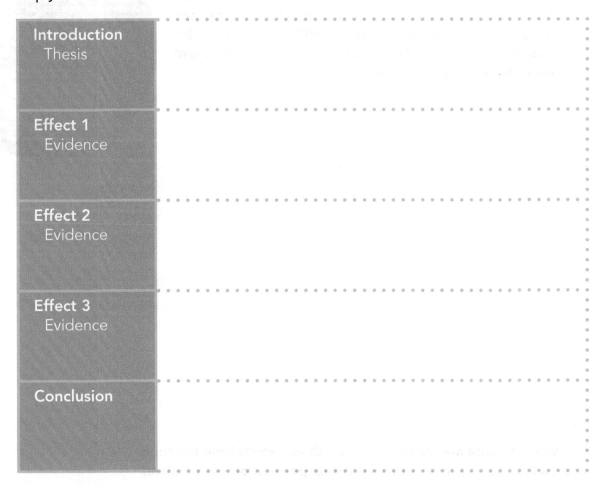

Introduction Thesis	
Effect 1 Evidence	
Effect 2 Evidence	
Effect 3 Evidence	
Conclusion	

Lesson 4 Writing Task: Consider Your Purpose and Audience With a partner, share your outline, your thesis statement, and the supporting evidence that you recorded from Lessons 1 through 4. Discuss whether your outline includes all of the relevant information you recorded. Then comment on your partner's outline.

Writing Task Using the outline you created in Lesson 3 and revised in Lesson 4, answer the following question in a five-paragraph explanatory essay: How did the environment affect the development of African empires and the trade networks that connected them to other lands, including Europe and Asia? As you write, remember to include a main idea with supporting details in each paragraph.

Essential Question **How do ideas grow and spread?**

Before you begin this topic, think about the Essential Question by completing the following activity.

1. The Renaissance, Reformation, and Scientific Revolution led to the spread of new ways of thinking about all aspects of life. List five ways in which you share ideas and learn, or pick up on new ideas. Keep in mind that such ideas might relate to any aspect of life, including family, community, government, science, religion, and economics.

Timeline Skills

As you read, write and/or draw at least three events from the topic. Draw a line from each event to its correct position on the timeline.

1400	1500

Map Skills

Using the map in your text, label the outline map with the places listed. Then color in bodies of water as well as the boundaries of the German States, Papal States, and Italian city-states, such as the Kingdom of Naples.

German States	Papal States	Venice	Florence
Naples	Rome	Wittenberg	Warburg
Nuremberg	Augsburg	North Sea	Adriatic Sea
Mediterranean Sea	Atlantic Ocean		

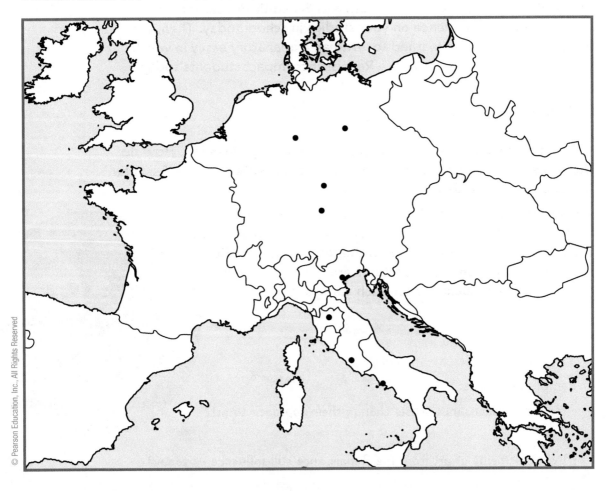

1600

Quest

Document-Based Writing Inquiry

Learning Through the Ages

On this Quest, you will explore primary and secondary sources about the ideas developed by artists, authors, and scientists who lived during the Renaissance, Reformation, and Scientific Revolution. You will examine their influence on your studies in school today. Then, you will use what you have learned to write an explanatory essay in which you explain how the ideas of the Renaissance impact students today.

1 Ask Questions

As you begin your Quest, keep in mind the Guiding Question: **How do the ideas of the Renaissance impact today's students?** and the Essential Question: **How do ideas grow and spread?**

What other questions do you need to ask in order to answer these questions? Consider the following aspects of life during the Renaissance, as well as during the Reformation and the Scientific Revolution. Two questions are filled in for you. Add at least two questions for each category.

Theme Art and Architecture

Sample questions:

• How did Renaissance artists change their approach to art?

• What elements of art from the Renaissance still influence us today?

Theme Literature and Literacy

Theme Religion and Philosophy

Theme Government and Society

Theme Science and Technology

Theme My Additional Questions

 INTERACTIVE

For extra help with Step 1, review the
21st Century Tutorial: **Ask Questions**.

② Investigate

As you read about the Renaissance, the Reformation, and the Scientific Revolution, collect five connections from your text to help you answer the Guiding Question. Three connections are already chosen for you.

Connect to Education

Lesson 1 Education in the Liberal Arts

Here's a connection! Study the infographic. Which subjects of study were valued during the Renaissance? How did they compare to subjects studied during the Middle Ages?

How do these subjects compare to the subjects you and other students study today?

Connect to John Calvin

Lesson 4 In-Text Primary Source John Calvin, *Institutes of the Christian Religion*

Here's another connection! Read the quotation. What does this connection suggest about Calvin's view on the purpose of education? Explain whether you agree or disagree with him.

How does this idea compare to modern views of education in the United States?

Connect to The Scientific Revolution

Lesson 6 The Scientific Method

Here's another connection! Study the diagram. What steps does it show for the scientific method?

Do these steps reflect the way you learn about science in school?

Now it's your turn! Find two more connections on your own. Fill in the title of your connections, then answer the questions. Connections may be images, primary sources, maps, or text.

Your Choice | Connect to

Location in text

What is the main idea of this connection?

What does it tell you about how Renaissance ideas influenced the subjects you learn today?

Your Choice | Connect to

Location in text

What is the main idea of this connection?

What does it tell you about how Renaissance ideas influenced the subjects you learn today?

NICCOLÒ MACCHIAVELLI

③ Examine Primary and Secondary Sources

Examine the primary and secondary sources provided online or that your teacher hands out. Fill in the chart to show how these sources provide further information about how Renaissance ideas influenced modern ideas and education. The first one is completed for you.

Source	What Renaissance ideas from these sources remain important today?
"On Noble Customs and Liberal Studies of Adolescents"	Learning must begin at an early age and continue throughout life.
Illustration from *The Nuremberg Chronicle*	
Oration on the Dignity of Man	
Letter to Augustinus Aemilius	
Plate from *On the Fabric of the Human Body*	

👆 INTERACTIVE

For extra help with Step 3, review the 21st Century Tutorials: **Analyze Primary and Secondary Sources** and **Analyze Images**.

4 Write Your Explanatory Essay

Now it's time to put together all of the information you have gathered and use it to write your explanatory essay in response to the Guiding Question: **How do the ideas of the Renaissance impact today's students?**

1. **Prepare to Write** You have collected connections and explored primary and secondary sources that show the lasting influence of Renaissance ideas about knowledge and education. Look through your notes, and identify the most important ideas that you want to include in your essay. Record your ideas in the table below. Be sure to write the source of each note.

Renaissance Ideas About Education, including Subjects Studied	
Modern Ideas About Education, including Subjects Studied	
Potential Benefits of Ideas and Subjects	

2. **Write a Thesis Statement** Review your notes in the table. What main idea ties together all the information? Write a one-sentence thesis statement in response to the Guiding Question.

3. **Write a Draft** On a separate sheet of paper organize your notes in an outline. Then, use your outline to write a draft of your explanatory essay. Remember to include your thesis statement and at least three paragraphs with evidence to support that statement. Your evidence should reference the sources and connections that you explored during the Quest.

4. **Revise and Finalize Your Essay** Share your completed draft with a partner. Take turns providing feedback to each other. Ask yourselves if each essay answers the Guiding Question clearly and cites appropriate evidence. Correct any grammatical or spelling errors. Then, finalize your essay.

5. **Reflect on the Quest** Think about your experience completing this topic's Quest. What did you learn about the influence of Renaissance ideas on modern schools? What questions do you still have about the lasting legacy of the Renaissance? How will you answer them?

 INTERACTIVE

For extra help with Step 4, review the 21st Century Tutorial: **Write an Essay**.

Take Notes

Literacy Skills: Analyze Cause and Effect Use what you have read to complete the chart. Record causes that led to the listed effects of the Renaissance. The first one has been completed for you.

Causes	Effect
• Trade and industry increased. • Towns grew. • Both peasants and nobles moved to towns.	Feudalism and manorialism weakened.
•	The Renaissance first developed in Italian city-states.
•	Florence became a center of Renaissance culture.
•	Church power and influence declined.
•	Renaissance ideas spread across Europe.

INTERACTIVE

For extra help, review the 21st Century Tutorial: **Analyze Cause and Effect**.

Practice Vocabulary

Word Map Study the word map for the word *mercantile*. Characteristics are words or phrases that relate to the word in the center of the word map. Non-characteristics are words and phrases not associated with the word. Use the blank word map to explore the meaning of the word *Renaissance*. Then make word maps of your own for these words: *patron, humanism, secularism, vernacular, individualism, satire,* and *utopia*.

Characteristics
selling, for profit, stores

Definition in your own words
related to trade

mercantile

Non-Characteristics
charitable, nonprofit

Picture or sentence
The store owner belonged to a mercantile group.

Characteristics

Definition in your own words

Renaissance

Non-Characteristics

Picture or sentence

Take Notes

Literacy Skills: Integrate Visual Information Use what you have read to complete the table. Beneath each heading, list key details from the lesson text, as well as from the primary source art and other images. Then, use your notes to synthesize what you learned from text and visual sources of information in the lesson. The first one has been partially filled in for you.

An Artistic Revolution	Great Artists of the Renaissance	Architecture Advances	Renaissance Literature
Text Details Renaissance artists often blended religious and secular themes or focused on secular themes entirely such as scenes from Greek mythology, portraits, landscapes.	**Text Details**	**Text Details**	**Text Details**
Visual Details The painting by Benozzo Gozzoli shows how Renaissance artists mix religious themes and realistic technique. • •	**Visual Details**	**Visual Details**	**Visual Details**

Synthesize: How does the Renaissance represent both a rebirth and a revolution?

 INTERACTIVE

For extra help, review the 21st Century Tutorial: **Synthesize**.

Practice Vocabulary

Words in Context For each question below, write an answer that shows your understanding of the **boldfaced** key term.

1. What kind of story does a **picaresque** novel tell?

2. What does **linear perspective** allow artists to do?

3. What are the characteristics of a **sonnet**?

4. How does **proportion** help architects to make pleasing designs?

5. How does an artist make an **engraving**?

Quick Activity Drawing in 3D

Leonardo da Vinci, like other Renaissance artists, used linear perspective to show depth and distance in his paintings. With a partner, research some of his paintings, such as *The Last Supper* or *The Annunciation*, and discuss what gives the paintings a sense of depth.

Da Vinci's paintings often had a vanishing point, to which your eye is naturally drawn, and a horizontal line, called the *horizon line*, that divides the top part of the image from the bottom. The perspective grid below provides a horizon line, a vanishing point, and other lines of perspective.

Team Challenge! Sit or stand across from a partner. Use the perspective grid to draw your partner and the surrounding environment. Begin by sketching your partner at the vanishing point. Then, add objects and people that appear on each side of him or her. Keep in mind that the farther away an object is, the smaller it appears. Use the lines on the grid to help. Generally, the sides of things will run straight up and down, while the tops and bottoms will angle toward the vanishing point. When you have finished, compare your 3D drawings!

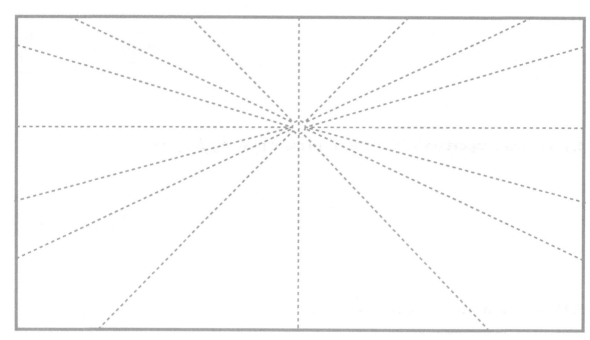

Take Notes

Literacy Skills: Identify Main Idea and Details Use what you have read to complete the charts. Write two main ideas from the lesson text. Then, list supporting details from the text for each main idea. The first one has been completed for you.

> **Main Idea**
> Renaissance culture changed the ways in which people thought about the world and shared ideas.

Detail

Authors began writing more books in the vernacular, increasing literacy.

Detail

Detail

Main Idea

Detail

Detail

Detail

INTERACTIVE

For extra help, review the 21st Century Tutorial: **Identify Main Ideas and Details**.

Practice Vocabulary

Word Map Study the word map for the term *movable type*. Characteristics are words or phrases that relate to the term in the center of the word map. Non-characteristics are words and phrases not associated with the term. Use the blank word map to explore the meaning of the word *censor*. Then make a word map of your own for the word *recant*.

Characteristics
Johann Gutenberg, printing press, metal type, individual letters, fast, many pages, less costly

Definition in your own words
individual letters made from metal that can be arranged and rearranged quickly to form words and sentences on a page

movable type

Non-Characteristics
block printing, handwritten, manuscript, wood blocks, slow, page by page, expensive

Picture or sentence
Movable type printing made it faster and easier to produce books.

Characteristics

Definition in your own words

censor

Non-Characteristics

Picture or sentence

Take Notes

Literacy Skills: Summarize Use what you have read to complete the chart. Write the actions associated with the movement in the center.

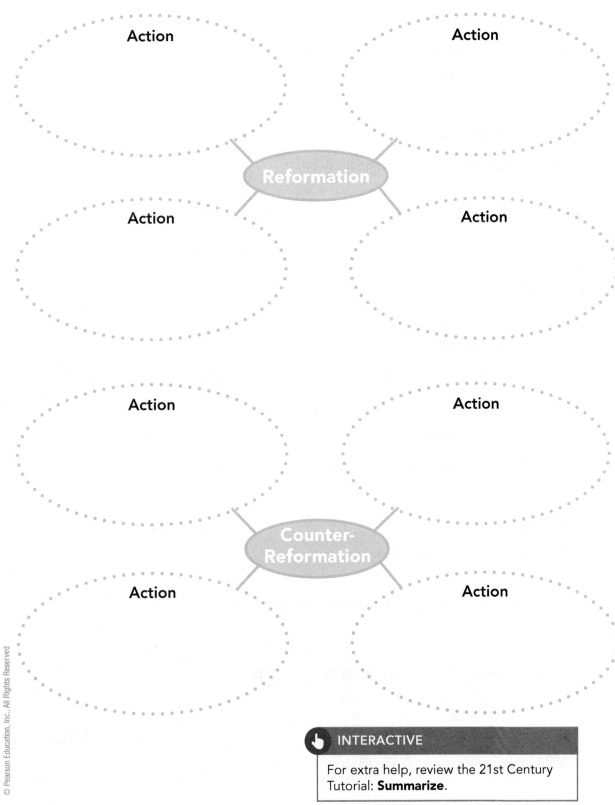

Action

Action

Reformation

Action

Action

Action

Action

Counter-Reformation

Action

Action

👆 **INTERACTIVE**

For extra help, review the 21st Century Tutorial: **Summarize**.

Practice Vocabulary

Sentence Builder Finish the sentences below with a key word from this section. You may have to change the form of the words to complete the sentences.

Word Bank

ghetto	indulgence	predestination	Reformation
sacrament	sect	theocracy	

1. People who believe in _____ think that God decided long ago who would gain salvation.

2. During the Counter-Reformation, Venice created a _____ to isolate Jews from the rest of the city.

3. Geneva was considered a _____ under John Calvin, because religious leaders governed the city.

4. Luther objected to the sale of _____ because he believed people could not buy forgiveness or salvation.

5. During the _____, Martin Luther and John Calvin founded Christian churches.

6. The spread of Luther's ideas increased the number of _____ in Europe, which means that many different types of Protestant churches sprang up.

7. Luther rejected five out of seven _____, including confession, as unnecessary for salvation.

Quick Activity Who Wrote What?

In this lesson, you have learned about historical figures who ignited the Protestant Reformation as well as leaders of the Catholic Church who responded with the Counter-Reformation. Read the excerpts below. Match the excerpt to one of the individuals listed, and explain your reasoning.

John Calvin	Ignatius of Loyola	Pope Innocent IV
Martin Luther	Pope Paul III	Teresa of Avila

"[W]ith God going before us in our deliberations, and holding before our minds the light of His own wisdom and truth,—we may, ... deliberate and discuss, execute and bring to the desired issue, speedily and happily, ... the integrity and truth of the Christian religion; the restoration of good and the correction of evil manners; the peace, unity, and concord both of Christian princes and peoples; and whatsoever is needful for repelling those assaults of barbarians and infidels, with which they seek the overthrow of all Christendom."

"In conformity, therefore, to the clear doctrine of the Scripture, we assert, that by an eternal and immutable counsel, God has once for all determined, both whom He would admit to salvation, and whom He would condemn to destruction. We affirm that this counsel, as far as concerns the elect, is founded on His gratuitous mercy, totally irrespective of human merit."

"And so it will profit nothing that the body should be adorned with sacred vestments, or dwell in holy places, or be occupied in sacred offices, or pray, fast, and abstain from certain meats, or do whatever works can be done through the body and in the body. ... [T]he soul can do without everything, except the word of God, without which none at all of its wants are provided for."

Team Challenge! Find a student with different matches. Discuss your ideas, and try to come to an agreement on the matches. Note that there are more people listed than you will have matches.

Take Notes

Literacy Skills: Sequence Use what you have read to complete the timeline. Record details about events that took place as a result of the Protestant Reformation. Be sure to draw a line from each box to the appropriate location on the timeline. The first one has been completed for you.

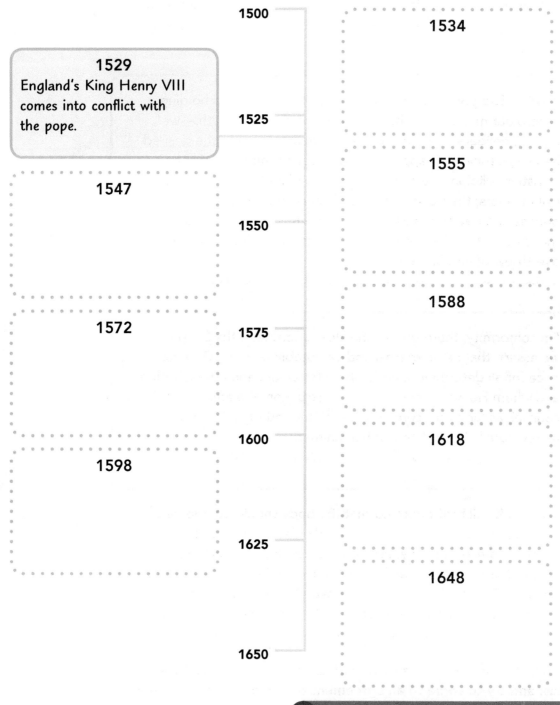

1500

1534

1529
England's King Henry VIII comes into conflict with the pope.

1525

1547

1555

1550

1572

1575

1588

1598

1600

1618

1625

1648

1650

👆 **INTERACTIVE**

For extra help, review the 21st Century Tutorial: **Sequence**.

Practice Vocabulary

Matching Logic Using your knowledge of the underlined vocabulary words, draw a line from each sentence in Column 1 to match it with the sentence in Column 2 to which it logically belongs.

Column 1	Column 2
1. King Henry VIII split from the Catholic Church when the pope refused to grant him an <u>annulment</u>.	The resulting battle, and loss, ended Spanish control of the seas.
2. Henry IV became king and issued the <u>Edict</u> of Nantes.	He officially declared the Catholic Church to be the church of France and granted French Huguenots the freedom to practice their religion.
3. King Philip sent an <u>armada</u> to attack England.	Such ideas entrusted greater power to local government.
4. Johannes Althusius drew on Calvinist ideas when he developed the idea of <u>federalism</u>.	He ended his marriage and started the Church of England.

Take Notes

Literacy Skills: Identify Main Idea and Details Use what you have read to complete the table. For each main idea, write details that support it. The first one has been partially filled in for you.

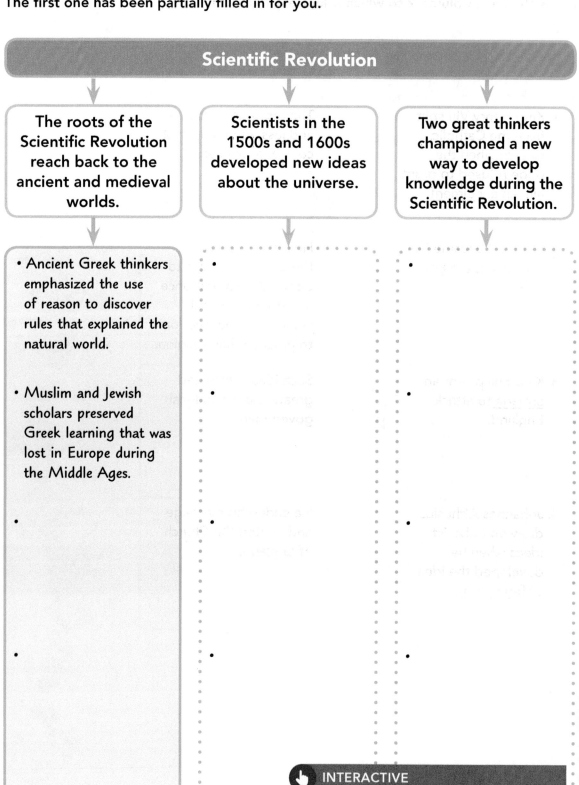

Scientific Revolution

The roots of the Scientific Revolution reach back to the ancient and medieval worlds.	Scientists in the 1500s and 1600s developed new ideas about the universe.	Two great thinkers championed a new way to develop knowledge during the Scientific Revolution.
• Ancient Greek thinkers emphasized the use of reason to discover rules that explained the natural world.	•	•
• Muslim and Jewish scholars preserved Greek learning that was lost in Europe during the Middle Ages.	•	•
•	•	•
•	•	•

INTERACTIVE

For extra help, review the 21st Century Tutorial: **Identify Main Ideas and Details**.

Practice Vocabulary

Vocabulary Quiz Show Some quiz shows ask a question and expect the contestant to give the answer. In other shows, the contestant is given an answer and must supply the question. If the blank is in the Question column, write the question that would result in the answer in the Answer column. If the question is supplied, write the answer.

Question

1.

2.

3. What is a belief that goes against the teaching of the Church called?

4.

5. What process is followed by using observation, experiments, and careful reasoning to gain new knowledge?

6. What is the theory that all knowledge is gained through experience and by making observations using the senses?

Answer

1. rationalism

2. heliocentric theory

3.

4. inductive reasoning

5.

6.

Writing Workshop Research Paper

As you read, gather information on a selected figure from the Renaissance, the Reformation, or the Scientific Revolution. Then, build a response to this question: **How did this individual contribute to the spread of new ideas in Europe?** The prompts below will help walk you through the process.

Lessons 1 and 2 Writing Task: Generate Questions to Focus Research
Make note of historical figures from the Renaissance, the Reformation, and the Scientific Revolution whom you might like to research. Make note of the movement with which each person is associated, and write three research questions for each figure. At the end of Lesson 2, circle the individual whom you plan to research.

Historical Figures	Movement	Research Questions

Lessons 3 and 5 Writing Task: Find and Use Credible Sources On a separate sheet of paper, list page references from the topic where you can find information on the individual you selected. Then, consider your research questions. List three other credible resources you will use to conduct additional research. These may be print or digital.

Lesson 4 Writing Task: Develop a Clear Thesis Using your research questions and your research, answer the question: **How did this individual contribute to the spread of new ideas in Europe?** Write one sentence in response to the question. You will use this response as a basis for your thesis statement. As you gather additional research, you may wish to revise your answer. Then, write your thesis statement.

Rough Response:

Thesis Statement:

Lesson 6 Writing Task: Pick an Organizing Strategy Consider how you will present the evidence to support your thesis statement. You might present information in chronological order, or you might examine several themes, influences, or effects of the individual's life and work. Then, on a separate sheet of paper, use your notes to prepare an outline. Remember that your paper must have an introduction and a conclusion. It should also include at least one, and no more than three, quotes.

Writing Task Use your thesis statement, evidence, quotes, and outline to answer the following question in a research paper: How did this individual contribute to the spread of new ideas in Europe?

When you have finalized your research paper, prepare a Works Cited page in which you list your sources. Be sure to attribute any quotes that you use.

👆 INTERACTIVE

For extra help, review the 21st Century Tutorials: **Search for Information on the Internet** and **Avoid Plagiarism**.

Essential Question What are the costs and benefits of human expansion?

Before you begin this topic, think about the Essential Question by completing the following activity.

1. List two positive aspects and two negative aspects of global expansion and contact.

2. Preview the topic by skimming lesson titles, headings, and graphics. Then place a check mark next to each person you predict will play an important role in global expansion during this era.

__Vasco da Gama   __Prince Henry the Navigator   __George Washington

__Ferdinand Magellan   __Hernán Cortés   __Genghis Khan

__Martin Luther   __Queen Isabella of Spain

Timeline Skills

As you read, write and/or draw at least three events from the topic. Draw a line from each event to its correct position on the timeline.

1400

1500

Map Skills

Using the map in your text, label the outline map with the places listed.
Then color in areas colonized by the Spanish.

Central America   New Spain   New Granada   Peru

North America   South America   Chile   Cuba

Hispaniola   Puerto Rico

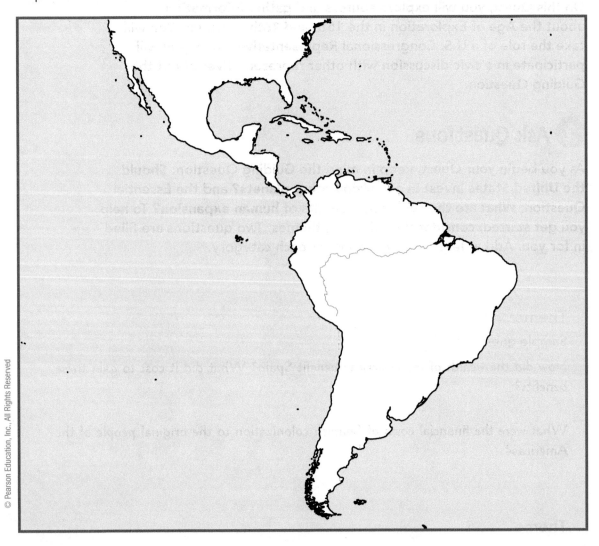

1600

1700

Quest
Discussion Inquiry

Colonizing Planets

On this Quest, you will explore sources and gather information about the Age of Exploration in the 15th and 16th centuries. You will take the role of a U.S. Congressional Representative. Then, you will participate in a civic discussion with other representatives about the Guiding Question.

 Ask Questions

As you begin your Quest, keep in mind the Guiding Question: **Should the United States invest in colonizing other planets?** and the Essential Question: **What are the costs and benefits of human expansion?** To help you get started, consider the following themes. Two questions are filled in for you. Add at least two questions for each category.

Theme Wealth

Sample questions:

How did the wealth of the Americas benefit Spain? What did it cost to gain these benefits?

What were the financial costs of Spanish colonization to the original people of the Americas?

Theme Food

Theme Disease

Theme Culture

Theme Technology and Knowledge

Theme My Additional Questions

 INTERACTIVE

For extra help with Step 1, review the 21st Century Skills Tutorial: **Ask Questions**.

2 Investigate

As you read about the Age of Exploration, collect five connections from your text to help you answer the Guiding Question. Three connections are already chosen for you.

Connect to Vasco da Gama

Primary Source Vasco da Gama, Journal

Here's a connection! What were the difficulties that Vasco da Gama and other early European sailors faced as they explored the oceans for new trade routes?

What dangers would face colonizers of space? How might they address these dangers?

Connect to Columbus's Voyages

Lesson 1 Explorers Find New Routes

Here's another connection! What do you think Ferdinand and Isabella considered to be the costs of supporting Columbus's voyages of discovery? What would they see as the benefits?

What do you think the costs and benefits of Spain's explorations would be to the people of the Americas?

Connect to Portugal's Global Empire

Lesson 4 How Did the Portuguese Empire Decline?

Here's another connection! Portugal's colonies faced many enemies and other obstacles. What opposition or obstacles might people of Earth face in colonizing other planets?

How might competition for resources lead to conflict between nations?

It's Your Turn! Find two more connections. Fill in the title of your connections, then answer the questions. Connections may be images, primary sources, maps, or text.

Your Choice | Connect to

Location in text

What is the main idea of this connection?

What does it tell about what the United States should consider as it debates colonizing other planets?

Your Choice | Connect to

Location in text

What is the main idea of this connection?

What does it tell about what the United States should consider as it debates colonizing other planets?

3 Examine Primary Sources

Examine the primary and secondary sources provided online or from your teacher. Fill in the chart to show how these sources provide further information about the costs and benefits of future colonization of other planets. The first one has been started for you.

Should the United States invest in colonizing other planets?

Source	Yes or No? Why?
"Founding Declaration of the Mars Society"	YES, because we can use comparative planetology to better understand the potential threat of global warming on Earth.
"Would It Be Ethical to Colonize Mars?"	
"Astronauts May Face Long-Term Brain Damage as a Result of Space Travel"	

INTERACTIVE

For extra help with Step 3, review the 21st Century Skills Tutorial: **Compare Viewpoints.**

 **FINDINGS**

4 Discuss!

Now that you have collected information and explored documents about the costs and benefits of human expansion, you are ready to discuss with your fellow Congressional Representatives the Guiding Question: **Should the United States invest in colonizing other planets?** Follow the steps below, using the spaces provided to prepare for your discussion.

You will work with a partner in a small group of representatives. Try to reach consensus, a situation in which everyone is in agreement, on the question. Can you do it?

1. **Prepare Your Arguments** You will be assigned a position on the question, either YES or NO.

   My position

   Work with your partner to review your Quest notes from the Quest Connections and Quest Sources.

   • If you were assigned YES, agree with your partner on what you think were the strongest arguments from the Mars Society.

   • If you were assigned NO, agree on what you think were the strongest arguments from Stemwedel and Gallego.

2. **Present Your Position** Those assigned YES will present their arguments and evidence first. As you listen, ask clarifying questions to gain information and understanding.

What is a Clarifying Question?

These types of questions do not judge the person talking. They are only for the listener to be clear on what he or she is hearing.

Example:	Example:
Can you tell me more about that?	You said [x]. Am I getting that right?

👆 **INTERACTIVE**

For extra help with Step 4, review the 21st Century Skills Tutorial: **Participate in a Discussion or Debate.**

While the opposite side speaks, take notes on what you hear in the space below.

3. **Switch!** Now NO and YES will switch sides. If you argued YES before, now you will argue NO. Work with your same partner and use your notes. Add any arguments and evidence from the clues and sources. Those *now* arguing YES go first.

When both sides have finished, answer the following:

Before I started this discussion with my fellow representatives, my opinion was that the United States	*After* I started this discussion with my fellow representatives, my opinion was that the United States
_____should invest in colonizing other planets. _____should not invest in colonizing other planets.	_____should invest in colonizing other planets. _____should not invest in colonizing other planets.

4. **Point of View** Do you all agree on the answer to the Guiding Question?

- ——Yes

- ——No

If not, on what points *do* you all agree?

Take Notes

Literacy Skills: Identify Cause and Effect Use what you have read to complete the chart. Read the event in the Cause column and write an effect in the Effect column. The first one has been completed for you.

Cause	Effect
Europe wanted to buy goods from Asia and Africa.	Europe sought a sea route to Asia that bypassed the Mediterranean Sea.
Bartolomeu Dias proved that Europeans could reach the Indian Ocean by sailing around the southern tip of Africa.	
Christopher Columbus sailed west to reach the East Indies.	
	Sailors could circumnavigate the globe.
	Sailors chose the best time of year to set sail.

INTERACTIVE

For extra help, review the 21st Century Skills Tutorial: **Analyze Cause and Effect**.

Practice Vocabulary

Sentence Builder Finish the sentences below with a key term from this section. You may have to change the form of the words to complete the sentences.

Word Bank

missionary   cartography   caravel   circumnavigate

1. European-built vessels with triangular sails and two or three masts are called

2. To sail completely around the world is to

3. The science of creating globes and maps is known as

4. People who attempt to convert others to a specific religion are known as

Quick Activity A Memorable Map

With a partner or small group, examine the nautical chart below.

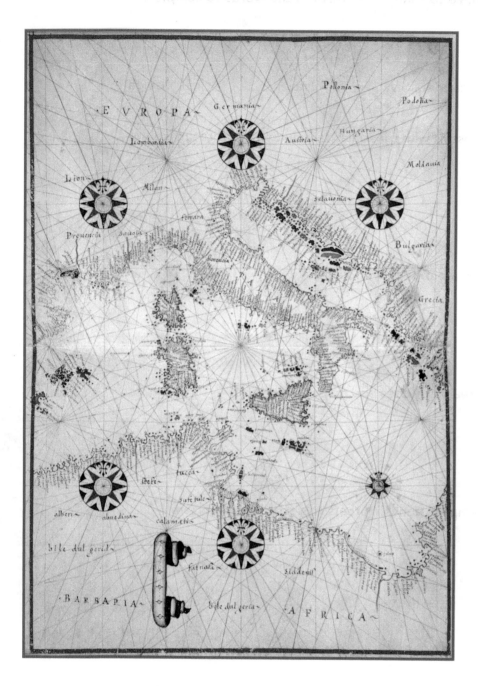

The technology of cartography has changed significantly over the past several hundred years, causing nautical charts to be more comprehensive and accurate. What advantages and disadvantages can you imagine for these new navigation tools?

Team Challenge! Draw a map of your school or area of your school. Include and label important details. Post the map in your classroom. Take a gallery walk to view everyone's ideas to see how the same idea can be mapped in different ways.

Take Notes

Literacy Skills: Sequence Use what you have read to complete the flowchart. In each space write an event to show how the Spanish conquered the Aztec Empire. The first one has been completed for you.

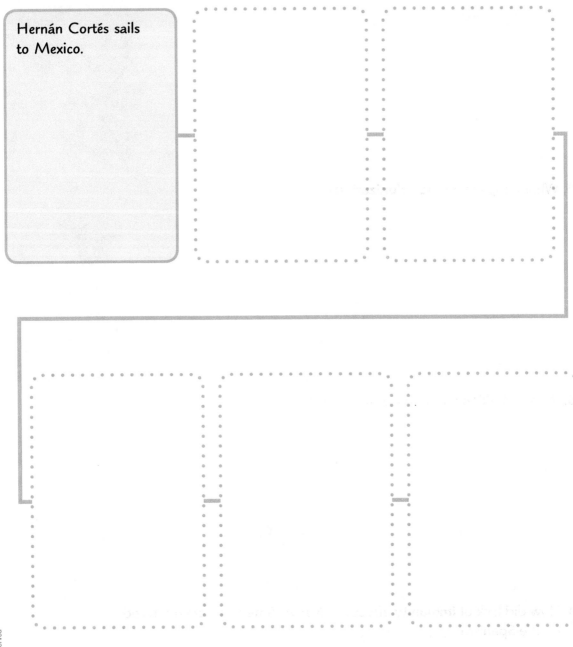

Hernán Cortés sails to Mexico.

INTERACTIVE

For extra help, review the 21st Century Skills Tutorial: **Sequence**.

Practice Vocabulary

Words in Context For each question below, write an answer that shows your understanding of the boldfaced key term.

1. Who were the **conquistadors**?

2. What happens during **colonization**?

3. What is **bullion** and why was it valued?

4. How did lack of **immunity** affect the Native Americans encountered by the Spanish?

Take Notes

Literacy Skills: Identify Main Idea and Details Use what you have
read to complete the table. In each space write four details under the
correct main idea. The first one has been started for you.

Effects of Spanish Rule in the Americas

Culture	Economy	Native Americans
• Hundreds of new towns and cities are built.		

INTERACTIVE

For extra help, review the 21st Century
Skills Tutorial: **Identify Main Ideas and
Details**.

Practice Vocabulary

Sentence Revision Revise each sentence so that the underlined vocabulary word is used logically. Be sure not to change the vocabulary word. The first one is done for you.

1. The <u>viceroy</u> of New Spain conquered territories in the Caribbean, Mexico, and South America.
The <u>viceroy</u> of New Spain governed territories in the Caribbean, Mexico, and South America.

2. <u>Peninsulares</u> were at the bottom of society in colonial Spain.

3. <u>Creoles</u>, who owned mines, ranches, and plantations, were African-born descendants of Spanish settlers.

4. <u>Mestizos</u>, who were of Native American and European descent, were among the wealthiest social groups in Spanish colonial society.

5. One of the primary purposes of <u>missions</u> was to teach sailing skills to Native Americans.

6. <u>Mulattoes</u> were of European and Mexican descent.

7. The <u>encomienda</u> system led to freedom for Native Americans.

Take Notes

Literacy Skills: Analyze Text Structure Use what you have read to complete the outline. Add details to explain the significance of Portuguese colonization during this era. The first entries are completed for you.

Significance of Portuguese Colonization

I. Brazil

    A. Politics and Wealth

        1. Portugal aimed to challenge Spain's position as the most powerful country in Europe, and Brazil's wealth would finance further colonial expansion.

        2. 4 million enslaved Africans brought to work; a new culture emerged blending European, Native American, African influences.

    B. Colonization Effect on Native Americans

        1. Death and illness were widespread since little immunity to European diseases.

        2. Portuguese converted many native people to Christianity.

II. Asia

    A.

        1.

    B.

        1.

        2.

III. Decline of the Portuguese Empire

    A.

        1.

        2.

        3.

 INTERACTIVE

For extra help, review the 21st Century Skills Tutorial: **Identify Main Ideas and Details.**

Practice Vocabulary

Matching Logic Using your knowledge of the underlined vocabulary words, draw a line from each sentence in Column 1 to match it with the sentence in Column 2 to which it logically belongs.

Column 1	Column 2
1. <u>Privateers</u> attacked cargo ships from the Americas.	Illegal smuggling was frequent in the colonies.
2. Early settlers discovered an important export—<u>brazilwood</u>.	This brought cinnamon, pepper, and other seasonings to European markets.
3. The <u>spice trade</u> was very profitable for Portugal and other countries.	The pope wanted to divide the non-European world between Spain and Portugal.
4. The <u>Treaty of Tordesillas</u> decided the location and terms of the <u>Line of Demarcation</u>.	The Portuguese named the South American colony after a tree which produced a valuable reddish-purple dye.

Take Notes

Literacy Skills: Summarize Use what you have read to complete the chart. In each space write details that elaborate on the main idea, then write a summary below. One detail has been entered for you.

Columbian Exchange	European Economy	Ming Dynasty
		Hongwu Emperor stimulated agricultural production.

Summary

INTERACTIVE

For extra help, review the 21st Century Skills Tutorial: **Summarize**.

Practice Vocabulary

True or False? Decide whether each statement below is true or false.
Circle T or F, and then explain your answer. Be sure to include the
underlined vocabulary word in your explanation. The first one is done
for you.

1. **T / F** The <u>Columbian Exchange</u> is the exchange of people, other living
things, and ideas between the Eastern and Western hemispheres.
True; The <u>Columbian Exchange</u> mainly took place across the Atlantic
Ocean between the Americas, Europe, Asia, and Africa.

2. **T / F** The economic policy of <u>mercantilism</u> promotes the expansion
of trade as a means of strengthening a nation.

3. **T / F** Under the economic system of <u>capitalism</u>, businesses are owned
by the government.

4. **T / F** <u>Inflation</u> occurs when there is an increase in available cash and
a decrease in prices.

5. **T / F** In a <u>traditional economy</u>, the exchange of goods is based
on custom.

6. **T / F** People engaged in <u>cottage industries</u> worked long hours
in factories.

7. **T / F** In a <u>market economy</u>, competition affects prices and the
distribution of goods.

Take Notes

Literacy Skills: Compare and Contrast Use what you have read to complete the Venn diagram. In each space write details that describe Jamestown, Plymouth, or both colonies. The first one has been started for you.

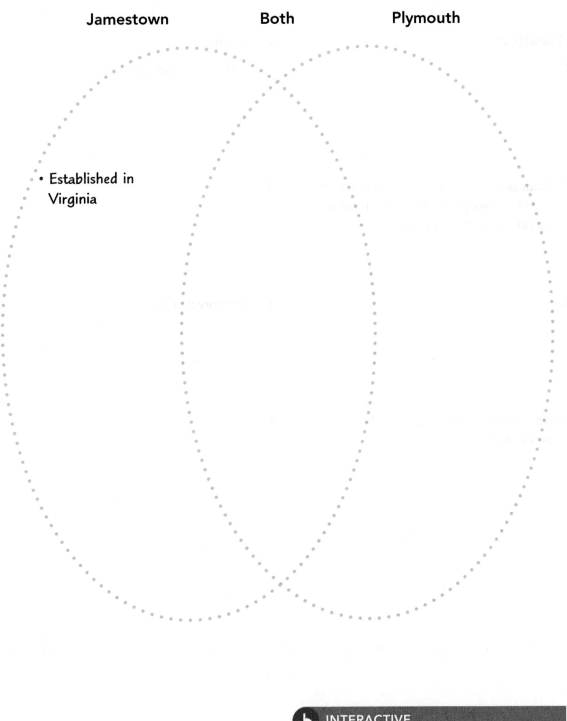

Jamestown   Both   Plymouth

- Established in
  Virginia

👆 **INTERACTIVE**

For extra help, review the 21st Century Skills Tutorial: **Compare and Contrast**.

Practice Vocabulary

Vocabulary Quiz Show Some quiz shows ask a question and expect the contestant to give the answer. In other shows, the contestant is given an answer and must supply the question. If the blank is in the Question column, write the question that would result in the answer in the Answer column. If the question is supplied, write the answer.

Question	Answer
1.	1. northwest passage
2. What is the term for the factors that motivate people to leave their homes and settle in a new place?	2.
3.	3. indentured servants
4. What agreement ended the Seven Years' War?	4.

Take Notes

Literacy Skills: Integrate Visual Information Use what you have read to complete the table. Write three visual elements from the lesson in the first column, the main idea of each visual element in the second column, and whether the visual element adds, clarifies, or repeats information presented in the text in the third column. One has been completed for you.

Visual Element	Main Idea	Adds, Clarifies, or Repeats Information
People from Burkino Faso making music, page 153	To show the survival of African culture in the face of slavery	Adds information

Select one visual element and explain why you think the author included the visual instead of simply using text to convey the message.

INTERACTIVE

For extra help, review the 21st Century Skills Tutorials: **Synthesize** and **Draw Conclusions**.

Practice Vocabulary

Use a Word Bank Choose one word from the word bank to fill in each blank. When you have finished, you will have a short summary of important ideas from the section.

Word Bank

chattel   Middle Passage   triangular trade   mutiny

The international trade network known as the ....

was formed by a three-way group of trade routes that crossed the Atlantic

Ocean. These three routes linked Europe, Africa, and the Americas. On

the first part of the journey, merchants shipped cloth and other goods

from Europe to Africa. On the second part of the journey, called the

...., African captives were sent across the

ocean to the Americas to be sold into slavery. Then, during the final

part of the journey, colonial products were sent to Europe. The enslaved

Africans, considered ...., had no rights.

However, fearful of a ...., the men operating

the slave ships would chain the male captives together.

Quick Activity The Middle Passage

With a partner or small group, read the following quotes.

> "The closeness of the place, and the heat of the climate, added to the number in the ship, which was so crowded that each had scarcely room to turn himself, almost suffocated us."
>
> — Olaudah Equiano, *The Interesting Narrative of the Life of Olaudah Equiano, or Gustavus Vassa, the African* (1815)

> "The [Africans] were chained to each other hand and foot, and stowed so close, that they were not allowed above a foot and a half for each in breadth."
>
> —Sir William Dolben, British Member of Parliament who proposed an act to regulate conditions on slave ships

Team Challenge! After Dolben's Act of 1788, British abolitionists, including Olaudah Equiano, continued to fight against the slave trade and the institution of slavery. In 1807, the slave trade was outlawed in the British empire, and in 1833, slavery was abolished in the empire. With your partner or group, put yourself in the place of a British citizen in 1805. Write a letter to your member of Parliament asking them to end the slave trade and slavery itself.

Writing Workshop Arguments

As you read, build a response to this question: **Was the impact of global convergence mostly positive or mostly negative?**
The prompts below will help walk you through the process.

Lesson 1 Writing Task: Introduce Claims Write one sentence stating your opinion of the impact of global convergence. This will be your claim for the argument you will write at the end of the topic.

Lessons 1 through 7 Writing Task: Support Claims List important facts and examples from the text that support or oppose your claim.

Support Claim	Oppose Claim

Lesson 3 Writing Task: Distinguish Claims from Opposing Claims
Write three sentences explaining how your claims are different from opposing claims.

Lesson 4 Writing Task: Use Credible Sources Think about credible sources from which you could gather additional evidence on global convergence. On a separate piece of paper, list these sources as well as the evidence each one provides.

Lessons 5 and 6 Writing Task: Shape Tone Review your main claim statement. Consider your audience and adjust the tone of your statement as necessary. Clarify relationships between your claim and the evidence by using transition words such as *for example, for instance, specifically, because, consequently, therefore, thus,* and *as a result.*

Lesson 7 Writing Task: Write a Conclusion Review your claim and evidence. Write a strong conclusion sentence to concisely sum up your argument on the impact of global convergence.

Writing Task Using the evidence you have gathered, write a five-paragraph essay arguing your claim. Your claim should be clear and supported by the evidence you have gathered.

17 Absolutism and Enlightenment Preview

Essential Question **What is the best form of government?**

Before you begin this topic, think about the Essential Question by completing the following activity.

1. What does it mean to you to be governed or have rules and laws?

....

2. Preview the topic by skimming lesson titles, headlines, and graphics. Place a check mark next to qualities that you predict will be true of European governments in the years leading up to the Enlightenment.

__powerful   __kind   __religious   __fair

__tolerant   __peaceful   __absolute   __wealthy

__democratic

Timeline Skills

As you read, write and/or draw at least three events from the topic. Draw a line from each event to its correct position on the timeline.

1500   **1600**

Map Skills

Using the map in your text, label the outline map with the places listed.
Then, color in the water.

Russia	Spain	England	Sweden
Austria	Poland	Prussia	France
Norway	Ottoman Empire	Mediterranean Sea	Baltic Sea

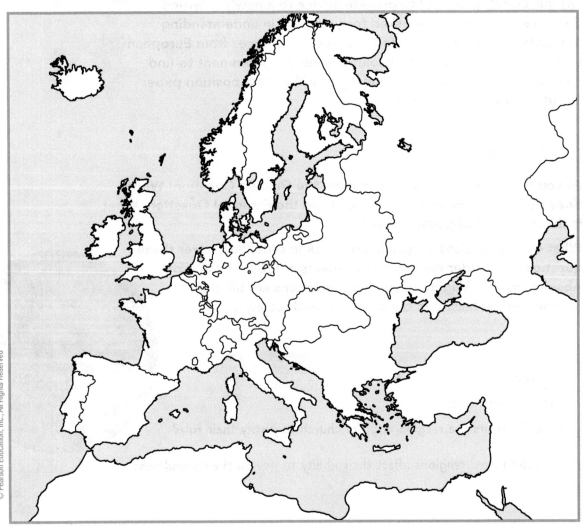

1700

1800

Quest

Document-Based Writing Inquiry

The Right to Rule

On this Quest, you need to provide advice to a newly crowned European queen who has asked for your help in understanding authority and government. You will examine sources from European thinkers during the age of Absolutism and Enlightenment to find examples. At the end of the Quest you will write a position paper about the ideal government.

1 Ask Questions

As you begin your Quest, keep in mind the Guiding Question: **Where does the right to govern come from?** and the Essential Question: **What is the best form of government?**

What other questions do you need to ask in order to answer these questions? Consider the following aspects of life in the age of Absolutism and Enlightenment. Two questions are filled in for you. Add at least two questions for each category.

Theme Religion and the Church

Sample questions:

How did rulers use religion and the church to justify their rule?

How did rulers' religions affect their ability to govern their kingdoms?

Theme Science, Art, and Humanism

Theme Government and the People

Theme Trade and Warfare

Theme My Additional Questions

 INTERACTIVE

For extra help with Step 1, review the
21st Century Tutorial: **Ask Questions**.

Quest CONNECTIONS

2 Investigate

As you read about Absolutism and Enlightenment, collect five connections from your text to help you answer the Guiding Question. Three are already chosen for you.

Connect to Bishop Jacques Bossuet

Primary Source Jacques Bossuet, *Politics Drawn from the Very Words of Holy Scripture*

Here's a connection! What does this Primary Source tell you about where Bishop Jacques Bossuet believed the right to govern comes from?

How do you think this works in practice?

Connect to John Locke

Primary Source John Locke, *Two Treatises of Government*

Here's another connection! What are John Locke's ideas about authority and the social contract?

How do you think these ideas affected Europe and the rulers who governed?

Connect to Baron de Montesquieu

Analysis Skills Draw Sound Conclusions from Sources

What does this connection reveal about Montesquieu's concept of authority?

What impact did this idea have on the history of the world?

It's Your Turn! **Find two more connections. Fill in the title of your connections, then answer the questions. Connections may be images, primary sources, maps, or text.**

Your Choice | Connect to

Location in text

What is the main idea of this connection?

What does it tell you about the ideal government or the right to rule?

Your Choice | Connect to

Location in text

What is the main idea of this connection?

What does it tell you about the ideal government or the right to rule?

③ Examine Primary Sources

Examine the primary and secondary sources provided online or from your teacher. Fill in the chart to show how these sources provide further information about where the right to govern comes from. The first one is completed for you.

Source	Explanation
Leviathan	In Leviathan, Thomas Hobbes explains that citizens should enter a social contract with an absolute ruler, because giving that ruler complete authority is the only true way to ensure protection and order.
Patriarcha	
The Social Contract	
Divine Right of Kings	
The Sun King	

👆 INTERACTIVE

For extra help with Step 3, review the 21st Century Tutorials: **Analyze Primary and Secondary Sources** and **Analyze Images**.

4 Write Your Position Paper

Now it's time to put together all of the information you have gathered and use it to write your argument. Absolute monarchs and Enlightenment thinkers had different ideas about where the right to govern comes from, as well as what those rights are, and who should have them. Use the steps below to outline your position on this issue and complete the writing process.

1. **Prepare to Write** You have collected connections and explored primary sources to learn more about where the right to govern comes from. On a separate piece of paper, summarize your position on this issue in one sentence. This will become the thesis statement for your argument.

2. **Outline Your Argument** Look through your notes for evidence that supports your thesis statement. Use the table below to begin to outline your argument.

Introduction Your thesis	
Evidence From primary sources	
Additional Evidence From primary sources	
Conclusion Restatement of your thesis	

3. **Write a Draft** Write a draft of your argument using your outline. Add transitional words and phrases to strengthen your argument and clarify your position.

4. **Share with a Partner** With a partner, correct any grammatical, spelling, or factual errors and make sure that your argument makes sense.

5. **Finalize Your Paper** Finalize your argument and use technology to publish your paper.

6. **Reflect on the Quest** Think about your experience in completing this topic's Quest. What did you learn about the different ideas about rights and where the right to govern comes from? What questions do you still have about absolute monarchs and the Enlightenment? How will you answer them?

Reflections

👆 **INTERACTIVE**

For extra help with Step 5, review the 21st Century Tutorial: **Publish Your Work**.

Take Notes

Literacy Skill: Cite Evidence Use what you have read to complete the table. Draw conclusions from the text, and support these statements with three pieces of evidence. One conclusion has been provided for you. Add evidence to support the conclusion, and then try one on your own.

> Charles V and Philip II were responsible for the golden age of Spain.

Charles V was hard-working and knew he had to answer to Spanish nobles.

Practice Vocabulary

Sentence Revision Revise each sentence so that the underlined vocabulary word is used logically. Be sure not to the change the vocabulary word. The first one is done for you.

1. The mighty Spanish <u>armada</u> fought many battles on land.
   The mighty Spanish <u>armada</u> fought many battles at sea.

2. As <u>absolute monarch</u>, Louis XIV wanted to share power with his people.

3. The idea of <u>divine right</u> meant that Louis XIV believed the people gave him the right to power.

4. Spanish <u>inflation</u> caused prices for goods and services to decrease.

5. An <u>assassin</u> gave birth to Henry IV.

Take Notes

Literacy Skills: Compare and Contrast Compare and contrast Russian reforms under Peter the Great and Catherine the Great.

Peter the Great   Both   Catherine the Great

INTERACTIVE

For extra help, review the 21st Century Tutorial: **Compare and Contrast**.

Practice Vocabulary

Word Map Study the word map for the word *tsar*. Characteristics are words or phrases that relate to the word in the center of the word map. Non-characteristics are words and phrases not associated with the word. Use the blank word map to explore the meaning of the word *serf*. Then make your own word map for the word *partition*.

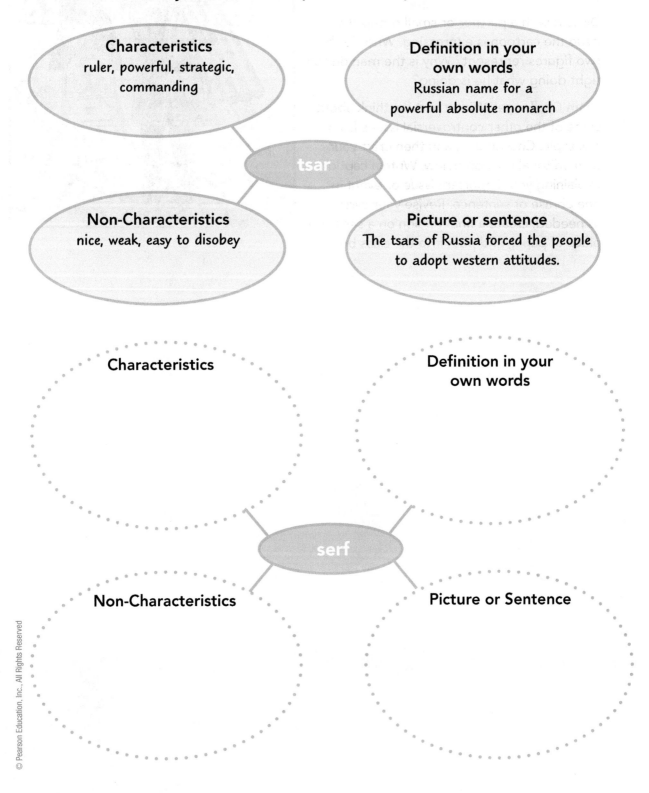

Characteristics
ruler, powerful, strategic, commanding

Definition in your own words
Russian name for a powerful absolute monarch

tsar

Non-Characteristics
nice, weak, easy to disobey

Picture or sentence
The tsars of Russia forced the people to adopt western attitudes.

Characteristics

Definition in your own words

serf

Non-Characteristics

Picture or Sentence

Quick Activity Editorial Cartoon

An editorial cartoon is an illustration that expresses a message, often about a controversial event or issue. Let's take a closer look at the editorial cartoon from your text.

Discuss with a partner or small group the issue the cartoon is expressing. Who do the two figures represent? Why is the man on the right doing what he is doing?

Team Challenge! With a partner, think about some of the other controversial issues from this topic. Choose one, and then draft your own editorial cartoon below. Write a caption explaining your important issue or event in one phrase or sentence. Revise your cartoon as needed, create a final version on a separate piece of paper, and post it to the class board.

Take Notes

Literacy Skills: Identify Cause and Effect Use what you have read to complete the chart. For each effect, identify three causes. The first has been completed for you.

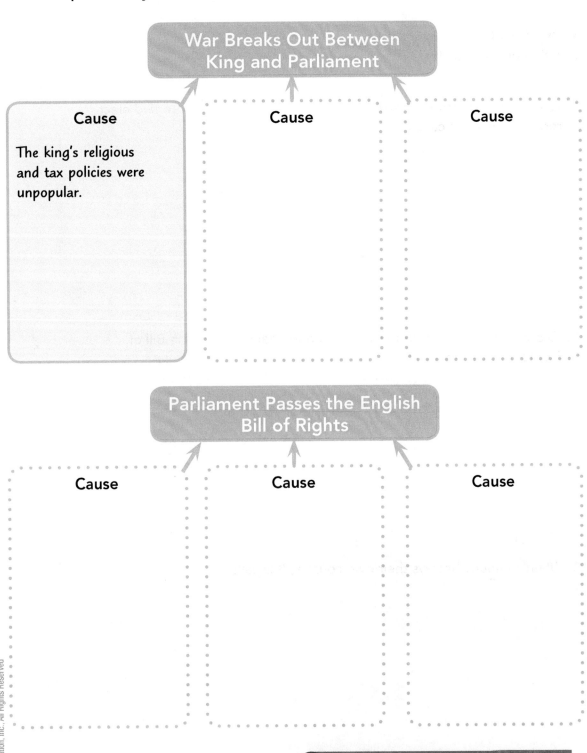

War Breaks Out Between King and Parliament

Cause

The king's religious and tax policies were unpopular.

Cause

Cause

Parliament Passes the English Bill of Rights

Cause

Cause

Cause

👆 **INTERACTIVE**

For extra help, review the 21st Century Tutorial: **Analyze Cause and Effect**.

Practice Vocabulary

Sentence Builder Finish the sentences below with a key term from this section. You may have to change the form of the word to complete the sentences.

Word Bank

constitutional monarchy   republic   treason

1. A form of government in which citizens have the right to vote and elect representatives is called a

2. To prevent absolutism from ever occurring again, the English Bill of Rights established a

3. When someone betrays their own country, it is called

Take Notes

Literacy Skills: Summarize Use what you have read to complete the table. Summarize the major ideas that came out of the Enlightenment.

Political Ideas	Social Ideas	Economic Ideas

Summary

INTERACTIVE

For extra help, review the 21st Century Tutorial: **Summarize**.

Practice Vocabulary

Matching Logic Using your knowledge of the underlined vocabulary words, draw a line from each sentence in Column 1 to match it with the sentence in Column 2 to which it logically belongs.

Column 1	Column 2
1. Voltaire argued that Christians should demonstrate <u>tolerance</u>.	If a government fails to protect them, the people should rebel and form a new government.
2. Montesquieu believed in <u>separation of powers</u>.	People agree to give up unlimited freedom in exchange for protection of their liberties.
3. John Locke believed that <u>natural rights</u> belong to all people.	Allowing others to hold beliefs different from one's own is essential for peace.
4. Many Enlightenment thinkers believed that a <u>social contract</u> was the basis of any government.	Having a legislative, judicial, and executive branch establishes a system of checks and balances.

Quick Activity In Your Own Words

Examine the quotes below from the Magna Carta, English Bill of Rights, and the Declaration of Independence. Discuss with a partner the similarities and differences between the quotes.

"(39) No free man shall be seized or imprisoned, or stripped of his rights or possessions, or outlawed or exiled or deprived of his standing in any way, nor will we proceed with force against him, or send others to do so, except by the lawful judgment of his equals or by the law of the land."

—*Magna Carta (1215)*

"The pretended power of dispensing with laws or the execution of laws by regal authority, as it hath been assumed and exercised of late, is illegal."

—*English Bill of Rights*

"We hold these truths to be self-evident that all men are created equal, that they are endowed by their Creator with certain unalienable Rights, that among these are Life, Liberty, and the pursuit of Happiness."

—*U.S. Declaration of Independence*

Team Challenge! With your partner, choose one of the quotes and rewrite the idea in your own words. Then, share your rewrite with the class.

Writing Workshop Arguments

As you read, build a response to this question: **Was the concept of an absolute monarchy doomed?** The prompts below will help walk you through the process.

Lesson 1 Writing Task: Introduce Claims Write a sentence that introduces your opinion about the question of whether or not the concept of absolute monarchy was doomed. This opinion will become the thesis statement of the argument that you will write at the end of the topic.

Lesson 2 Writing Task: Support Claims Now add details from the lessons to support your claim.

Lesson 1:	
Lesson 2:	
Lesson 3:	
Lesson 4:	

Lesson 3 Writing Task: Clarify Relationships with Transition Words
Referring to your claim and evidence, brainstorm transition words and phrases that will help you clarify the relationships between your evidence and your claim.

Lesson 4 Writing Task: Write a Conclusion Draft a conclusion statement for your argument. Your conclusion should revisit the claim of your argument and should complete your thoughts about whether the concept of absolute monarchy was doomed.

Writing Task Using your thesis, evidence, some transition words, and your conclusion, answer the following question in a five-paragraph argument: Was the concept of an absolute monarchy doomed? Expand your thesis into an introduction paragraph. Each supportive paragraph should have an introductory sentence, two or three details, and a conclusion sentence. Expand your conclusion statement into a conclusion paragraph that ends with a thought-provoking or challenging question.

TOPIC 18   A Revolutionary Era Preview

Essential Question   What forces can cause society to change?

Before you begin this topic, think about the Essential Question by completing the following activities.

1. Think about your society. This might include your community, your state, and your nation. What are some changes that you have observed in your society? List cultural, economic, political, and social changes below.

Timeline Skills

As you read, write and/or draw at least three events from the topic. Draw a line from each event to its correct position on the timeline.

1750	1800

Map Skills

Using the map in your text, label the outline map with the countries and dates of independence listed. Then, label the Pacific Ocean and the Atlantic Ocean. Finally, color in water and land areas.

Peru (1824)   Haiti (1804)   Paraguay (1811)   Chile (1818)

Colombia (1819)   Mexico (1821)   Bolivia (1825)   Uruguay (1828)

Venezuela (1830)   United States (1776) Brazil (1822)   Ecuador (1822)

Dominican Republic (1844)   Argentine Confederation (1816)

Guatemala, Honduras, El Salvador, Nicaragua, and Costa Rica (1838)

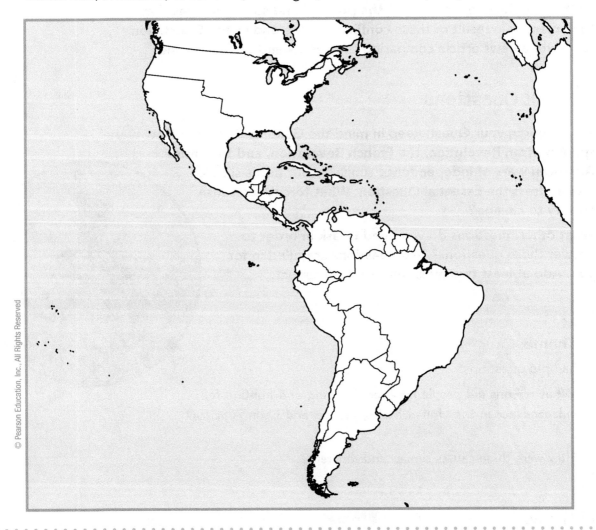

1850   **1900**

Quest
Document-Based Writing Inquiry

Dateline: Revolution

On this Quest, you will explore similarities and differences between the revolutionary wars in the United States and France and the wars for independence in Latin America. You will examine sources from all three regions to learn about the political and social changes that took place as a result of these conflicts. At the end of the Quest, you will write a news article comparing the events and their outcomes.

1 Ask Questions

As you begin your Quest, keep in mind the Guiding Question: **How were the American Revolution, the French Revolution, and the Latin American wars of independence similar?** Your notes should also address the Essential Question: **What forces can cause society to change?**

What other questions do you need to ask in order to answer these questions? Two questions are filled in for you. Add at least two questions for each aspect.

Theme Causes

Sample questions:

What reasons did people have for declaring and fighting for independence in the United States, France, and Latin America?

How were these causes similar and different?

Theme Territory and Government at Beginning of Conflict

Theme Key People and Events During the Conflict

Theme Changes to Government

Theme Changes to Economy and Society

Theme My Additional Questions

 INTERACTIVE

For extra help with Step 1, review
the 21st Century Skills Tutorial:
Ask Questions.

2 Investigate

As you read about the revolutions in the United States and France and the wars for independence in Latin America, collect five connections from your text to help you answer the Guiding Question. Three connections are already chosen for you.

Connect to the Declaration of Independence

Lesson 1 Breaking Away from Britain

Here's a connection! Read about the American Patriots' Declaration of Independence and the ideas behind it. What ideas and events led to the American Revolution?

How did the Enlightenment influence the Patriots?

Connect to the French Revolution

Lesson 2 How Did the French Revolution Begin?

What does the excerpt from the Declaration of the Rights of Man and the Citizen suggest about the reasons behind French independence? Paraphrase the statement in your own words, and explain how it compares to the Declaration of Independence.

How does the excerpt reflect a significant change in French society?

Connect to the Americas

Lesson 5 How Did Nationalism Spread?

Here's another connection! Read about the spread of nationalism in the Americas. How were the wars in Latin America similar to the revolutions in the United States and France?

How were the outcomes of the wars for independence similar to and different from the outcomes of the revolutions in the United States and France?

It's Your Turn! **Find two more connections. Fill in the title of your connections, then answer the questions. Connections may be images, primary sources, maps, or text.**

Your Choice | Connect to

Location in Text

What is the main idea of this connection?

What does this connection tell you about similarities and differences between the conflicts in the United States, France, and Latin America?

Your Choice | Connect to

Location in Text

What is the main idea of this connection?

What does this connection tell you about similarities and differences between the conflicts in the United States, France, and Latin America?

③ Examine Primary Sources

Examine the primary and secondary sources provided online or from your teacher. Fill in the chart to show how these sources provide further information about the causes, events, and effects of the revolutions in the United States and France and the wars for independence in Latin America.

Source	What impact of revolutionary movements does this source demonstrate?
Common Sense	
The Tennis Court Oath	
The Reign of Terror, 1793–1794	
Letter from Jamaica	
Revolutionary Leaders: George Washington and Simón Bolívar	

INTERACTIVE

For extra help with Step 3, review the 21st Century Skills Tutorials: **Analyze Primary and Secondary Sources** and **Analyze Images**.

4 Write Your Article

Now it's time to put together all the information that you gathered, and write your article.

1. **Prepare to Write** Remember that you are a news correspondent reporting on the similarities and differences among the revolutions in the United States and France and the wars for independence in Latin America. You have collected connections and explored primary and secondary sources related to these events. Look through your notes. Identify major similarities and differences between the causes, events, and effects of the conflicts. Record details here.

How do the major causes for the revolutions and wars for independence compare?	
How were events in the United States, France, and Latin America similar or different?	
How do the major changes caused by the conflicts compare?	

2. **Outline Your Ideas** You may choose to focus on one aspect (such as the causes) of the conflicts, or you may narrow your comparison to two out of the three conflicts. In any case, your article should include an introduction that identifies its main idea, a body of three to five paragraphs that explores your topic, and a conclusion that restates your main idea. Use a separate sheet of paper below to outline your ideas.

3. **Write a Draft** Use your notes and your outline to write a draft of your article. Remember to answer Who? What? Where? When? Why? and How? in your article and to compare and contrast events in the United States, France, and Latin America in the late 1700s and early 1800s. Your first paragraph should capture readers' interest and state the main idea of your article. Be sure to use details from the Quest Connections. You should quote at least three sources in your discussion.

4. **Share With a Partner** Exchange drafts with a partner. Tell your partner what you like about his or her draft, and suggest any improvements.

5. **Finalize Your Article** Revise your draft based on your partner's feedback.

6. **Reflect on the Quest** Think about your experience completing this topic's Quest. What did you learn about this pivotal time in the history of the United States, France, and Latin America? What questions do you still have about these events? How will you answer them?

Reflections

Take Notes

Literacy Skills: Analyze Cause and Effect Use what you have read about the American Revolution to complete the chart. Record the correct causes and effects in the appropriate column. The first one has been completed for you.

Causes	Effects
Britain places a number of heavy taxes on the colonists and does not allow colonists to elect representatives to the British Parliament.	Colonists try to persuade Parliament to change its policies, and some colonists take part in violent protests.
A group of colonists stages a protest known as the Boston Tea Party.	
Thomas Paine writes *Common Sense*, arguing that the colonies should not be ruled by a government located across the ocean.	
	The French government is convinced that the colonists can defeat Britain, and it forms an alliance with the Americans.
Under the Articles of Confederation, individual states have more power than the central government.	
At the Constitutional Convention, large states and small states argue over representation in the legislature.	
	The Framers of the Constitution divide power among the national government and state and local governments.

INTERACTIVE

For extra help, review the 21st Century Skills Tutorial: **Analyze Cause and Effect**.

Practice Vocabulary

Sentence Builder Finish the sentences below with a vocabulary term from this section. You may have to change the form of the words to complete the sentences.

Word Bank

alliance   boycott   constitution

massacre   militia

1. Early battles of the American Revolution were fought by armies of citizen volunteers who trained to fight during emergencies, or

2. Delegates from the states met in Philadelphia in 1787 and wrote a document that lists the basic principles and structure of a government, called a(n)

3. The killing of a large number of helpless people is called a(n)

4. France and the American colonies formed a(n)

5. To show disapproval by refusing to buy certain goods is a(n)

Take Notes

Literacy Skills: Sequence Use what you have read about the French Revolution to complete the chart. Add details about events that took place during the dates listed.

The French Revolution

May 1789:

July 14, 1789: Parisians storm the Bastille.

August 1789:

1791: The National Assembly ends the monarchy's absolute power with the Constitution of 1791. France declares war on Prussia.

1793:

1794:

1799:

1804:

1804–1810: Napoleon creates a strong central government, writes the Napoleonic Code, and invades almost all of Europe.

1812:

1814–1815:

INTERACTIVE

For extra help, review the 21st Century Skills Tutorial: **Sequence**.

Practice Vocabulary

Words in Context For each question below, write an answer that shows your understanding of the boldfaced vocabulary term.

1. What were the main characteristics of the three **estates** that French society was divided into before the French Revolution?

2. How did **radicals** cause the Reign of Terror during the French Revolution?

3. Why do many scholars believe that Napoleon's most important achievement was the **Napoleonic Code**?

4. Why did Napoleon **abdicate** in 1814?

Quick Activity Who Am I?

With a partner or in a small group, read and discuss the facts provided below. Identify the historical figure from the topic who fits the facts. Write his or her name in the center oval.

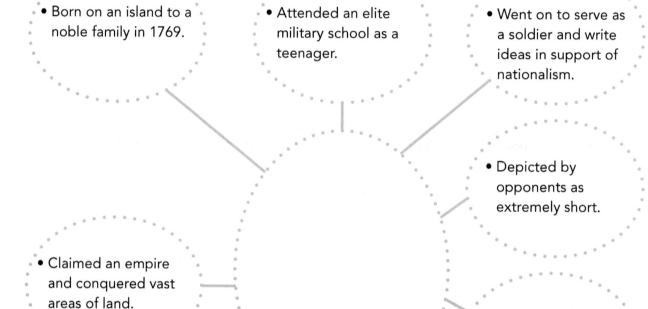

- Born on an island to a noble family in 1769.

- Attended an elite military school as a teenager.

- Went on to serve as a soldier and write ideas in support of nationalism.

- Depicted by opponents as extremely short.

- Claimed an empire and conquered vast areas of land.

- Became a great military leader who organized and led a massive army.

- Codified a system of law that protected citizens' freedoms.

- Made a grave mistake that cost many people's lives.

- Fell from power twice.

Team Challenge! With your partner or group, write a short response to the question: **Why do I matter?** from the perspective of the person described above. Consider how the person would describe his or her achievements and defend his or her mistakes. Select one student to read aloud your response to the class.

Take Notes

Literacy Skills: Classify and Categorize Use what you have read about nationalism in Europe to complete the chart. Categorize events based on the country in which they occurred. The first one has been completed for you.

Germany	Italy
In the early 1800s, German-speaking peoples were divided into many separate states.	In the early 1800s, Italy was divided into separate city-states and kingdoms.

INTERACTIVE

For extra help, review the 21st Century Skills Tutorial: **Categorize**.

Practice Vocabulary

Word Map Study the word map for the term *nation-state*. Characteristics are words or phrases that relate to the term in the center of the word map. Non-characteristics are words and phrases not associated with the term. Use the blank word map to explore the meaning of the word *nationalism*. Make your own word map for the term *social welfare*.

Characteristics
shared interests, one culture, one religion, one language, one system of law, state and nation together

Definition in your own words
a state in which the people are united by a shared identity

nation-state

Non-characteristics
state without nation, nation without state, empire, diversity, many cultures, many ethnic groups, many languages

Picture or sentence
The French and American Revolutions led to the formation of new nation-states.

Characteristics

Definition in your own words

nationalism

Non-characteristics

Picture or sentence

Take Notes

Literacy Skills: Analyze Cause and Effect Use what you have read about the Industrial Revolution to complete the chart. Record the effects of the changes listed below.

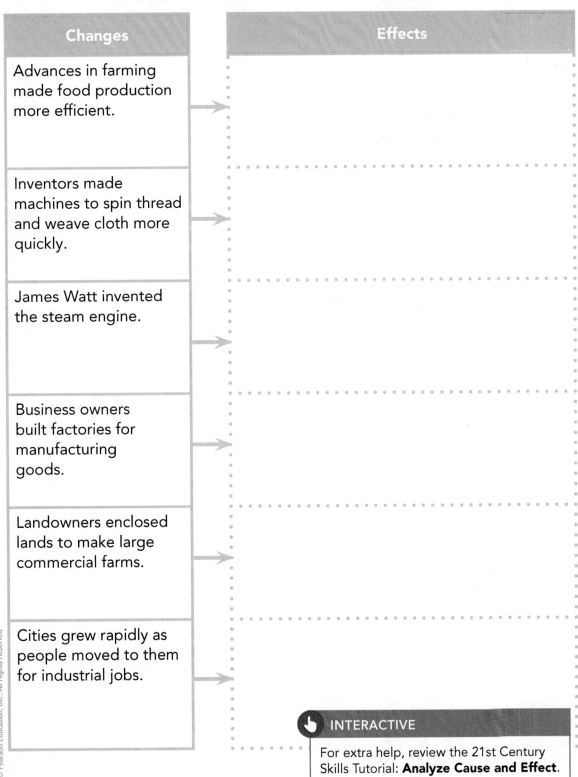

Changes	Effects
Advances in farming made food production more efficient.	
Inventors made machines to spin thread and weave cloth more quickly.	
James Watt invented the steam engine.	
Business owners built factories for manufacturing goods.	
Landowners enclosed lands to make large commercial farms.	
Cities grew rapidly as people moved to them for industrial jobs.	

👆 INTERACTIVE

For extra help, review the 21st Century Skills Tutorial: **Analyze Cause and Effect**.

Practice Vocabulary

Vocabulary Quiz Show Some quiz shows ask a question and expect the contestant to give the answer. In other shows, the contestant is given an answer and must supply the question. If the Answer column is blank, write the correct answer to the question. If the answer is provided and the Question column is blank, write the question that would produce that answer.

Question

Answer

1. What economic system called for workers to own the means of production and to distribute goods?

1.

2.

2. enclosure

3. What economic system called on the government to own all property and make all economic decisions?

3.

4. What period of change in the late 1700s and early 1800s used new sources of energy to power machines?

4.

Quick Activity Before and After Industrialization

What was daily life and work like before and after industrialization in Europe? Study the images below. With a partner, identify key differences between the two scenes. Then, brainstorm a list of other differences between pre-industrial society and industrialized society.

Team Challenge! Write a paragraph letter or journal entry for a pre-industrial worker and an industrial worker. The two accounts should highlight differences in their living and working environments, their methods and tools, their output, and their personal experience of the work. Be creative! Give your workers names, and include personal characteristics. Take turns sharing your writings with a partner or in a small group.

Take Notes

Literacy Skills: Analyze Text Structure Use what you have read about imperialism and nationalism to complete the chart. Record the main idea and supporting details for each heading in the lesson. The first one has been completed for you.

Causes of Imperialism	Carving Up the World	Southeast and East Asia	Spread of Nationalism
Main Idea: Many factors helped European nations and the United States gain colonies around the world.	**Main Idea:**	**Main Idea:**	**Main Idea:**
Details: need for raw materials; nationalist rivalries; racism and feelings of cultural superiority; desire to spread Christianity	**Details:**	**Details:**	**Details:**

👆 INTERACTIVE

For extra help, review the 21st Century Skills Tutorial: **Identify Main Ideas and Details**.

Practice Vocabulary

Word Bank Choose one word from the word bank to fill in each blank. When you have finished, you will have a short summary of important ideas from the section.

Word Bank

concessions   gunboat diplomacy   imperialism

European empires controlled most of the world by the 1800s.

This control of foreign lands by stronger states is called

.... There were many reasons for European

domination of the world. One was industrialism. Europe needed raw

materials for its factories. Another reason was nationalism. The British, in

particular, were eager to expand their empire.

The European empires carved up the world among themselves. In China,

different European nations had separate spheres of influence. When

the Chinese tried to stop Great Britain's opium trade to China, the two

countries went to war. Britain won, and the Chinese were forced to offer

.... , or trading rights, to Europeans.

Japan, alarmed by events in China, restricted contact with the West.

However, in 1853, the United States sent Matthew Perry to Japan to

demand diplomatic relations and trading rights. Fearful of bombardment

by the guns on Perry's ship, the Japanese agreed. Western powers

often used this .... to threaten the use of

firepower to win various terms.

Take Notes

Literacy Skills: Use Evidence Use what you have read about the Second Industrial Revolution to complete the chart. Identify evidence from each of the sections of text to support the conclusions listed below. The first one has been started for you.

The Second Industrial Revolution

Innovations gave rise to new types of industries and businesses.

- Power and Productivity New sources of power, such as electricity, and new methods, such as the assembly line, spurred industrial growth.

- New Inventions

- Big Business

Societies experienced great changes in their ways of life and work.

- Higher Standard of Living

- People on the Move

The many changes caused challenges that led to popular calls for reform.

- Workers in the Age of Industry

- Forming Unions

- Child Labor Laws

- Education and Health

- Women's Suffrage

INTERACTIVE

For extra help, review the 21st Century Skills Tutorial: **Identify Evidence**.

Practice Vocabulary

Words In Context For each question below, write an answer that shows your understanding of the boldfaced vocabulary term.

1. What benefit does a business gain from practicing **vertical integration**?

2. How does an **assembly line** work?

3. What happens when employees go on **strike**?

4. What did women who demanded **suffrage** want?

5. What were **tenements**, and where were they located?

6. What is the purpose of a **union**?

Writing Workshop Research Paper

As you read, build a response to this question: **How did revolutionary movements affect society and daily life during this era? The prompts below will help walk you through the process. You will conduct additional research to complete this writing workshop.**

Lesson 1 Writing Task: Narrow Your Topic After you read Lesson 1, skim the other lessons, and note possible research topics. When you have finished, highlight the topic you want to research. Confirm your topic with your teacher before you begin conducting research.

Lesson 2 Writing Task: Generate Questions to Focus Research On a separate sheet of paper, list questions that you have about your chosen topic. Use these questions to guide your research and writing. You may wish to add questions to your list as you move through the lessons.

Lesson 3 Writing Task: Find and Use Credible Sources Conduct independent research to find historical sources in the library, on the Internet, and in academic periodicals. Online, you should search for information on specific topics, such as the effect of unification on German farmers and workers. On a separate sheet of paper, write complete source citations for your sources according to directions given by your teacher. Begin investigating your research questions.

Lessons 4 and 5 Writing Tasks: Develop a Clear Thesis and Support Ideas with Evidence Customize the research paper prompt to suit your topic. For instance, if you chose to focus on the French Revolution, you would change the question to: "How did the French Revolution affect French society and daily life?" Then, answer this question in one or two sentences. Your answer is your thesis. Write it in the box below. Then write down the strongest three pieces of evidence from the appropriate lesson and your research.

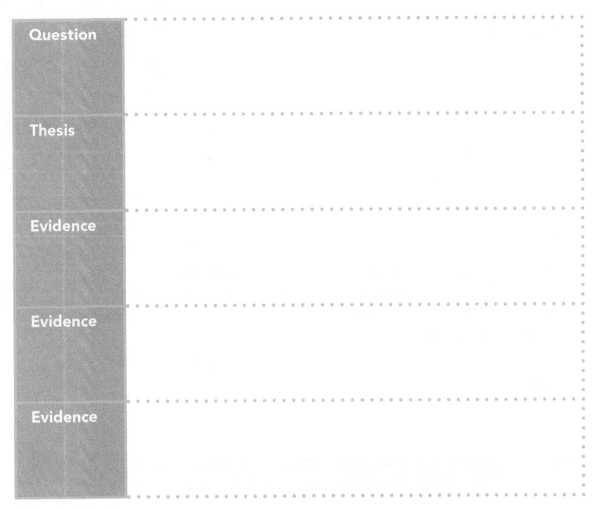

Question	
Thesis	
Evidence	
Evidence	
Evidence	

Lesson 6 Writing Task: Draft Your Research Paper Use your thesis, your notes, and your outline to write a draft of your research paper. Remember to include appropriate citations for the information that you include. When you have finished, exchange drafts with a partner and provide feedback. Revise your draft based on his or her feedback.

Writing Task: Research Paper Read aloud your draft a final time to check for misspellings, grammatical errors, and other problems. Make any needed revisions. Finally, be sure that your revised draft answers the following question: **How did revolutionary movements affect society and daily life during this era?**

Essential Question What are the costs and benefits of technology?

Before you begin this topic, think about the Essential Question by completing the following activities.

1. List two positive aspects and two negative aspects of technology.

2. Preview the topic by skimming lesson titles, headings, and graphics. Then place a check mark next to the areas where you think technology will play an important role.

__medical equipment   __religion   __workplace

__politics   __military warfare   __transportation

__poetry   __communication   __tradition

Timeline Skills

As you read, write and/or draw at least three events from the topic. Draw a line from each event to its correct position on the timeline.

1900	1930	1960

Map Skills

Using the map in your text, label the outline map with the places listed.
Then color in the countries with access to the Bay of Bengal:

Afghanistan	Pakistan	India	Arabian Sea
Bay of Bengal	South China Sea	Myanmar (Burma)	Thailand
Laos	Cambodia	Vietnam	Malaysia
Sri Lanka	Philippines	China	

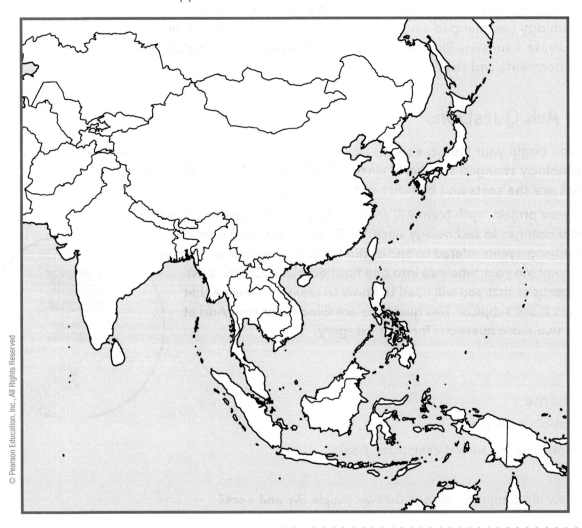

1990	2020	2050

Quest
Project-Based Learning Inquiry

Science/Technology Timeline

On this Quest, you will work with a team to create a technology timeline. You will examine sources to find examples of how technology has changed since 1900. At the end of the Quest, you will create a timeline illustrating several important technological advancements and their impact.

1 Ask Questions

As you begin your Quest, keep in mind the Guiding Question: **How has technology changed the world since 1900?** and the Essential Question: **What are the costs and benefits of technology?**

For your project, each team will collect information to create a timeline about changes to technology since 1900, with each team member identifying events related to one of the themes listed below. Then you will combine your timelines into one finished piece. Create a list of questions that you will need to know to create a timeline that covers these subjects. Two questions are filled in for you. Add at least two more questions for each category.

Theme Computers

Sample questions:

How were the earliest computers used?

How did computers change the way people live and work?

Theme The Internet and Social Media

Theme Warfare

Theme Medicine

Theme My Additional Questions

 INTERACTIVE

For extra help with Step 1, review
the 21st Century Skills Tutorial:
Ask Questions.

② Investigate

As you read about changes in technology, collect five connections from your text to help you answer the Guiding Question. Three connections are already chosen for you.

Connect to World War I

Primary Source Life in the Trenches

Here's a connection! Read about trench warfare in your text, and look at the accompanying photographs. Do armies fight each other from trenches today?

How did changes in military technology affect World War I? What changes in military technology have occurred since then?

Connect to the Cold War

Primary Source Winston Churchill, "Iron Curtain" Speech

Here's another connection! Read Winston Churchill's speech. How did people in 1946 hear about Churchill's speech?

How might today's technology affect the way people learn about and react to such a speech?

Connect to the Information Revolution

Lesson 8 Revolutions in Information Technology

How would communicating with others be different without the Internet?

How would you get news and information or access entertainment?

It's Your Turn! **Find two more connections. Fill in the title of your connections, then answer the questions. Connections may be images, primary sources, maps, or text.**

Your Choice | Connect to

Location in text

What is the main idea of this connection?

What does it tell you about how the world has changed since 1900?

Your Choice | Connect to

Location in text

What is the main idea of this connection?

What does it tell you about how the world has changed since 1900?

③ Conduct Research

Form teams based on your teacher's instructions. Meet to decide who will create each part of the timeline.

You will research further only the subject that you are responsible for. Use the ideas in the connections to further explore the subject you have been assigned. Pick what you will include, and find more sources about that subject.

Be sure to find valid sources, and take good notes so you can properly cite your sources. Record key information about your subject, and brainstorm ways to enhance your points with visuals.

Team Member	Subject	Changes to/Impacts of Subject
	Computers	
	The Internet and Social Media	
	Warfare	
	Medicine	

> **↓ INTERACTIVE**
>
> For extra help with Step 3, review the 21st Century Skills Tutorials: **Work in Teams** and **Interpret Sources**.

4 Create Your Timeline

Now it's time to put together all of the information you have gathered and make your part of the timeline.

1. **Prepare to Write** Review the research you've collected, and make sure you've identified the key changes related to your subject and their impacts.

Key changes, with dates:

Impacts of those changes:

Sources to cite:

Possible visual/visuals to support your changes:

2. **Write a Draft** Draft four to five key events in the development of your subject and any impacts that resulted from those changes. Each timeline entry should have a date and one sentence or phrase telling what happened.

3. **Share with a Partner** Once you have finished your draft, ask one of your team members to read it and provide comments on the clarity and flow of the information. Revise the text based on the comments you receive, and comment on your team member's timeline, if possible.

4. Create a Visual Now that you have the text for your part of the timeline, find or create visuals to support two or three of your entries.

5. Put Together Your Timeline Once all the team members have written and revised their segments, brainstorm a way to put them together. You may choose to create a web site with a tab for each subject or each decade, or create one large illustrated timeline, either digitally or on paper. Consider color-coding the different subjects, with one color for computers, one for the Internet and social media, and so on. Place the images near the appropriate text.

6. Share Your Timeline Share your timeline with other groups. Read what each person has written, taking notes on the information he or she shared. Pay close attention to how the information is presented.

7. Reflect After you have examined the other timelines, discuss your thoughts on your group's timeline and those created by others. Reflect on how each group presented the information. Reflect on the project and what you learned about technology since 1900.

Reflections

INTERACTIVE

For extra help with Step 4, review the 21st Century Skills Tutorials: **Sequence**.

Take Notes

Literacy Skills: Identify Main Ideas and Details Use what you have read to complete the chart. In each space write one main idea and two details. The first one has been started for you.

Causes of World War I

Imperialism and Nationalism

• There is competition for raw goods.

Effects of World War I

Practice Vocabulary

Vocabulary Quiz Show Some quiz shows ask a question and expect the contestant to give the answer. In other shows, the contestant is given an answer and must supply the question. If the blank is in the Question column, write the question that would result in the answer in the Answer column. If the question is supplied, write the answer.

Question	Answer
1. What was the first truly global conflict?	1.
2. Who fought against Russia on the Eastern Front?	2.
3.	3. trench warfare
4.	4. militarism
5.	5. propaganda
6. What is the name of the radical socialist group led by Vladimir Lenin?	6.
7. What did French leader Georges Clemenceau want Germany to pay after World War I?	7.

Take Notes

Literacy Skills: Summarize Use what you have read to complete the chart. List details under each heading. Then write a summary statement based on those details. The first one has been started for you.

Soviet Union	Germany	Japan	Italy
Stalin took control over Soviet agriculture.			

Summary

Practice Vocabulary

Use a Word Bank Choose one word from the word bank to fill in each blank. When you have finished, you will have a short summary of important ideas from the section.

Word Bank

Great Depression   mandates   totalitarianism

New Deal   fascism

When World War I ended, the Allies created a system of

_____ that they claimed would help certain

countries become independent. However, these countries simply became

colonies of Allied powers. Economic issues and feelings of betrayal and

discontent boiled up in these colonized regions, including the Middle

East, sometimes leading to protests and revolts. When the U.S. stock

market collapsed in 1929, it sent the United States into a massive

economic downturn, known as the _____.

President Roosevelt's _____ gave many

Americans employment through federal programs. Europe was also in

the midst of economic troubles, but extremist political leaders used

this as an opportunity to seize control over their people. Germany

and the Soviet Union were just two of the countries that fell to

_____. In Italy, nationalist pride led to

_____, a political system that stresses military

might and the belief that the state is more important than the individual.

Quick Activity Evidence of Totalitarianism

With a partner or small group, list the characteristics of totalitarian governments. Then, analyze how these characteristics affect people under this type of leadership. Use the images on this page to help you.

Do you think people under totalitarian rule are happy? Do you think they have the right to free speech and the power to make important decisions regarding their lives? How are people dealt with if they disagree with their leaders?

Team Challenge! With a partner, write a speech against totalitarian rule. Imagine what you might say to leaders regarding changes you want made to the government and your own life. Read your speech aloud to the class to compare and contrast what your classmates would say and how they would want to see society changed.

Take Notes

Literacy Skills: Sequence Use what you have read to complete the chart. In each box, write at least one event in the sequence of events before, during, and after World War II. The first one has been completed for you.

Japan, Italy, and Germany follow a policy of military aggression in the 1930s.

INTERACTIVE

For extra help, review the 21st Century Skills Tutorial: **Sequence**.

Practice Vocabulary

Sentence Revision Revise each sentence so that the underlined vocabulary term is used logically. Be sure not to change the vocabulary term. The first one is done for you.

---

1. The <u>Axis powers</u> included the United States, Great Britain, and France.
The <u>Axis powers</u> included Germany, Japan, and Italy.

---

2. A German <u>blitzkrieg</u> always began with a ground assault.

3. Adolf Hitler and Joseph Stalin signed a <u>nonaggression pact</u> in which both sides committed to fighting each other until the end of World War II.

4. To avoid German aggression, European leaders chose <u>appeasement</u>, a policy in which weaker countries attack the aggressor first.

5. During the <u>Holocaust</u>, the Japanese military murdered 6 million of Europe's Jews and 5 million others.

6. The Nazis' Final Solution was a plan to commit <u>genocide</u>, the exile of an ethnic, racial, or religious group.

Quick Activity Propaganda Posters

With a partner or small group, examine these U.S. propaganda posters from World War II.

What is the purpose of these posters? How are these two posters the same? How are they different? Do you think the images and words work together to get the message across? Why or why not?

Team Challenge! Work with your team or partner to create your own World War II propaganda posters. Use what you learned in Lesson 3 and the images on this page to guide you. Decide how your choice of images, words, and colors can make your message clear. Hang the posters in your classroom. View everyone's posters to see how the ideas were expressed in different ways.

Take Notes

Literacy Skills: Sequence Use what you have read to complete the chart. In each box, write one event in the sequence of events before, during, and after the Cold War. The first one has been completed for you.

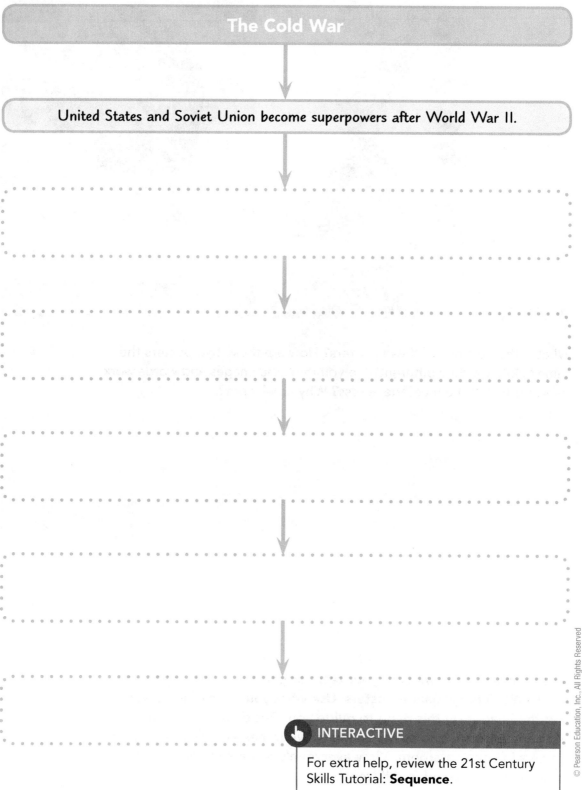

The Cold War

United States and Soviet Union become superpowers after World War II.

> **INTERACTIVE**
>
> For extra help, review the 21st Century Skills Tutorial: **Sequence**.

Practice Vocabulary

True or False? Decide whether each statement below is true or false. Circle T or F, and then explain your answer. Be sure to include the underlined vocabulary term in your explanation. The first one is done for you.

1. **T / F** The U.S. and Soviet conflict from 1945 to 1991 is known as the <u>Cold War</u>.
True; the <u>Cold War</u> began after World War II.

2. **T / F** A <u>superpower</u> is a country that is able to influence world events because it wields much political, economic, and military strength.

3. **T / F** <u>Glasnost</u> was a policy in which open discussion about the Soviet political system was punishable by imprisonment.

4. **T / F** <u>Free enterprise</u> is an economic system that allows business owners to make economic decisions.

5. **T / F** Under Communist <u>command economies</u>, owning private property was encouraged.

6. **T / F** President Truman's policy of <u>containment</u> attempted to keep the Soviet Union from expanding beyond areas already under its control.

7. **T / F** <u>Détente</u> ended in 1979 when the United States invaded the Soviet Union.

Take Notes

Literacy Skills: Analyze Cause and Effect Use what you have read to complete the chart. Write causes in the first column and effects of that cause in the second column. The first one has been completed for you.

Cause	Effect
1. Colonies were expensive to defend.	1. Imperialism ends.

INTERACTIVE

For extra help, review the 21st Century Skills Tutorial: **Analyze Cause and Effect**.

Practice Vocabulary

Matching Logic Using your knowledge of the underlined vocabulary words, draw a line from each sentence in Column 1 to match it with the sentence in Column 2 to which it logically belongs.

Column 1	Column 2
1. Kwame Nkrumah favored <u>pan-Africanism</u>.	He believed all people on the continent should cooperate to make progress.
2. Gandhi was assassinated by a Hindu <u>extremist</u>.	Some governments were forcibly overthrown, usually by the military.
3. With independence of African nations, <u>coups d'etat</u> became common.	Some Muslims and Hindus turned to violence after the subcontinent was split into India and Pakistan.

Take Notes

Literacy Skills: Synthesize Visual Information Use what you have read
to complete the table. Write three visual elements from the lesson in
the first column, the main message of each visual element in the second
column, and whether the visual element adds, clarifies, or repeats
information presented in the text in the third column. One has been
completed for you.

Visual Element	Main Idea	Adds, Clarifies, or Repeats Information
People in street, p. 849	Arabs protested, wanting greater freedom.	Repeats, Adds

INTERACTIVE

For extra help, review the 21st Century
Skills Tutorial: **Analyze Images**.

Practice Vocabulary

Sentence Builder Finish the sentences below with a key term from this section. You may have to change the form of the words to complete the sentences.

Word Bank

fundamentalism   terrorism

recognize   nationalization

1. A system of beliefs based on literal interpretation of sacred texts is known as

2. When other countries officially treat a nation as a legitimate state with a legitimate government, that state has been

3. When violence is employed as a means of achieving political goals and creating fear, it is called

4. Government takeover of businesses or property is known as

Take Notes

Literacy Skills: Summarize Use what you have read to complete the table. List details under each heading. Then write a summary statement based on those details. The first one has been started for you.

India	United States	Latin America
• Sikhs demanded independence.		

Summary

© Pearson Education, Inc., All Rights Reserved

INTERACTIVE

For extra help, review the 21st Century Skills Tutorial: **Summarize**.

Practice Vocabulary

Word Map Study the word map for the word *segregation*. Characteristics are words or phrases that relate to the word in the center of the word map. Non-characteristics are words and phrases not associated with the word. Use the blank word map to explore the meaning of the word *apartheid*. Then make a word map of your own for *Tiananmen Square*.

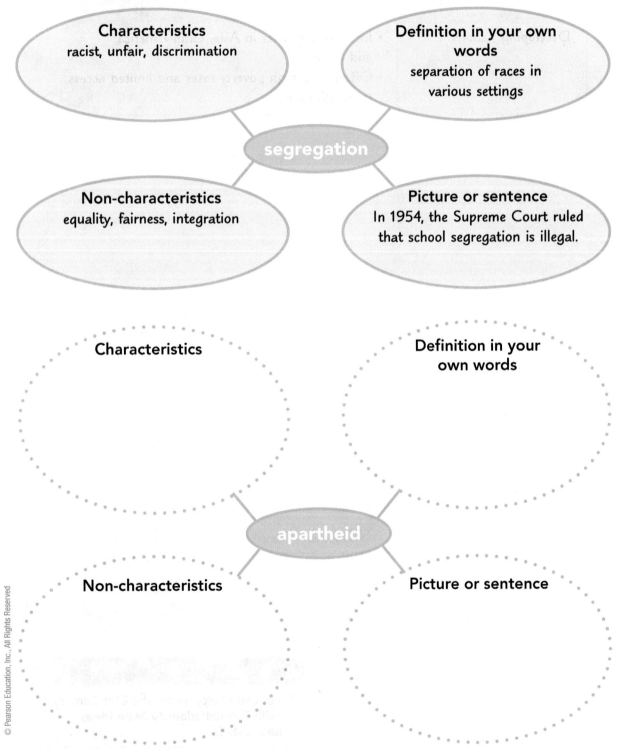

Characteristics
racist, unfair, discrimination

Definition in your own words
separation of races in various settings

segregation

Non-characteristics
equality, fairness, integration

Picture or sentence
In 1954, the Supreme Court ruled that school segregation is illegal.

Characteristics

Definition in your own words

apartheid

Non-characteristics

Picture or sentence

Take Notes

Literacy Skills: Identify Main Ideas and Details Use what you have read to complete the table. In each space, write one main idea and two details. The first one has been completed for you.

Main Idea	Details
Developing nations	• Includes countries in Asia, Latin America, and Africa • Often have high poverty rates and limited access to health care

INTERACTIVE

For extra help, review the 21st Century Skills Tutorial: **Identify Main Ideas and Details**.

Practice Vocabulary

Use a Word Bank Choose one word from the word bank to fill in each blank. When you have finished, you will have a short summary of important ideas from the section.

Word Bank

inflation	free trade	deforestation
desertification	globalization	genetic engineering
import	climate change	

After Soviet and other Eastern European Communist

governments fell in 1991, the switch to a market economy caused

_____, a rise in prices, and the standard

of living fell. Once the economy adjusted, the situation improved.

_____ refers to the increasing links between

the world's people and economies. A key feature is a move toward

_____, trade among nations without taxes

or tariffs. An _____ is a good or service

produced in one country and sold in another.

Technology has also helped, moving science and medicine

forward. _____ has led to new drugs

for treating diseases, such as cancer. However, there are new

concerns such as _____, or long-term

changes in weather patterns, including rainfall and storm frequency.

_____, the clearing of woodlands, is occurring

on a large scale and creating droughts. These droughts may lead to

_____, which forces people to migrate.

Writing Workshop Narrative Essay

As you read, build a response to this assignment: **Write a series of diary entries, written by a person who is more than 100 years old, that describes the changes he or she has seen in the world.** The prompts below will help walk you through the process.

Lessons 1 and 2 Writing Task: Introduce Character and Establish Setting On a separate piece of paper, write a one-paragraph introduction to your character. Include the character's current age and physical description and some historical background. To establish setting, introduce the character's current home and environment and perhaps some sights and sounds that will change in the course of your essay.

Lesson 3 Writing Task: Organize Sequence of Events In the table below, record some political, social, economic, and/or technological changes the character has seen throughout his or her life.

Decide if your character thinks the changes made life better or worse. Determine in what order you plan to present these changes in the diary entries. Place numbers next to the changes you added to the table below to indicate the order in which they will appear.

Change	Type of Change	Better or Worse

Lesson 4 Writing Task: Use Narrative Techniques Consider the tone your character will use when telling about how life has changed. Write possibilities here.

Lessons 5, 6, 7, and 8 Writing Task: Draft the Diary Using Sensory Language and Supporting Details Research credible sources to find factual supporting details about changes your character experienced and how your character's generation first responded. Draft your diary using sensory language to describe what your character saw, heard, and felt when experiencing these changes. End with a strong diary entry that reflects on a lifetime of changes and sums up your character's current thoughts and feelings about those changes.

Writing Task Using your notes and your draft, finalize your narrative essay, which features a series of diary entries, written by a person who is more than 100 years old, that describes the changes he or she has seen in the world.

Acknowledgments

Photography

COVER:

CVR Sino Images/Getty Images

002 World History Archive/Alamy Stock Photo; **004** E&E Image Library Heritage Images/Newscom; **005** Will Steeley/Alamy Stock Photo; **006** The Irish Image Collection/Design Pics Inc/Alamy Stock Photo; **007** Debu55y/Fotolia; **009** Clement Philippe/Arterra Picture Library/Alamy Stock Photo; **010** Zev Radovan/BibleLandPictures/Alamy Stock Photo; **011** Ann Ronan Picture Library Heritage Images/Newscom; **018T** Pierre Andrieu/Staff/AFP/Getty Images; **018B** Mike Greenslade/Alamy Stock Photo; **021** Ancient Art & Architecture Collection Ltd/Alamy Stock Photo; **028** Interfoto/Personalities/Alamy Stock Photo; **029** Image Asset Management/World History Archive/Age Fotostock; **030** Photo Researchers, Inc/Alamy Stock Photo; **031** Pictures From History/The Image Works; **054** Peter Horree/Alamy Stock Photo; **057** Michael DeFreitas Middle East/Alamy Stock Photo; **059** Akg Images/Franois Gunet/Newscom; **061** David Keith Jones/Images of Africa Photobank/Alamy Stock Photo; **062** Sylvain Grandadam/Age Fotostock; **063** Efesenko/Fotolia; **066T** Santiago Urquijo/Moment Open/Getty Images; **066B** Stuart Gleave/Moment Open/Getty Images; **069T** Fatih Kocyildir/Shutterstock; **069B** Mary Evans Picture Library/Alamy Stock Photo; **074** Roger Bacon/Reuters/Alamy Stock Photo; **076** Twinsterphoto/Fotolia; **077** Godong/Alamy Stock Photo; **079** M.A.Pushpa Kumara/EPA/Newscom; **081** Saiko3p/iStock/Getty Images; **086TL** World History Archive/Alamy Stock Photo; **086TR** CM Dixon/Heritage Image Partnership Ltd/Alamy Stock Photo; **086BL** Peter Horree/Alamy Stock Photo; **086BR** Robert Harding Productions/Alamy Stock Photo; **102** Weerapong Pumpradit/Shutterstock; **104** Paul Springett 10/Alamy Stock Photo; **105** Snark/Art Resource, NY; **106** Danita Delimont/Gallo Images/Getty Images; **107** Zhuhe2343603/Shutterstock; **109** BL/Robana/Robana Picture Library/Age Fotostock; **111** Hung Chung Chih/Shutterstock; **116** BnF, Dist. RMN-Grand Palais/Art Resource, NY; **128** Zack Frank/Fotolia; **130** Erich Lessing/Art Resource,NY; **133** Fine Art Images/Heritage Image Partnership Ltd/Alamy Stock Photo; **135** Richard Osbourne/Alamy Stock Photo; **136** Anatoly Vartanov/Fotolia; **158** Nito/Shutterstock; **160** Atlaspix/Alamy Stock Photo; **161** Cliff Owen/AP Images; **165** Alessandro0770/123RF; **166** Dmitry Naumov/123RF; **167** World History Archive/Alamy Stock Photo; **180** Peter Horree/Alamy Stock Photo; **183** Akg Images/Newscom; **184** David Ball/Alamy Stock Photo; **185** Interfoto/Personalities/Alamy Stock Photo; **187** Erich Lessing/Art Resource,NY; **208** Pictures From History/Akg Images; **211** North Wind Picture Archives/The Image Works; **212** Charlemagne and his paladins in battle against the Saracens, miniature from 'Charlemagne and his paladins' (vellum), French School, (13th century)/Private Collection/Index/Bridgeman Images; **215** Jeff Greenberg/The Image Works; **229T** Photo 12/Alamy Stock Photo; **229B** Duncan1890/E+/Getty Images; **234** Pictures From History/Akg Images; **232** Fine Art Images/Heritage Image Partnership Ltd/Alamy Stock Photo; **235** Loading Goods on to a Ship, from the manuscript 'Justiniano Institutiones Feodorum et Alia', c.1300 (vellum), Bolognese School, (14th century)/Biblioteca Nazionale, Turin, Italy/Index/ Bridgeman Art Library; **256** Zurijeta/Shutterstock; **258** Philippe Lissac/Photononstop/Getty Images; **259** PeopleImages/E+/Getty Images; **260** Mediacolor's/Alamy Stock Photo; **261** Jorg Hackemann/Shutterstock/Asset Library; **263** Emad Aljumah/Moment/Getty Images; **265** Raga Jose Fuste/Prisma Bildagentur AG/Alamy Stock Photo; **268T** Wigbert Röth/ImageBroker/Alamy Stock Photo; **268C** The box studio/Alamy Stock Photo;

268B Evgenyvasenev/IStock/Getty Images; **280** Mary Evans Picture Library/Alamy Stock Photo; **282** World History Archive/Alamy Stock Photo; **283** Age Fotostock; **284** Hiroshi Higuchi/Photographer's Choice/Getty Images; **288** JTB Media Creation, Inc./Alamy Stock Photo; **308** Peter Groenendijk/Publisher Mix/Getty Images; **311** Pedrosala/Shutterstock; **320T** Robert Wyatt/Alamy Stock Photo; **320B** Peter Horree/Alamy Stock Photo; **330** Sébastien Cailleux Corbis Historical/Getty Images; **332** Bruno Morandi/Robertharding/Alamy Stock Photo; **333** J.D. Dallet/Age Fotostock/Alamy Stock Photo; **334** Jan Wlodarczyk/Alamy Stock Photo; **335** Michael Macintyre/Eye Ubiquitous/Alamy Stock Photo; **337** DEGAS Jean-Pierre/hemis.fr/Alamy Stock Photo; **338** Abraham Cresques/Getty Images; **339** Paul Springett B/Alamy Stock Photo; **352** Franz Marc Frei/LOOK Die Bildagentur der Fotografen GmbH/Alamy Stock Photo; **354** World History Archive/Alamy Stock Photo; **355** Jean-Leon Huens/National Geographic Creative/Alamy Stock Photo; **356** Prisma/UIG/Getty Images; **357** World History Archive/Alamy Stock Photo; **359** Wjarek/Shutterstock; **360** Prisma Archivo/Alamy Stock Photo; **361** Jonathan Littlejohn/Alamy Stock Photo; **378** Bildarchiv Steffens/Henri Stierlin/Diego Rivera/akg-images; **381** Prisma Archivo/Alamy Stock Photo; **382** Vasco da Gama's Ships Rounding the Cape (gouache on paper), English School, (20th century)/Private Collection/Look and Learn/Bridgeman Art Library; **383** North Wind Picture Archives/Alamy Stock Photo; **385** Interfoto/History/Alamy Stock Photo; **390** Paris Pierce/Alamy Stock Photo; **406** 3dsculptor/Fotolia; **408** Detail of the Grille d'honneur depicting fleur de lys and the emblem of Louis XIV (1638–1715) (gilded iron), French School, (17th century)/Chateau de Versailles, France/Bridgeman Art Library; **409** Sergei Bobylev/TASS/Getty Images; **410** Lebrecht Authors/Lebrecht Music and Arts Photo Library/Alamy Stock Photo; **411** Alex Segre/Alamy Stock Photo; **413** Jan Luyken/AKG Images; **414** Fine Art Images/Heritage Image Partnership Ltd/Alamy Stock Photo; **415** Alex Segre/Alamy Stock Photo; **420** Anonymous Person/AKG Images; **428** Everett Collection Inc/Alamy Stock Photo; **430** Hulton Archive/Stringer/Archive Photos/Getty Images; **431** Timewatch Images/Alamy Stock Photo; **432** Christie's Images Ltd/Superstock; **433** SuperStock/Alamy Stock Photo; **437** Napoleon Crossing the Alps, c.1801 (oil on canvas), David, Jacques Louis (1748–1825) (workshop of)/Tokyo Fuji Art Museum, Tokyo, Japan/Bridgeman Art Library; **447T** Sotk2011/Alamy Stock Photo; **447B** Sotk2011/Alamy Stock Photo; **454** Mikeledray/Shutterstock; **456** Milos Luzanin/Alamy Stock Photo; **457** Mary Altaffer/AP Images; **458** Hulton Deutsch/Corbis Historical/Getty Images; **459** Bettmann/Getty Images; **461** Bettmann/Getty Images; **462** Greg Balfour Evans/Alamy Stock Photo; **468B** Everett Collection Inc/Alamy Stock Photo; **468T** Fine Art Images/Heritage Image Partnership Ltd/Alamy Stock Photo; **471L** John Parrot/Stocktrek Images, Inc./Alamy Stock Photo; **471R** War posters/Alamy Stock Photo

Text

Harvard University Press Xenophon in Seven Volumes by E. C. Marchant and G. W. Bowersock. Copyright © Harvard University Press 1925. **Africaine Editions** The Epic Of Sundiata by D.T. Niane. Copyright © Presence Africaine Editions. Used by Permission. **Cambridge University Press** Corpus of Early Arabic Sources for West African History edited by Nehemia Levtzion and JFP Hopkins. Copyright © Cambridge University Press 1981. **Marcus Wiener Publishers** Ibn Battuta in Black Africa by S Hamdun and N King. Copyright © Marcus Wiener Publishers 1998. **Pearson** The Epic of Sundiata by D.T. Niane. Copyright © Pearson. Used by permission.